Ayn Rand

Novelist with a Vision and Philosophy

Ayn Rand

Novelist with a Vision and Philosophy

Anuradha

Prestige Books International

Delhi : Sydney

Published by
Prestige Books International
New Delhi 110 060
email: prestigebooks@gmail.com

Associate Office
10, Folkard Street,
North Ryde, NSW 2113, Australia

ISBN: 978-93-82186-41-0

Printed in India

Contents

Foreword

Russia has a rich cultural heritage and is embodied in the city of Moscow. Russian culture is a hybrid one. It is formed from the cultures of different nationalities of this multinational state and the result of development over several epochs. Russian literature has greatly influenced world literature. In *Reference Guide to Russian Literature* (1998), Neil Cornwell and Nicole Christian rightly say: "In the eyes of the world Russian literature is perhaps the chief cultural glory of Russian culture. What the world knows above all as the classic Russian novel, whose great age was amazingly brief—a mere quarter century, all within reign of Alexander II (1855-1881), which saw the publications of the best works of Tolstoy, Dostoevsky, Turgenev, and Goncherov." (3) The famous Russian writers are: Alexander Pushkin, Leo Tolstoy, Fyodor Dostoevsky, Anton Chekhov, Vladimir Mayakovski, Boris Pasternak, Joseph Brodsky, Maxim Gorky and Vladimir Nabokov.

Among Russian writers Ayn Rand is distinctive for promulgating Objectivism. Fascinated by her works, I chose her for my doctoral research. The first chapter "Ayn Rand and the Evolution of Russian Literature" provides the evolution of the history of the Russian literature and gives a bio-critical account of women writers in Russia. In providing the evolution of women's literature, scholars and critics usually consider African women writings, Afro American women writings, West Indian women writings, Asian American women writings etc. But the writings of Russian women writers fail to hold attention due to traditional negligence. In the light of this perception, this chapter gives the bio-critical information about the women writers in general and Ayn Rand in particular. A synoptic view of the themes of all her works is provided specifying the reason in considering the study of some of her important novels.

The second chapter "The demise of Communist Tyranny" reviews Rand's *We the Living*. One can find biographical resonance between the events of Rand's early life and the theme of the novel. There are many parallels between Rand's early life under communism and that of her novel's heroine, Kira. Barbara Branden says about the experience of Rand in *The Passion for Ayn Rand*: "When she first heard the communist slogan-shrilled in the Bolshevik's every speech and article and plastered on the walls throughout the city—that man must live for the state, she knew that this was the horror at the root of all the other horrors taking place around her." (21)

Rand was twelve when she rejected indignantly the ideology which she witnessed on the posters everywhere. This is very much similar to the experience of Kira: "Kira looked at the words on the bare plaster walls of the station. The plaster had crumbled off dark blotches that made the walls look skin-diseased. But fresh signs had been printed upon them. Red letters announced: "LONG LIVE THE DICTATORSHIP OF THE PROLETARIAT! WHO IS NOT WITH US—IS AGAINST US!" (29)

Until the time of revolution, Rand had lived very comfortably. But after three years of exile in the Crimea, when she returned with her family to Leningrad, it was a nightmare for her. Kira too lives with her family in Petrograd until the Civil War in Russia which drives them out of their home: "It had been four years since the Argounov family left Petrograd. Four years ago Argounov textile factory on the outskirts of the capital was nationalized in the name of the people. In the name of the people the banks were declared national property. Argounov's safe-deposit boxes were broken open and emptied." (21)

Like Kira in *We the Living*, Ayn Rand hated the sordidness of Soviet life, the never-ending search for bare necessities. She suffered from near starvation for many years. She lived under the constant threat of fatal diseases such as typhoid and cholera. Like Kira, Rand too witnessed political purges during her university years. She narrowly escaped being purged from Leningrad University. Her heroine is not that fortunate. When an outspoken fellow student was exiled to Siberia, Ayn Rand felt outraged and could not keep silent. She told a communist that one day, all of them would hang from lampposts of the city. For this dangerous indiscretion, she paid the price of terror. For a long time afterwards, she waited for the knock at the door that could send her and her family to Siberia, but it never came.

The third chapter "Theory of Human Nature" analyses Rand's novel *Anthem*. Rand's working title for this short novel was *Ego*. She writes to one correspondent: "I used the word in its exact meaning." The ego constitutes the essential identity of a human being. In his introduction to the novel, Leonard Peikoff writes: "It is obvious why Ayn Rand exalts man's ego. In doing so she is (implicitly) upholding the central principles of her philosophy and her heroes: reason, values, volition, individualism. Her villains, by contrast, do not think, judge, will; they are second-handers, who show themselves to be run by others." (v) Thus by renouncing their mind, they are, in a literal sense, self-less. The novel depicts a world of the future, a society so collectivized that even the word 'I' has vanished from the language.

Though the book was published a decade before Orwell's *1984*, it provides a good introduction to Rand's philosophy of Objectivism, built on individuality, freedom and reason. Paul Meier is an excellent choice for the novel's first person narrator. He manages to maintain urgency in his voice. The story of *Anthem* carries the collectivist program to its logical conclusion. In the society people are simply numbered units and are subject to state control and planning. The story's origins lie in Rand's own experience of communism in Russia, but its significance is far more autobiographical. It is a critique of many of the world's most influential books, ideas, and intellectual movements.

It is said that throughout *Anthem*, Rand associates the corrupt ideology of the collectivists with religion. For example, she describes the daily City Council meetings in the format of church services. Even the word Anthem itself has a religious connotation.

Rand consciously chose to describe her story using traditional religious images, hoping to replace God with exalted view of man.

The fourth chapter "Liberation as Idealism" deals with Rand's other novel *The Fountainhead*. Rand says in the introduction: "My purpose . . . is the portrayal of Howard Roark . . . as an end in himself." (vii) She sets her hero against the collective ideas that existed—and to some degree continue to exist—in the United States. Ellsworth Toohey, the villain in the novel, is a Marxist intellectual. He preaches socialism to the masses and holds that an individual has no value in himself but exists only to serve his brothers. As Peekskill comments that the successful philosophical or a political novel is a rarity. *War and Peace* and *Zen* and *The Art of Motorcycle Maintenance* present philosophical ideas, but none of them is a novel in the traditional sense. The secret of success in the novel, *Fountainhead* is to present the ideas through the media of sympathetic characters and a compelling narrative. Rand's characters are mouthpieces for specific points of view. It shows that Rand is not a conventional writer.

One may doubt what the problems were supposed to be in relation to the architecture of the time. This was the age of Art Deco and of Frank Lloyd Wright and surely a golden age in American architecture. It was the era of Wall Street Crash, the great depression and Roosevelt's New Deal which was the best advertisement from laissez-faire economics. But Rand wrote the novel in 1930s when collectivism was engulfing the world. The communists took over her native Russia, then Fascists came to power in Italy, then Hitler and the National Socialists took political control of Germany. Rand wrote *The Fountainhead* to prevent their recurrence in America.

While setting forth her philosophy, Rand has also given a novel with a well developed plot. The readers' interest is held as the novel provides enough twists to provide surprises. The book can be enjoyed both as a novel and as a philosophical statement. The Broadway Hollywood department store has a modern style annexe just to the west of it built in the 1930s. It is said that the young Rand viewed the building of that addition and it became the basis of her research in construction techniques and workers found within the novel. Architect Richard Neutra, who designed the international styled Laemmle Building (1932) across Hollywood Boulevard to the north, is said to be the man on whom she modelled Roark.

The fifth chapter "Creating a Different Utopia" examines in an analytical way Rand's novel *Atlas Shrugged*. The novel is about Rand's objectivist philosophy that the individual is free to pursue his or her own happiness without bowing to God or society. Objectivism shows that the full laissez-faire capitalism as the only philosophy that can protect humankind's freedom to think, to be inventive and to live productively. The novel succeeds in establishing the essence of business, as a profoundly moral activity.

It is apt to quote Nathaniel Branden's comment in *The Literary Method of Ayn Rand*: "*Atlas Shrugged* is an action story on a grand scale, but it is a consciously philosophical action story, just as its heroes are consciously philosophical men of action. To those who subscribe to the soul-body dichotomy in literature, *Atlas Shrugged* is an anomaly that defies classification by conventional standards." (4) The novel obviously shows the significance of industrialists and mental work to society. Rand uses this conflict to draw wider philosophical conclusions. This is made clear in the plot and from the statements of the characters.

The sixth chapter "Capitalism as Morality" gives a detailed account of Rand's non-fiction writing "Capitalism: The Unknown Ideal." There may be certain flaws in Rand's Objectivist philosophy, but this book remains a brilliant and unique defence of freedom and capitalism. Moreover, history has proved Rand to be a profound thinker who was correct in many of her analyses. The book ranks among the very best of her non-fiction works. It is highly engaging, thought-provoking and often quite amusing. It concludes with an index and a bibliography listing titles by Henry Hazlitt, Isabel Paterson, Ludwig von Mises and others.

All the essays are worth serious consideration. However, four essays stand out for their contemporary application: "What is Capitalism?" "The Roots of War," "Gold and Economic Freedom"

(Greenspan), and "Conservatism: An Obituary." All the articles in the book were written and copyrighted in the 1960s and the book itself as collection of these articles was first published in 1967. Rand believes that man's mind is his basic means of survival—his only means of gaining knowledge. Men can learn from one another, but learning requires a process of thought. If some men do not choose to think, they can survive only by imitating and repeating a routine work discovered by others.

Capitalism is a social system based on the recognition of the individual rights, including property rights, in which all property is privately owned. In a capitalist society, all human relations are voluntary. In history, the tribal notion of the common good has served as the moral justification of most social systems—and of all tyrannies—in history. As Soviet Russia, a country professedly dedicated to the common good where, with the exception of a minuscule clique of rulers, the entire population has existed in subhuman misery for over two generations.

The social application of an objective theory of values is represented by the free market. On a free market, it is the purveyor of the best product at the cheapest price who wins the greatest financial rewards in that field. In the alternative of free market, the tribal society, all men throw their efforts, values, ambitions, and goals into a common pot, then wait hungrily at its rim: "The most consistent example of such a system is the union of Soviet Socialist Republics. . . . Today, Soviet Russia is still unable to feed her people—while the rulers scramble to copy, borrow, or steal the technological achievements of the West." (29) America's abundance was not created by public sacrifices to the common good, but by the productive genius of the free men who pursued their own personal interests.

The seventh chapter "Spawning Criticism" examines Rand's objectivism and shows how Rand has treated anti-feminist and anti-Marxist and also about the reality in it. The study makes an attempt to go beyond Objectivism in order to evaluate Rand's works. I substantiate that objectivism is incomplete without proper understanding of her works. I apply different techniques of literary criticism: Postmodernism, New Historicism, Marxism, Postcolonialism and Feminism in order to gain true knowledge of her writings. While applying feminism to Rand, I have provided the background of feminist literary criticism for the critical understanding of her works.

Rand differs from other philosophers by limiting the scope of ethics in deriving principles needed in all contexts, whether one is alone or with others. She writes in "The Virtue of Selfishness": "The greatest of all philosophers, Aristotle, did not regard ethics as an exact science; he based his ethical system on observations of what the noble and wise men of his time chose to do, leaving unanswered the questions of: why they chose to do it and why he evaluated them as noble and wise." (14) Thus the morality of Objectivism is that one's own choices and actions are the instruments to maintain and to enhance one's life, and therefore one's happiness. Rand writes that man is a rational being, but rationality is a matter of choice. Nature offers him the alternatives—rational being or suicidal animal. By choice man has to be a man and has to hold his life as a value. By choice he has to learn to sustain it, discover the values it requires and practise his virtues. Thus, through my research I paved the way for a serious understanding of the chosen works of Ayn Rand.

Vijayawada **Anuradha**

Ayn Rand and the Evolution of Russian Literature

Russian literature includes the literature of Russia or its émigrés, and of several independent nations which were once a part of Russia or the Soviet Union. Before the nineteenth century, the global recognition for Russian Literature was very insignificant. Writers faced a great difficulty in adapting to and being accepted in a new environment. It was because their language is the instrument of creativity and by its nature a foreign and inaccessible element. A few Russian writers have flourished on American soil. These include Vladimir Nabokov who switched from Russian to English in the late 1940s and produced many novels, including the very popular *Lolita* (1958), and the short story writer Nina Berberova. From around the 1830s, Russian literature underwent a golden age. It had begun with the poet Alexander Pushkin and culminated in two of the greatest novelists in world literature, Leo Tolstoy and Fyodor Dostoevsky, and the playwright Anton Chekhov.

What Neil Cornwell and Nicole Christian say about Pushkin in his *Reference Guide to Russian Literature* is true: 'My argument, in brief, will be that Pushkin, Byron and Shakespeare, as creative writers and personalities, represented a crucial chronicle in the period 1824-26; and furthermore, that being English, these figures offered the "Frenchman" Pushkin a choice of romantic personality versus "romantic" art, but romantic art defined in a special, non or "anti-Byronic way."' (18) Thus, Pushkin is compared to Shakespeare. Old Russian literature had several masterpieces written in Russian language. Anonymous works of this nature include *The Tale of Igor's Campaign* and the *Praying of Daniel the Immured*. Lives of saints formed a popular genre of the Old

Russian literary monuments like *Zadonschina*, *Psychologist*, *Synopsis* and *A Journey beyond the Three Seas*. Bylinas.

In the tenth century after the introduction of Christianity from Byzantium, Russian literature was first produced. "The written masterpiece of Russian literature was *The Song of Igor's Campaign*, which towered above the general cultural desolation under Tatar domination. A few notable sermons and lives of saints were written in this period, and in the early 15th century. The priest Sophonia of Ryazan wrote the epic *Beyond the River Don* to commemorate the victory over the Tatars at Kulikoyo (1380). Athanasy Nikitin (1472) wrote a distinguished account of his journey beyond Three Seas to distant lands." In the mid-17th century, the Russian Church was influenced by the great schism which produced the memorable autobiography of the archpriest, Avvakum (martyred 1682), the first work in colloquial Russian.

Western influence was manifest in the 17th century in numerous translations and in the establishment (1682) of the first theatre in Russia. Prince Antioch Kantemir (1708-44) blended the syllabic system common to French and Polish. The founder of Russian drama, A. P. Sumarokov, combined European forms with Russian themes in his fables and plays. The influence of European Enlightenment was seen on literature during the reign of Catherine II. In his plays, D.I. Fonzivin (1745-92), and the author of Russia's first truly national drama, *The Minor* (1782), combined satire with realistic modes. Sentimentality in the drama was developed by Vladislav Ozerov (1769-1816. It was also seen in Nikolai Karamzin, the principal prose exponent who initiated the Russian short story.

The critic, V.G. Belinsky, the leader of Westernizers, stressed the importance of the relationship of literature to national life. He thus helped the development of Russian literary realism. Neil Cornwell and Nicole Christian in *Reference Guide to Russian Literature* rightly say: "The career of Aleksandr Ostrovskii (1823 1886) thoroughly exemplifies the new sense of realism. He is unique among front-rank Russian playwrights in writing for the theatre alone, his 50 plays constituting a broad study of contemporary Russian life centred on the middle class, such as it was, or classless people." (11) At mid-century, I.A. Goncherov developed a merciless realism, not devoid of humour and A. N. Ostrovsky was the first to make the merchant world a subject of Russian literary works. He wrote a vast number of plays most of which are no longer performed.

In prose literature, the works of Russia's golden age were written against a background of a czarist autocracy. With the rise of symbolism, a reaction against realism manifested. Symbolism flourished from the 1890s to about 1910 in the works of Feodor Sologub, V. K. Brynsov and I. F. Annesnsky. The Russian symbolist movement is divided at two generations of writers. The first was "decadent" generation which includes the poets Konstantin Batmont (1867-1941), Valerov Bryurov (1893-1924), Zinader Hippius (1869-1945), and Dmitry Merezhkvsky (1865-1941). The second, mystic generation includes Andrev Beliy (1880-1936), Alexander Blok (1880-1921) and Vycheslav Ivanov (1866-1949). The rise of Decadence as an idealistic-artistic movement can be traced to the 1890s. The philosophical ideas of A. Bergson, I. Kant, and the Neo-Kantists had a significant influence on the decadence movement as they were modernized and applied in the atmosphere of the times.

In Russian Literature, the recurrent theme is suffering, often shown as a means of redemption. Dostoevsky in particular is noted for exploring suffering in works such as *Notes from the Underground*, *Crime and Punishment*. Christianity and Christian symbolism are also important themes, notably in the works of Dostoevsky, Tolstoy and Chekhov. In the 20th century, suffering as mechanism of evil was explored by the authors such as Solzhenitsyn in The Gulag Archipelago. It shows that Russian literature is devoted to the description of unsuccessful love affairs. Anna Akhmatova's brief lyrics brought her fame at the outset of her career, but later in life she produced longer works such as *Requiem*. It was written from 1935 to 1940, but published in Russia only in 1989, her memorial to the victims of Joshed Stalin's purges.

Most of the writers who began publishing immediately after the 1917 revolution turned to prose, particularly the short story and the novella. The writers who had been by the revolution and the subsequent Russian Civil War (1918-1920) were Boris Pilnyak (*The Naked Year*, 1922), Isaak Babel (*Red Cavalry*, 1926) and Mikhail Sholokov. Sholokov was awarded the Nobel Prize for literature in 1965. The short stories of Mikhail Zoshchenko, the comic novels of IIya and Yevgeny Petrov, and the short novel *Envy* (1927) by Yury Olesha and others described life in the new Soviet Union with varying degrees of mordant sarcasm. Among the communities of anticommunist exiles in Germany, France, Italy, and the United States, writing in Russian flourished.

The role played by women in the literate culture of medieval Russia and the images of women in Old Russian writings is an interesting study. What Neil Cornwell and Nicole Christian write in *Reference Guide to Russian Literature* is true: "Russian women have been writing, in the broader sense, if not producing literature, for many centuries. Female signatures have been found on some of the earliest documents in the Russian language—the letters written on birchbark by inhabitants of Novgorod in the 11th, 12th, 13th centuries." (35) After observing variety of texts, one can understand that certain types of female characters had enduring popularity, though they did not conform to the code of feminine virtue prescribed by the Russian Orthodox Church.

In *Women Writers in Russian Literature*, Margaret Ziolbowsky in her essay, "Women in Old Russian Literature" gives a good reference: "In 1051 Anna Iaroslavna, one of the daughters of the renowned Kievan ruler Iaroslav the Wise (1036-1054), married Henry I of France. As queen and later regent, Anna was the signatory of several documents; on one the name 'Anna Regin' appears in Cyrillic characters." Iaroslav's sister predslava is known to have correspond with her brother. In the 11th century, a convent was founded by the daughter of Vsevolod I (1078-93), Ianka. These details show that in early Russia female literacy was common among the princely families. The life of the twentieth-century abbess and convent founder, Evfrosiniia who was the daughter of a prince of Polotsk, mentions that she copied manuscripts.

Russian cities have numerous inscriptions composed by and for women. What Neil Cromwell and Nicole Christian write in *Reference Guide to Russian Literature* is true: "Accordingly in the late 18th and early 19th centuries a number of women, mostly well-educated aristocrats, did indeed begin contributing to the development of Russian letters. Several of them were the sisters, daughters or wives of male writers. Ekateina Sumarokova (1746-97) was the daughter of the poet and playwright Aleksandr Sumerakov; Elizaveta Kheraskova (1740-1809) and Ekaterina Urusova (1747-1817) the wife and cousin respectively of Mikhail Kheraskov, author of the epic Rossiiada."

At the beginning of the 18th century, in the course of debates about the character of the Russian literary language, the writer Nokolai M. Karamzin (1766-1826) and his followers crystallized ideas and assumptions about women's influence on literature and language that first appeared at the beginning of the century. Women's taste and language were made the standard of literary and linguistic excellence by the Karamzinists. Thus women were awarded such authority over Russian language and literature that later scholars have spoken of a feminization of Russian culture. In the general outline it accompanied the rapid Westernization and secularization of Russian society that took place in the 18th century.

It was not until the second half of the 18th century that women began contributing to the secular westernized tradition of literature such as—that is, writing as more than purely functional communication—which had been established in Russia for about a hundred years. However, from 1750s various factors combined positively to encourage women's participation in literature. Thus writers now started writing for a society transformed by the presence of aristocratic women, who had formerly been sequestered.

In *A History of Women's Writing in Russia* (2002), Adele Marie Barter and Jehanne M. Gheith write: "Outstanding among these, both in terms of opportunity and of availability, was Catherine II, whose lively comedies of the 1770s, such as Ovremial (O temporal and mores!), spicing didacticism with humour, are among the better eighteenth-century excursions in the vernacular style; Catherine's Shakespearian histories were interesting attempts to break the neoclassical mould, if scarcely classics of the stage." (55) Encouraged by the example of the first active generation of prose women writers, many women started writing and continued refining their craft through the decades.

The plot based on lover's vicissitudes was standard from the moment the earliest fiction by Russian women appeared in the late 1770s. From the late 1850s, they showed their heroines taking part in the work of social reconstruction then under way." In her essay, "Women's Prose Fiction in the Age of realism," in the book, *Women Writers in Russian literature* Mary F. Zirin says: "The lives of these writers reflect the handicaps the women had to overcome in order to establish independent careers. Almost all of them came from the miniscule (3 percent) gentry's class. Under Russian autocracy, nobody enjoyed full autonomy, but women suffered under a double burden: to the restrictions on civil freedom imposed to a greater or lesser degree on everyone was added a concomitant tutelage by men." (77) Thus, by the late 1840s, women writers were shaking off the spell of Romanticism and beginning to depict the constraints of women's situation and the domestic milieu in sober and muted terms.

In the latter half of the century, women's autobiographies depict the girls from the traditionally patriarchal merchantry and peasantry and also from supposedly Westernized gentry's family. The feminist scholars were engaged in a massive project of recovering and reinterpreting the autobiographical writings of women over the last two decades. They outlined the recurrent patterns in women's texts, or in the most ambitious cases, a poetics of women's autobiography by exposing the privileges and silences of patriarchal cultures, challenging traditional norms of genre and canon.

In the field of drama, it has been noted that the Russian votes with this theatre ticket, but dramaturgy is mostly a one-party system that rarely elects women. Though there has been no dearth of women writing plays, their legacy is scant. Even among the most prolific female writers for the stage, playwriting tends to be a phase in a women's career rather than an area of her major emphasis. However, it is not entirely Russian phenomenon. In Women Writers in Russian Literature, Malissa T. Smith says in her essay, "Waiting in the Wings: Russian women Playwrights in the Twentieth Century": "The influential Soviet Plyriohgt Aleksei Arbuzov has offered the view on women and drama that in *The Passion According to Barbara*, Olga Pavlova-Kuchkina has decided on a fairly brave move—only women has chosen as her craft dramaturgy—the most merciless, most masculine form of literature. Here, besides talent, the dramatist must have a strong will, unyielding character, a defensive reaction against literary failures and life's misfortunes." (189) Thus, women playwrights have a double burden not known to the non-dramatist writers.

Ultimately, their works must stand both as works of literature and as material for stage production. Apart from them, as it is said in *Reference Guide to Russian Literature*: "Though some late 18 and early 19 century women poets were no more than dilettante rhymesters, some for example Urusova and Kheraskova, later Aleksandr Sandra, Murginova and Aleksandr Magnitskaia (active in 1790s), Maria Pospelova (1780-1805), and Anna Volkova 91781-1834), were genuinely talented individuals, the best of whose work displays intelligence, wit and technical, facility." (Cornwell and Christian, 35) Here, the authors say about the plight of the women poets.

The subject of Russian women writers in emigration has not yet been seriously discussed by literary critics. The cataclysms in 20th century Russia have forced many talented Russian women writers to flee from their homeland and seek asylum in many countries and on all continents. They wholeheartedly rejected Bolshevik or Soviet tyranny in exchange for independence and spiritual freedom beyond their homeland's borders. They aptly followed the dictum of Pythagoras of Samos, one of European civilization's most ancient exiles: For a reasoning man it is immoral to remain under the authority of a tyrant.

After the exodus of 1918-1925, cultural centres emerged in the entire diaspora, with the most significant in Paris, Berlin, Prague, Riga and Revel, Sofia and Warsaw, and the far East—Harbin and Shanghai. Their contribution to literature includes all the existing genres from poetry, fiction, and drama to literary criticism, Journalism prose, and philosophic-religious treatises. But little is known about most of the women among American Slavists. In American scholarship, famous writers like Zinaida Gippius, Nadezhda Teffi, Marina Tsetaeva have received attention, but only some of émigré women writers are included in scholarly anthologies and the available literary handbooks and dictionaries.

What is written in *Reference Guide to Russian Literature* is true: 'After 1930s, when Stalin declared the "women question" solved, and closed down the Zbenotdel, its activists disappeared from fiction, but the "new women" continued to be popular figure until the mid-1930s, when increasing disapproval of extramarital intercourse and other such "promiscuous" behaviour meant that fiction like ideology, began to place a new emphasis on women's duties as wives and mothers. In the late 1930s and 1940s, the main characters of factory-and-collective-form novels by writing such as Keravaeva, Antonina Kopriaeva (b. 1909), Galina Nickolaeva (real name Volianskaia), (1911-63), and Vera Panova (1905-73) were often women in full-time employment and taking an active role in Party business who nonetheless managed to work the "second shift" of domestic duties smilingly and uncomplainingly.' (Cornwell and Christian, 38) Thus the era of new women started.

In the chain of feminine poetic consciousness, Bliznetsova's lyrical persona embodies a contemporary link. A new generation of young women poets whose poetry embraces ever larger themes and methods are represented by Blitznetsova's modern, complex, and intellectually charged work.

Among the women writers, Ayn Rand is the most prolific writer. She was the first woman who dared to write against communism. Rand was born in Saint Petersburg, Russia. She was the eldest daughter of Zinovy Zacharovich Rosenbaum, agonistic and largely non-observant ethnic Jews. 'Ayn Rand' is not her birth name she used most of her life. She adopted that name when she left the Soviet Union. Rand's Russian birth name can be translated into English as 'Alisa Zinovievna Rosenbaum'. In a letter to a fan, Rand wrote that Ayn is both real name and an invention. The original of it is a Finnish feminine name. This Finnish name is pronounced in Russia as I-na and would be written as Aino in English. Rand shortened this to a single syllable 'Ayn'. How she chose 'Rand' as last name is not clear. There are many contradictory speculations about it.

Rand had two younger sisters. One was Natasha, born in 1907, and the other was Eleanora, born in 1910 and known as Nora. During World War II, all of her family except Nora died and Rand was not aware of the fact that her sister was still alive until 1973. After they rediscovered one another, a brief visit to the US by Nora and her husband went badly and the two sisters were estranged. After returning to Russia, Nora survived her sister's death until March 15, 1999. It is said that her father was a chemist and a successful pharmaceutical entrepreneur who earned the privilege of living outside the Pale. From an early age, Alisa displayed interest in literature and film. Throughout her youth, Rand read the novels of Sir Walter Scott, Alexander Dumas, Pere and other Romantic writers of whom Victor Hugo was her favourite. Rand was an advocate of rational individualism and laissez-faire capitalism, and she vehemently opposed socialism, altruism, and other contemporary philosophical trends, as well as religion. Her controversial ideas have altered both enthusiastic admirers and scathing denunciators. Rand was taught French by her mother who subscribed to a magazine featuring stories for boys where Rand found her first childhood hero Cyrus Paltons, an Indian army officer in a Rudyard Kipling-style story by Maurice Champagne, called *The Mysterious Valley*.

Rand wrote that an ideal educational curriculum would be: Aristotle in Philosophy, Von Mises in Economics, Montessori in education, Hugo in literature. At the time of Russian Revolution,

Rand was twelve and her family life was disrupted by the rise of the Bolshevik party. The Soviets confiscated her father's pharmacy and their family fled to Crimea to recover financially. In 1921, as Crimea fell to Bolsheviks, Rand burned her diary which had vitriolic anti-Soviet writing. On October 2, 1921, Rand returned to Saint Petersburg to attend the University in Petrograd. Then she was sixteen. Petrograd was the new name of St. Petersburg. Three years later, on October 13, 1924, she received her degree from the newly renamed University of Leningrad. She studied social pedagogy and specifically majored in history and minored in philosophy.

Mimi Reisel Gladstein writes about Rand's studies in his *The New Ayn Rand Companion* (1999): "Rand left Russia in 1926. She had graduated from the University of Petrograd two years earlier and then attended the State Institute of Cinema Arts, where she studied acting and screenwriting. Her twenty-first birthday was spent in transit to the United States. The occasion for her leaving was an invitation from her Portnoy family relatives to visit them in Chicago." (8) After reading Friedrich Nietzsche's works, she admired his depiction of a heroic and independent individual who embraces egoism and rejects altruism in *Thus Spake Zarathustra*, but when discovered more about his writings later, she rejected the other aspects of his philosophy. She graduated in 1924 and arrived in the United States at the age of 21. Later United States became her home.

In an article in the newspaper, *The Hindu*, it is written how America was once treated as the shining city upon a hill. In the 19th century and up to the end of the Second World War there was a superpower. It was not America but Britain. The British Empire sprawled across five continents, taking up more than a third of the globe. Britons were admired, envied and disliked overtly and covertly. Britain was hated by the countries it colonized and by other colonizers—France, Holland and America: "The Americans were never racists, though Afro-Americans in the U.S., faced insurmountable odds. But a superiority complex lies at the root of the American mentality and culture. America was from the beginning a New World for everyone to start from scratch when he fled the Old World with its preconceptions, social barriers and other age-old problems. The majority of Americans still believe in the American Dream, which gives an impetus to the native conviction that America is best." (*The Hindu*, 3 Nov. 2008) Ayn Rand too started from scratch after coming to America.

Mimi Reisel Gladstein explains in *The New Ayn Rand Companion*: "She moved to Los Angeles. And in a scene straight out of a Hollywood movie, she met Cecil B. De Mille on second day in town, after her only lead for work in Hollywood had fizzled. He offered her a job as an extra on the set of his movie *The King of Kings*." (9) As the movie was being completed, De Mille offered her a job for preparing synopses of works that might be adapted for films. Gladstein continues: "Success did not come to Ayn Rand early. She worked as an extra and junior screenwriter, on and off, until De Mille closed his independent studio in 1928. She then did odd jobs such as wait at tables and stuff envelops until she got a position in the wardrobe department of RKO pictures." (10) Branden here gives the details about how initially Rand struggled in Hollywood to pay her basic living expenses.

At RKO Studios, Rand worked as the head of the costume department. While working on the film, she intentionally became an aspiring young actor and met Frank O'Connor, who caught her eye. When he and Rand met, O'Connor was an actor. Later in course of his life he did various jobs, including running the Couple's California reach when they lived there and designing floral arrangements. Then he was an amateur painter. Rand and O'Connor got married on 15 April 1929. In *The New Ayn Rand Companion*, Gladstein writes: "Whatever the realities of Frank O' Connor's public persona, in him Ayn Rand found a spiritual soulmate, a man who remained devoted and supportive through a fifty-year marriage," (10) until O'Connor's death in 1979 at the age of 82.

Rand is mostly referred to as Miss Rand, never even thought she was married. During Ayn Rand's lifetime, 'Miss' and 'Mrs.' were standard courtesy titles for women. Mrs. was used with any variation of a woman's married name, then 'Miss' would be appropriate. While still running the wardrobe department, in 1934, Rand made her first professional writing sale; a movie screenplay namely *Red Pawn* which was never produced. She got $1,500 from that sale and with it, she quit the wardrobe department. From that point forward she worked primarily as a professional writer. In 1934, when *Night of the January 16th* (1934) was to be produced on Broadway, Rand moved to New York city.

The royalties from *The Fountainhead* (1943) freed her from the financial need to do any work other than writing. After the publication of *Atlas Shrugged* (1957) years later, Rand was in demand as a public speaker. She delivered annual speeches at the Ford Hall Forum in Boston, and also spoke at colleges, universities and other forums. From 1961 to 1976, she acted as editor and publisher for a series of magazines devoted to discussing Objectivist ideas, for which she also wrote numerous essays. Rand became a naturalized American citizen in 1931. As a thinker, Rand has occupied a remarkably polarized status in American culture. Her novels and collections of nonfiction essays have for decades attracted a large popular readership, worldwide.

Rand is celebrated for her substantial contribution to the revival of classical liberal thought which is a revival that has gained broad visibility and influence through such organizations as the Reason Foundation and the Cato Institute in the past two decades. Rand's philosophy was debated in scholarly journals even during her lifetime, and her ideas have begun to be dealt with in the academy. A number of them have entered the teaching ranks. Recently, beginning with the publication of Chris Matthew Sciabarra's *Ayn Rand: The Russian Radical* (1995), by Penn State Press, serious Rand studies have accelerated. Éntries on Rand have also been appearing in philosophic reference works such as the *Routledge Encyclopedia of Philosophy*. In addition, the *Journal of Ayn Rand Studies*—the first peer-reviewed journal devoted to Rand's life and thought, founded in 1999—has begun, under Sciabarra's editorship, to establish a dialogue with scholars outside the sphere of Rand's philosophic influence." (www.aristos.org.com) Thus after the death of Rand, her ideas have begun to be included in widely used philosophy textbooks and anthologies on ethics and politics compiled by non-Objectivist scholars.

Major books review media, in print or on air, have been reluctant to deal with a serious book about Ayn Rand's ideas. The first exception is the review of Roger Kimball's *What Art Is* in 2001 issue of the *Public Interest.* To promote broader appreciation of Rand's work and thought in academia, as well as by the public at large, through diverse publications, lectures, seminars, and other activities, two organizations are working—*The Ayn Rand Institute* founded in 1985 and the Objectivist Centre founded in 1990, at the *Institute for Objectivist Studies.* Academic projects are research courses for undergraduate and doctoral students, and publishing. Due to these efforts, many young scholars well-versed in Objectivism have been entering the academic teaching ranks in such fields as Philosophy, History, Psychology and Political Science.

Rand feels proud of the United States. In later years she said to the graduating class at West Point that she could say—not as a patriotic bromide, but with full knowledge of the necessary metaphysical, epistemological, ethical, political and aesthetic roots—that the United States of America was the greatest, the noblest and, in its original founding principles, the only moral country in the history of the world. Gladstein says in *The New Ayn Rand Companion*: "Rand had always dreamed of America; she considered New York City greatest city in the world. Its skyline was indicative to her of the wonders that the human mind was capable of creating." (8) In 1960, Rand became a visiting lecturer at several universities such as Yale University, Princeton University and Columbia University. In 1963, she received an honorary doctorate from Lewis & Clark College.

Later her close associate, Branden established the Nathaniel Branden Institute. As Gladstein writes in *The New Ayn Rand Companion:* "The Nathaniel Branden Institute was a business with a purpose; that purpose was changing the world. Objectivism was the foundation upon which this new world was to be erected. During the 1960s Objectivism, which Rand characterized as an intellectual movement, grew phenomenally. Its influence was far-reaching."

(16) In 1974, Rand underwent surgery for lung cancer. Though she had planned to write another novel, *To Lorne Dieterling*, she did not get far in her notes. It is said: "Rand died of heart failure on March 6, 1982 at her 34th Street home in New York city, years after having successfully battled cancer, and was interred in the Kensico Cemetery, Valhalla, New York. Rand's funeral was attended by some of her prominent followers, including Alan Greenspan. A six-foot floral arrangement in the shape of a dollar sign was placed near her casket." http://www.wikipedia.com

Rand professed that epistemology, the theory of knowledge, was fundamental to philosophy and she defined reason as the faculty that identifies and integrates the material provided by man's senses. In order to defend and explain her position on reason, she developed a theory of sense-perception that distinguishes between the form and object perception. The sense-perception holds that the form in which an organism perceives is determined by its physiological means of perception but that in whatever form it perceives, what it perceives, the object of its perception, is reality. She strongly rejected the Kantian dichotomy between things as we perceive them and things as they are in themselves. She professed rational selfishness. In *The Virtue of Selfishness* (1964) she gave an original validation of her moral code. She claims that the moral code has bridged the infamous gap between "Is" and Ought" or between facts and values. She holds that all living organisms act as gain values, i.e., the items their survival requires.

Rand says that the purpose of a moral code is to provide a standard of value and a code of virtues. A man can achieve the values his survival requires and which enhance his life by reference to that code of virtues. The standard of value for Rand is: Man's life qua rational being. Independence, integrity, honesty, justice, productiveness, and pride are the derivative virtues of her Objectivist morality. She explains each of them in some detail in *The Objectivist Ethics.* The political views of Rand were strongly individualist and hence anti-statist and anti-Communist. Rand strongly opposed mysticism and religion. She believed they fostered crippling culture which acts against individual human happiness and success.

Gladstein says in *The New Ayn Rand Companion*: "Her family was normally Jewish, but here father, Zinovy Zcharovich (proxy), was nonreligious and her mother, Anna Borisovna, only perfunctorily so. There is little evidence that Rand received any traditional religious upbringing. Early in life she developed an antipathy to all religions which were branded as mysticism. By the age of fourteen she had declared herself an atheist." (1) Many prominent liberal and conservative politicians of her time such as prominent anti-Communist, such as Harry S. Truman, Ronald Reagan, Hubert Humphrey, and Joseph McCarthy were detested by Rand. Though she rejected libertarianism and the libertarian movement, she is treated as one of the three founding mothers along with Rose Wilder Lane and Isabel Paterson of modern American libertarianism.

Though Rand strongly denounced pacifism, she opposed U.S. involvement in World War I, World War II, and the Korean War too. Rand also believed that unilateral American withdrawal would be a mistake of appeasement as it would embolden communists and the Soviet Union. During the 1973 Arab-Israeli War, Rand supported Israel. She took it as an attack by a primitive society on a government that supported individual rights: "The Arabs are one of the least developed cultures. They are typically nomads. Their culture is primitive, and they resent Israel because it's the sole beachhead of modern science and civilization on their continent. When you have civilized men fighting savages, you support the civilized men, no matter who they are." (48)

Rand had enthusiasm for the economic thought of Ludwig von Mises and Henry Hazlitt. The Ludwig von Mises Institute notes that it was largely the result of Any's efforts that the work on von Mises began to reach its potential audience. Rand holds that a writer should be an active intellectual leader of his time, but not passive follower riding any current and this is the essence of the Romantic school of literature which is vanished from the scene. It leaves her contemporary writers at the dead end. Naturalism believes that a writer must be a passive photographer or reporter who must transcribe uncritically whatever he observes around him. On the other hand, Romanticism says that a writer must present things, not as they are at any given moment, but, to quote Aristotle, as they might be and ought to be.

Rand feels that contemporary literature in general is philosophically immoral. Her favourite is Mickey Spillane because of his being a moralist. In a primitive form, that form of a detective novel, he presents the conflict of good and evil, in terms of black and white. He does not present nasty gray mixture of scoundrels indistinguishable on both sides. He presents an uncompromising conflict. As a writer, he is brilliant which Rand considers most important. Faulkner is a good stylist, but cannot be read practically which made her read very little of him. In *Anthem* (1938), Rand's protagonist declares: "It is my will which chooses, and the choice of my will is the only edict I respect." (94) It does not indicate that one's own will is the only law one must respect, but it means one's own rational judgment.

Rand says that during World War II, any free nation had the right to invade Nazi Germany and that any free nation today has the moral right, though not the duty, to invade Soviet Russia, Cuba, or any other slave pen. Martin Mo Quillan writers in his *Paul de Man* how by the start of 1942 the Nazis persecuted the Jews. In January, the Nazis made plans for the extermination of European Jews, including the 43000 Jews resident in Belgium. Germany had invaded the Soviet Union the previous year and America entered the war in December 1941. With the surrender of the German army at Stalingrad in February 1943, the course of the war turned. This is the final defeat of Germany. A dictatorship—a country that violates the rights of its own citizens—is an outlaw and can claim no rights.

Rand does not say that the United States should invade Cuba or the Soviet Union. She would only say that which the Soviet Union fears above all else: economic boycott would advocate a blockade of Cuba and an economic boycott of Soviet Russia; and one would see both those regimes collapse without the loss of a single American life. Rand rejects the idea that she is a conservative and she never describes her position in terms of negatives. She resents the modern method of never defining ideas, and lumping totally different people into a collective by means of derogatory terms. She detests Governor Rockefeller's smear tactics such as his refusal to identify specifically who and what he meant. What is wrong with them is that they don't seem to have any specific and clearly defined political philosophy.

She says that they still have a chance to reform their society or to put it on a better road so long as there is no censorship. Imposition of censorship is the sign that men should go on strike intellectually. By this she means one should not cooperate with the social system in any way whatsoever. She believes that ideas determine social trends that create or destroy social systems: "Rand's views on gender role are controversial. While her books champion men and women as intellectual equals, she thought that physiological differences between the sexes led to fundamental psychological differences that were the source of gender roles. Rand denied endorsing any kind of power difference between men and women. According to Rand, for a woman qua woman, the essence of femininity is hero-worship—the desire to look up to man. Rand's theory of sex is implied by her broader ethical and psychological theories. Far from being a debasing animal instinct, she believed that sex is the highest celebration of our greatest values." (http://www. encyclopedia.stateuniversity. com) Therefore, the right ideas, the right philosophy, should be advocated and spread.

In an interview with McCall's magazine, Rand states that women are competent to be President, but no rational women should seek that position; she later explains that it would be psychologically damaging to the woman. Rand holds that women had the right to choose an abortion since a child cannot acquire any rights until it is born. The living has preference over the not yet living or the unborn. Another controversial view of Rand is about homosexuality: "Rand stated at the Ford Hall Forum at Northeastern University in 1971, that homosexuality is immoral and disgusting. Specifically, she stated that there is a psychological immorality at the root of homosexuality because it involves psychological flaws, corruptions, errors, or unfortunate premises." (http://encyclopedia.stateuniversity.com) But Rand's views were in accordance with the views of the general public at that time.

Rand had an obvious passion for discussing ideas. She used to discuss regularly philosophy, economics and other topics with friends and even strangers. During the 1940s and early 1950s, most of these discussions were with prominent conservatives like Isabel Patterson and Henry Hazlitt. Nathaniel Branden writes about his own discussions with her in *My Years with Ayn Rand:* "Ayn's entire social existence was now confined—almost without exception—to the people in this room. The eldest person present, apart from Frank, was more than 20 years her junior. But we all had one attribute in common—absolute devotion to Ayn and her work." (152) In respect of race, Rand opposed ethnic and racial prejudice on moral grounds. In the essays like "Racism" and "Global Balkanization," she argues for the right of individuals and businesses to act without government intervention.

During the Second Red Scare, in 1947 Rand testifies and a friendly witness before the United States House Un-American Activities Committee where she says about the disparity between her personal experiences in the Soviet Union and the fanciful portrayal of it in the *Song of Russia*, a 1943 film. Rand argues that the film totally misrepresented the socio-economic conditions in the Soviet Union and portrayed life in the USSR as being much better than it actually is. As Robert Mayhew writes in *Ayn Rand and Song of Russia:* "She had been born in Russia and lived there until she was a young woman. And she testified that she had seen a picture MGM made called 'The Song of Russia' and that it showed Russian children smiling, which was a phenomenon she had never observed during her years in the Soviet Union." (164)

Rand asks if we have good reason, why we should not tell the truth. Mayhew explains this: "The ubiquitous smiling in 'Song of Russia' is an attempt to create the same thing the soviets wanted, a lie-picture of Russian people as happy, when in fact they were consciously following, or even knew about, this Soviet form of propaganda is beside the point. The goal—and morality—of the propaganda is sense approval of their system. And she was right." (165) When Rand was asked about her feelings on the effectiveness of their investigations, she described the process as futile. Within academic philosophy, Rand's ideas have found some recognition. Clemson University and the University of Texas at Austin have established chairs or centres which involve the study of Rand's views.

Her books continue to be widely read, with 25 million copies sold as of 2007, and 800,000 more sold each year. After the death of Rand, continued conflict within the objectivist movement led to establishment of independent organizations: 'In 1985, Leonard Peikoff, a surviving member of "The Collective" and Ayn Rand's legal heir, established. "The Ayn Rand Institute: The Centre for the Advancement of Objectivism" (ARI). The Ayn Rand Institute works to introduce young people to Ayn Rand's novels, to support scholarship and research based on her ideas, and to promote the principles of reason, rational self-interest, individual rights ad lissez-faire capitalism to the widest possible audience.' (http://www.encyclopedia.stateuniversity. com) In 2008 the Ayn Rand Centre for Individual Rights (ARC) in Washington, D.C. to specialize in issues of public policy was opened by The Ayn Rand Institute.

"Another schism in the movement occurred in 1989, when Objectivist David Kelley wrote *A Question of Sanction*, in which he argued for a more tolerant view in regard to moral judgment than that associated with such Ayn Rand writings as *The Cult of Moral Grayness*, and *How Does One Live a Rational Life in an Irrational Society?"* (http://www.encyclopedia.stateuniversity. com) As Peikoff denounced Kelley's views, he expelled Kelley from his organization, and Kelley founded The Institute for Objectivist Studies. Now it is known as The Atlas Society, which has its own website that is focused on attracting readers of Ayn Rand's fiction. The associated Objectivist Centre division deals mostly with academic ventures. The Atlas Society/Objectivist Centre also publishes *The New Individualist* (formerly *Navigator*).

Four of her books are placed on the 100 Best Novels list by a poll during 1998 and 1999 by Modern Library. *Atlas Shrugged* (1957), *The Fountainhead*, *Anthem* and *We the Living* (1936) were in first, second, seventh, and eighth place, respectively; and one on the 100 Best Nonfiction list (*The Virtue of Selfishness*, in first place), with books about Rand and her philosophy in third and sixth place. Ayn Rand also appears on 33 cent U.S. postage stamp, which debuted April 22, 1999 in New York City. The Ayn Rand Society, founded in 1987 and affiliated with the American Philosophical Association, has been active in sponsoring seminars. In 2006, Cambridge University Press Published *Ayn Rand's Normative Ethics: The Virtuous Egoist*. It is a volume on Rand's ethical theory written by ARI-affiliated scholar Tara Smith, a philosophy professor at the University of Texas at Austin. Rand's ideas and *Atlas Shrugged* in particular, are generally dismissed by Academic philosophers as preachy, and not original.

"Although Ayn Rand was born a century ago, and died a generation ago, her philosophy of Objectivism is among the most vital influences on contemporary American culture—and, increasingly, on contemporary global culture. That is all the more impressive in light of the rabid opposition that Rand's ideas initially drew from both the Right and Left. During her own lifetime, moreover, hostility to Rand's ideas seemed only to intensify as her detractors confronted Rand's uncompromising and often undiplomatic responses to criticism. But truth will be out, and with the passage of time, Rand's philosophy of Objectivism has proved its enduring insightfulness, thereby winning admiration even from many former sceptics." (http://www.objectivistcentre.com) The cultural impact of Ayn Rand began in 1943 with *The Fountainhead* and burst forth after the publication of *Atlas Shrugged*. This can be attributed mostly to the ways in which she differed from others on the Right and also because she presented her philosophy in the form of powerful novels.

The most famous of Rand's innovations is her defence of self-interest and in *Atlas Shrugged*, one of the chapters is titled "The Utopia of Greed." Late she would produce a collection of essays called *The Virtue of Selfishness*. Perhaps Rand dared critics to misunderstand. By depicting Rand's hero a blind pleasure-seeker, her critics ignored her insistence that one's true self-interest is rational, not a thoughtless whim moving from one superficial desire to another. She says: "Think deeply to feel deeply." "Many critics have tried to downplay Rand's importance and influence. William F. Buckley, for example, claims that he and his magazine *National Review* purged Rand from the conservative movement but Rand never considered herself to be a conservative. In 2003 Buckley published a novel, supposedly based on facts, of how the Objectivist movement was marginalized and consigned to irrelevance in the American political scene and society. The book was fiction through and through. That Rand's ideas have indeed become part of our culture is now indisputable." (http://objectivistcentre.com) This is proved by the fact that long after her death, her books continue to sell hundreds of thousands of copies every year. Huge posters of the cover of *Atlas Shrugged* hang in major bookstores.

It is a fact that Rand has changed the American political scene in no small measure: "The political policies she advocated are no longer considered as radical as they were in her own day. For example, before most free market advocates imagined it possible, Rand envisioned shutting down entire government agencies, especially those that had to do with controlling the economy. Today, the oldest regulatory agency, the Interstate Commerce Commission, has ceased to exist, along with most government regulations of the airline and trucking industries." (http://objectivistcentre.com) Several individuals heavily influenced by Ayn Rand including Bob Poole, a regulatory expert who later became known as the father of the privatization movement, founded the *Reason* magazine. The founders of Cato Institute Edward Crane and David Boaz are also Rand admirers.

When Steve Moore, a member of the *Wall Street Journal*'s editorial page, was asked, by which book he was influenced in his early years, his answer was *Atlas Shrugged*. A long-time senior editor at the *Readers' Digest* Howard Dickman is an Objectivist who recently joined Moore on the editorial staff of the Journal. Many government officials are admirers of Rand: "The most famous is recently retired Federal Reserve Chairman Alan Greenspan, an early associate and lifelong friend of Rand who wrote and lectured under her auspices during the 1960s. Today, the highest-ranking government official who has been influenced by Ayn Rand may be Supreme Court Associate Justice Clarence Thomas." (http://www.objectivistcentre.com) He can quote his favourite parts of *Atlas Shrugged* from memory. Congressman Edward Royce, Republican of California, says that Ayn Rand is one of the three thinkers who influenced him early. The other two were F.A. Hayek and H.L. Mencken.

Many of those officials may not be Objectivists, and most of them reject Rand's atheism, but all have taken something from her. Rand's influence does not stop at America. For example, the head of Junior Achievement in Argentina, Eduardo Marty, has been a long-time admirer of Rand and he facilitated new translation of her works into Spanish. Andrei Illarionov, until recently a top economic advisor to Russian President Vladimir Putin, keeps *Atlas Shrugged*, a Russian language version, in his office. In India too, interest in Rand is thriving. The major figures in its Bollywood film industry are fans of Rand. By using Rand's name as an epithet, the critics of freedom, personal responsibility, and a rational culture demonstrate Rand's influence. Rand's works have gained a significant place in the literature of the U.S. The first postcolonial society to develop a national literature was the U.S.

Rand approves of certain philosophical positions, including some of Baruch Spinoza and St. Thomas Aquinas. She also respected Brand Blanshard, the 20th Century American rationalist. Like Rand, Blanshard believed that there had been no period in the past two thousand years when both reason and rationality have undergone a bombardment so varied, so competent, so massive and sustained in the last half-century: "Rand's greatest philosophy reflects an Aristotelian epistemology and metaphysics—both Aristotle and Rand argued that there exists an objective reality that is independent of mind and that is capable of being known. Although

Rand was ultimately critical of Aristotle's ethics, others have noted that her egoistic ethics is of the eudemonistic type, close to Aristotle's own, a system of guidelines required by human beings to live their lives successfully, to flourish, to survive as man qua man. Her philosophy diverges from Aristotle's by considering essences as epistemological and contextual instead of as metaphysical. She envisions Aristotle as a philosophical intuitivist who declared the existence of essences within concretes." (http://www.encyclopedia.stateuniversity. com)

Aristotle, states Rius in *Max for Beginners* (1977), found Plato's ideas ridiculous. He considered the senses as the only sources of truth: "His teachings about ethics were that the goal of life was happiness. So he admitted that anyone lucky enough to have money or power or humour was bound to be happy." (52) Ayn Rand agreed with John Locke, when he conceptualized the ideas that individuals own themselves, have a right to the products of their own labour. Rand admired the work of Friedrich Nietzsche in her early life, and she shared Nietzsche's reverence for human potential and his loathing of Christianity and the philosophy of Immanuel Kant. But eventually, she became critical of his philosophy as it emphasizes emotion over reason. Certain aspects of Nietzsche's views are exemplified in the characters from *The Night of January 16th Bjorn Faulkner and Karen Andre*.

In *We the Living*, there is a passage which Rand has omitted from the 1959 reprint. In it, the heroine entertains (though finally rejects) sentiments that can be attributed to Nietzsche about the justice of sacrificing the weak for the strong. In *The Fountainhead*, the destruction of Gail Wynand is an example of her later view, a rejection of Nietzsche that the great cannot succeed by sacrificing the masses. Rand disagrees with many of Nietzsche's ideas, but still the introduction of the 25th anniversary edition of *The Fountainhead* concludes with Nietzsche's statement that the noble soul has reverence for itself. Rand also strongly opposes the philosophy of Immanuel Kant, Hegel's great predecessor. Hegel is the Campion of an idealist philosophy which arose as the exact opposite of 17th century materialist philosophy. His most liked about work is the *Critique of Pure Reason*.

As Rius in his *Marx for Beginners* says, Hegel seeks to justify the idea of god. Kant separates science from religion. Hegel wants to make religion into a science. He was an idealist. For him the essence of reality is not material, but spiritual or mental and therefore independent and thus free: "Hegel's advice to any worker exploited by his boss would be: Don't worry yourself about material oppression, but only about the 'spiritual' kind. By obeying the state (God's representation on earth) you will find happiness and freedom of the Spirit)" (Rius, 7).

On almost every philosophical issue, Rand disagreed with Kant and this divergence is greatest in metaphysics and epistemology. Kant says that the phenomenal world is not real because reality perceived by man's mind is a distortion. Kant holds that man's basic concepts are not derived from experience of reality. They come from an automat of system of filters in his consciousness labelled categories and forms of perception which impose their own design on his perception of the external world and make him incapable of perceiving it in any manner other than the one which he perceived. According to Kant this proves that man's concepts are only a collective delusion which no one has the power to escape. His argument amounts to a negation, not only of man's consciousness, but of consciousness. The essence of his argument is that man is blind because he has eyes, deaf, because he has ears, deluded, because he has a mind and the things he perceives do not exist, because he perceives them.

In contrast, Rand believed that man can have full, direct awareness of reality. She rejects Kant's idea that morality has nothing to do with happiness. Kant says that an action is moral only if one has no desire to perform it, but performs it out of a sense of duty and derives no benefit, either material or spiritual, out of it. For Kant a benefit destroys the moral value of an action. According to Rand, Kant is the chief destroyer of the modern world and his philosophical system, Objectivism embraces objective reality in metaphysics, reason in epistemology, and rational egoism in ethics.

The Passion of Ayn Rand , a 1986 bestselling biography demonstrates her continuing influence on people both in America and abroad. Ayn Rand, one of the few systematic philosophers who have used imaginative literature to develop their ideas, is the founder of the Objectivist school of philosophy.

By the late Sixties, Rand has become an international figure with a devoted following which remains to this day. Ayn Rand served as editor-in-chief of *The Objectivist*, a monthly journal from 1962 to 1971 which was devoted to the propagation of her philosophy. After the publication of *The Objectivist* ceased, she began *The Ayn Rand Letter* which she continued until 1976. It is said that she had her first literary success with the sale of her screenplay *Red Pawn* in 1932 to Universal Studios: Von Sternberg later considered it for Dietrich, but Russian scenarios were out of favour and the project was dropped. Then in 1934, Rand wrote the play *The Night of January 16th* which was produced on Broadway. The play was a courtroom drama in which a jury chosen from the audience decided the verdict, leading to one of two possible endings. In 1936, Rand published the novel *We the Living*. As Stephen Cox, at The Objectivist Centre, observed *We the Living* was published at the height of Russian socialism's popularity among leaders of American opinion.

Rand then wrote the short novel *Anthem*. It is a novella in the style of the psychological surrealism of Anna Kavan or Anais Nin. Like *A Canticle for Liebowitz* this story takes place in the future. In order to complete *Atlas Shrugged* Rand returned to New York. *Atlas Shrugged* took thirteen years for her to research and write. As predicted its publication created a storm of controversy which never abated in her lifetime, and it continues to this day. *The Ayn Rand Lexicon: Objectivism from A to Z* (1986) is an invaluable compilation of quotations from Rand, collected from her essays, fiction, and lectures, on issues and concepts as diverse as the Min-Body Dichotomy and Implicit Knowledge. Entries are organized and cross-referenced according to concepts of philosophy, psychology, and economics and includes general topics as well. Though Rand's *We the Living* is basically post-Tolstoyan, it is developed in her own direction. After this novel, Rand's work moves more towards the novel of ideas, reaches a peak of quality in *The Fountainhead*, then becomes strongly, overtly, and perhaps less artistically didactic in *Atlas Shrugged*.

The Fountainhead is Rand's best and most approachable novel. Through the book had mixed reviews, it was praised by some critics like Lorine Pruette. Pruette, writing for the *New York Times Books Review*, observed that Rand is a writer of great power, and she compared the novel to such classics as Thomas Mann's *The Magic Mountain* and Henrik Ibsen's *The Master Builder*. *The Fountainhead* was the only novel of ideas written by an American woman that she could recall. Inspired by the death of the "Match King," Ivar Krueger Rand wrote a play *Night of January 16th*. The play was first published in 1934 and it centred on a murder trial. It was a hit of the 1935-36 Broadway season. The play deals with issues of a man's ability to regard oneself as important and exist in a society where moral decay is prevalent. The story is about the issue of love, loyalty and betrayal. Specifically, what is interesting is a feature of the play which picks members of the audience to take on the role of jury members each night. Depending on whether the Jury finds the defendant of the case guilty or not guilty, the play would have different endings.

She began to publish and edit a newsletter, *The Objectivist Newsletter* (name later changed to *The Objectivist* and *The Ayn Rand Letter*). This provided her with a continuing venue to expand on her philosophy of self-interest. Rand published six fiction books and plays and six non-fiction works. The major non-fiction works she produced during this time are: *For the New Intellectual* (1961); *The Virtue of Selfishness: A New Concept of Egoism* (1964); *Capitalism: The Unknown Ideal* (1966); *The Romantic Manifesto: A Philosophy of Literature* (1969); *The New Left: The Anti-Industrial Revolution* (1971); and *Philosophy: Who Needs It* (1982). *For the New Intellectual* (1961) is Rand's own collection of significant philosophical passages from her novels and earlier writings. This is a collection useful for understanding Rand, but Rand's reputation is damaged by the title essay. In that essay Rand broadly labels numerous historical philosophers as mystics, Attilas, and witch doctors. Yet, she shows no sign of knowing the slightest thing about any of these phenomena.

The Virtue of Selfishness is a provocative title. It is an equally provocative thesis about ethics. Traditional ethics has always been suspicious of self-interest, praising acts that are selfless and calling the acts that are motivated by self interest immoral. According to Rand, self-interest if it is rightly understood is to see oneself as an end in oneself. *Capitalism: The Unknown Ideal* has articles by Rand and her approved associates. It is Rand's best statement of her political and economic ideas, and the ideas of her followers that apparently had her blessing. *The Romantic Manifesto* is essays by Rand on her aesthetics. Rand advocated Romanticism in artistic work seriously concerned with the struggle for lofty values. It can be considered one of the most provocative artistic manifestoes of the 20th century. The first four essays of this volume constitute the core of Rand's theory of art, which is examined in depth in *What Art Is* by Louis Torres and Michelle Marder Kamhi. The remaining essays are about her philosophy of literature and her analysis of contemporary popular culture.

Voice of Reason (1990) is an excellent collection of essays that should be included in the library of every fan of Objectivism. This book contains several great essays by Ayn Rand, which include her thoughts on abortion, the Apollo missions, Vietnam and working for the government. This collection also includes several insightful higher level philosophical essays including the topic: "Who is the Final Authority in Ethics?" where Ayn Rand clarifies that morality ultimately stems from facts of reality, not from a religious, political or legal authority "The Sanction of the Victims" where Ayn Rand emphasizes the importance of never voluntarily relinquishing any of our rights or accepting unearned guilt. I suppose the contributions in this volume that are not by Rand are also incredibly valuable.

The New Left: The Anti-Industrial Revolution is Rand's views against New Left sloppy anti-industrial thinking. It consists mainly of reprints from her magazine *The Objectivist*. In 1998 under the title *Return of the Primitive: The Anti-Industrial Revolution*, the second expanded edition with additional essays by Rand and Peter Schwartz was published. Rand comes out in favour of polluting smokestack industrialism. Still, Rand scores many excellent points against the sloppy thinkers of the 1960s. *An Introduction To Epistemology* (1979) is an expansion of articles originally published in *The Objectivist* in 1966-67; the first edition was published in 1977. The book includes an analysis of concept-formation and a discussion of principles of definition. Rand presented her new theory of concepts and her solution to the age-old problem of universals. Her theory holds that concepts (abstract ideas) are classifications of existents that possess commensurable characteristics. She holds things that are similar have the same characteristic, but in different measure or degree. After seeing many links between concepts and mathematics, her theory of concepts uses such mathematical terms as unit, measurement, and common denominator.

The Passion of Ayn Rand (1986) is the only full-length life of Rand available. It is balanced and definitive. Barbara Branden was the wife of Nathaniel Branden and an intimate of Rand. Nathaniel first met Rand in person in 1950. Branden describes it in *Many Years with Ayn Rand*: "I met her a month before I turned twenty. She was forty five. I was studying psychology, at UCLA. She was already famous as the author of *The Fountainhead* and was now engaged in writing a new novel, *Atlas Shrugged*, which would make her still more famous—and more controversial—not only as a novelist but also as a philosopher." (1) After a name change and marriage, the Brandens went on to found the Nathaniel Branden Institute to deliver lectures on Rand's ideas. In 1962, Rand and Nathaniel Branden began co-publishing *The Objectivist Newsletter* (later *The Objectivist*), with Barbara Branden as the managing editor.

In 1968, Rand publicly broke all ties with the Brandens. She accused Nathaniel of deliberate deception of several persons, failing to keep up with his duties at *The Objectivist* and financial impropriety regarding loans of money from *The Objectivist* to Nathaniel Branden Institute. Branden explains it in *My Years with Ayn Rand*: "At the time of break, neither she nor I (for different reasons) chose to disclose to the world its actual cause. In her case, she chose to withhold the truth even from her closest friends." (1) Branden is a therapist and author of a number of books on psychology and how to improve one's own self-esteem. His books include *The Psychology of Self-Esteem, Honouring the Self, The Six Pillars of Self-Esteem* and *Taking Responsibility*. Barbara Branden admired and respected Rand and she tells Rand's story sympathetically.

Nathaniel Branden repudiated this book in the 1970s. She gave a radically incomplete picture of its subject just like Andre Maurois' *Ariel, ou La Vie de Shelley*, but it was very enjoyable. One feels that life should be like this. Branden was a close intellectual soul mate to Rand. In 1999, he reissued and altered the book under the title *My Years with Ayn Rand* from Jossey-Bass Publishers in San Francisco. The volume of *Journals of Ayn Rand* (1997) does not contain direct relevance to Rand's philosophy of art. It offers much illuminating material about her fiction and the development of her overall philosophy. These letters shed much light on Rand's character, personality, and thought. *The Early Ayn Rand* (1984) was a collection which includes the fiction Rand never sold, the synopsis of an original 1932 screenplay, *Red Pawn*. It also contains unpublished and yet charming short stories which she wrote in the late 1920s and early 1930s while she was still learning English, and also mature works such as the stage plays *Think Twice and Ideal* and scenes cut from the published edition of *The Fountainhead*. She wrote and narrated another short story about the functioning of an artist's creative process in her *The Simplest Thing in the World*.

During her lifetime, three screen plays of Rand were produced: *Love Letters* (1945), an adaptation of a novel by Christopher Massie; *You Came Along* (1945), Rand credited as a co-writer for revising a script originally written by Robert Smith. Both were made into films in 1945. *The Fountainhead* (1949) is an adaptation of her novel. In addition to these three, Rand also worked on the screenplay for *The Conspirators*. It is said that Rand also began unproduced screenplays for four other movies. One was called Red Pawn. Three other were written while she was under contract with

Hal Wallis in the 1940s. One is *The Crying Sisters*, based on a novel by Mabel Seeley and the other one is *House of Mist*, based on a novel by Maria Luisa Bombal. The third is *Top Secret*, an original script about the development of the atomic bomb. Most of her books including *We the Living* and *The Fountainhead* are made into films. A film adaptation of *Atlas Shrugged* is pre-production as of early 2008, with Angelina Jolie cast in the role of Dagny Taggart.

In 1999, *The Passion of Ayn Rand*, an independent film about her life, was made starring Helen Mirren as Ayn Rand, Eric Stoltz, Julie Delpy and Peter Fonda. This film was based on Barbara Branden's book. Rand presented her theory of aesthetics more fully in her 1969 book, *The Romantic Manifesto: A Philosophy of Literature*. Tim Woods in his *Beginning Post Modernism* writes how Somer Brodribb in her *Nothing Mat(t)ers: A Feminist Critique of Post Modernism* produced an excoriating critique of attempts to ally feminism with postmodernism, which she perceives as an incorporation of feminism within a masculinist theory. By neglecting Rand, feminists have lost some substantial values. The most obvious is an integrated philosophy on which they found their theories. Rand's female heroes, especially Dagny Taggart who succeeds romantically as well as in the business world, are unrivalled in their inspirational power for women.

Rand says that when women were regarded exclusively as mothers, there was no need to make them into heroes. Their power of giving life is more than sufficient and no heroically individual achievement was expected of them. But Dagny Taggart is heroically individual and a productive achiever. Michelson claims that Dagny Taggart is the first fully individuated woman in Western epic literature. She acts like the men of previous epics and so Dagny Taggart is as great a value as feminists could have. Though she is a liberated woman who competes with men in the commercial sphere, she does not compete with men as such. Objectivist psychological theories have rarely sought differences between men and women, which is certainly an improvement over the neo-Freudianism of the feminine mystique. Therefore, feminism can gain from Objectivist morality and psychology from Rand's fiction. The two male protagonists, Leo and Andrei in *We the Living* show opposed character traits that the heroine, Kira, transcends. From a feminist perspective, these are interesting since Rand's patterns of synthesis centre on her female protagonist, rather than on her two male characters that remain dyadic and fractured.

In Rand's second novel *The Fountainhead*, the skyscrapers, supermodels, and strange attractors and the architecture are an instance of an information-age aesthetic. In the information age, what is beautiful will be what works, and what works will be beautiful, Roark's buildings are an example of this new, harmonious approach. Rand's architectural aesthetic can be compared with the aesthetic views of Naomi Wolf, whose first book, *The Beauty Myth*, was an attack on the fashion and modelling industries. This replicates the beauty and utility dichotomy that Rand had broken down and in the information age, that is out-of date. Thus, Rand provides a superior aesthetic for feminists in the information age. Rand's objection to a woman becoming a president is that she wants to look up to a man, but the president cannot look up because all others are his inferiors.

She managed to alienate, both sides of the political spectrum in her philosophical pronunciations. It is surprising that she had a great deal of satisfaction in teaching. But in novelist Erika Holzer's new book *Ayn Rand: My Fiction-Writing Teacher* (2005), we find another facet of Rand's personality, i.e. a caring mentor and a scrupulous tutor. Ms. Holzer's memoir is distinctive in that she has taken her relationship with Ayn Rand, Ms. Rand's teaching skills, and the writing of her two novels. Erika Holzer's two novels were both well received. Her first novel, *Double Crossing* (1920), focused on the theme of human rights and it was written during the miasmatic period of détente. Her second novel, *Eye for an Eye* (1993) was so popular that Paramount Pictures bought the rights and made a movie version.

In *Atlas Shrugged*, Ayn Rand glorified the right of individuals to live entirely for their own interest. Rand's message was attacked by intellectuals who argued that individuals should also work in the service of others. But the book attracted a number of fans and some of them are top corporate executives, who dared not speak of its impact except in private. One of Rand's most famous devotees, the former chairman of the Federal Reserve Alan Greenspan calls it complete. When Mr. Greenspan met Rand in the 1950s he was 25 and working as an economic forecaster. He was very much attracted to her moral defence of capitalism. He eventually became a lecturer for the Nathaniel Branden Institute and a contributor of articles to *The Objectivist Newsletter*. In 1977, he received Ph.D. in economics from New York University.

Greenspan served on various commissions and councils for President Nixon, Ford and Reagan and in 1987, he was appointed by Reagan to be chairman of the Federal Reserve Board. By succeeding presidents he was repeatedly reappointed to this position until his retirement in early 2006. However, Rand's idea of the virtue of selfishness is a harsh phrase for the Buddhist idea that we have to take care of ourselves. Some business leaders may be unsettled by the idea that the only thing members of the leadership class have in common is their success. James M. Kilts, who led turnarounds at Gillette, Nabisco and Kraft, find her writing reassuring because it makes success seem rational. John P. Stack is one of the business executives who have taken Rand's ideas to heart. He was chief executive of Springfield Remanufacturing Company and also created an "open book" company in which employees were transparently working in their own interest. Mr. Stack says his free market replaced all that with rational behaviour.

A machinist knew the cost of slacking off exactly as he knew what his working hour contributed to the bottom line. Mr. Stack said that this was a manifestation of the philosophy of objectivism in *Atlas Shrugged*. People are guided by reason and self-interest. Rand draws out the inner self within us. The book stresses the importance of growing and bettering ourselves without hindering other people. The continuing flow of works by and about Rand is a proof of a virtual renaissance in Rand scholarship. The publication of two new books is the evidence of this growth in Rand studies.

Rand's *Russian Writings on Hollywood* (1990), which features translations of Rand's work on the American cinema, is the first official release from the *Ayn Rand Archives*.

The books, published in 1925 in Leningrad and Moscow under the name, A. Rosenbaum, opens with a facsimile and translation of Rand's *Pola Negri*. This monograph was part of a series about movie stars. Rand also wrote *Hollywood: American City of Movies* captivated by the power of the American cinema. Without Rand's permission it was published in St. Petersburg in 1926, after her American emigration. In this book, Rand examines the origins of the Hollywood studios, their intense competition and most prominent producers, directors, and stars, but remains critical of Hollywood's scenarists, who are more likely to adapt existing works. The other one *Ayn Rand's Movie Diary* is a compendium of the author's ratings of various films, with their actors and directors noted. The diary, begun in 1922, was copied by her sister Nora and mailed to Rand approximately one month after her emigration.

Upto March 1929, Rand continued the diary and provided an almost daily rendering of her film-viewing activities, including notations on the movie houses she visited. She eventually worked with some of her favourite actors, including Joseph Schildkraut, who apparently flirted with her on the set of *The King of Kings* and Walter Pidgeon, who would star in the Broadway production of *Night of January 16th*. Some critics criticize Rand's rating of any particular film, for example, her not even 0 grade for Lon Chaney's classic *Phantom of the Opera*. But she certainly recognizes the greatness of some of the most important silent films ever made, for example *The Indian Tomb*, *The Isle of Lost Ships*, *Intolerance*, *Ben-Hur*, *The Big Parade* and *Metropolis*. The book concludes with a ranking of Rand's favourite actors, headed by Conrad Veidt and Gary Cooper who would eventually portray Howard Roark in the film version of *The Fountainhead* and her favourite actresses, headed by Greta Garbo and Pola Negri.

Russian Writings on Hollywood provides some interesting research possibilities for scholars. It gives Rand's life-long fascination with film, a book-length scholarly examination of the impact of the cinema on her fiction and overall aesthetic seems long overdue. It is rightly pointed out; "Although Rand's influence has been greatest in the United States, she has a growing international following. Her books were international bestsellers, and they continue to sell in large numbers. For example, *Atlas Shrugged* is consistently in the top few hundred bestsellers at Amazon.com; 185,000 copies were sold in 2007, fifty years after it was first published. Many individuals have acknowledged that Rand significantly influenced their lives, including Harry Binswanger, Nathaniel Branden, Barbara Branden, Chris Cox, Allan Gotthelf, David Kelly, Leonard Peikoff, Ronald Reagan, Tara Smith, Margaret Thatcher, Vine Vaughn, Jimmy Wales, and many others. Rand's philosophy of Objectivism continues to influence works in the arts, business and science." (http://www.encyclopedia.stateuniversity.com)

The Demise of Communist Tyranny
We the Living

We the Living, Ayn Rand's first novel, is a story about a young woman who never gives up on herself, the people she loves, and her dreams. One cannot decide who would be better suited to Kira: Leo because of her love for him and Andrei because of his love for her. The novel was published in 1936, reissued by Random House in 1959, and 400,000 paperback copies were issued by NAL in 1960. Rand is popular with her later novels, *The Fountainhead and Atlas Shrugged*. From internal evidence, one would guess her to be a middle-class White Russian living in exile in America. *We the Living* is boldly a counter-revolutionary novel and it may annoy the readers Reddish sympathies. She writes, often graphically, about the life in Leningrad in the nineteen twenties. She wishes to show the corruption of the communism as she witnessed in Russia.

Barbara Branden illustrates about Rand in *The Passion of Ayn Rand:* "The events seething in the world outside her barely penetrated Alice's consciousness in the years from 1914 to 1916. Children should not know about the terrible carnage in the world, her protective parents believed, the war rarely was discussed in the presence of The Rosenbaum children; nor were they permitted to read newspapers. But perhaps more relevantly, her major focus continued to be on her writing. 'I was writing in every spare moment. I felt I was preparing for the future, for the world I would enter when I grew up.' Nothing could be allowed to distract her from the dedicated singleness of purpose that was to guide her life for the next forty years" (16) Hence, *We the Living* is a story of life in post-revolutionary Russia.

Rand lived for twenty one years under the Soviets: "The novel is unique in that it displays the talents of a younger Rand pointing out the vagaries of socialism without saying on the soapbox for twenty pages at a time. Largely based on her childhood and young adulthood in Soviet Russia, Rand claims that the book's female protagonist, Kira Argounova, is 'the closest to an autobiography that my readers will find . . . the events of her life are not mine, but her ideals and philosophies are.' (http://www.everything2.com)

The novel starts with a group of pale faces and greasy overcoats waiting for the train. Kira Argounova enters Petrograd on the threshold of a box car. Kira is the centre of the passengers' attention. For lack of space her feet rest on her father, Alexander Dimitrievitch Argounova's lap. Crushed against his elbow, Galina Petrovna, his wife manages to hold her body erect. Lydia, their eldest daughter, has to sit in the aisle.

Four years ago, the Argounov family left Petrograd when their textile factory was nationalized in the name of people. The leave for Crimea. The year nineteen twenty-one sees the end of the struggle of Revolution in Russia. The red banner rises. In 1922, the family takes the train back to Petrograd to start life all over again. Kira is eighteen years old and Lydia, twenty-eight. People around Kira speak about Petrograd, New Economic Policy (NEP) and private stores. A crowd awaits the train in Petrograd. She touches the boards of the platform in Petrograd. Station buildings are disinfected against the diseases like cholera that pour into the city. The Argounov's family crowds into one cab and turns into the Nevsky Prospect. Petrograd has seen five years of revolution. Four of the years have closed its every artery and every store in the name of nationalization. The state's NEP allows small private stores to reopen timidly. Galina has a sister, Maria Petrovna.

When they reach her house, Maria is surprised to see them and embraces Galina. She has always been the beauty of the family. Now, she looks older than Galina. Galina's niece, Irina, a girl of eighteen, comes flying into anteroom and her sister, Asia waddles in slowly. Galina kisses them and her brother-in-law, Vasili Ivanovitch. Before the revolution, Vasili has owned a prosperous fur business. Galina sees the changes in the dining room. The rusty nails on the wall show the places where old paintings have hung.

Victor, Vasili's son arrives. Victor is studying Electrical Engineering in the Institute of Technology. Alexander announces that he will open a store. Vasili says gloomily that it is only until the government squashes it under its heel. But Victor says: "The days of confiscations are past. The Soviet government has a most progressive policy outlined." (39)

Maria asks about the plans of the girls. Lydia says that she is not going to study as too much education is unfeminine. Kira answers calmly that she will go to the Technological Institute. Victor remarks that her attitude is antisocial. She should be useful to society in a more feminine capacity. Victor says that society is a stupendous whole. Kira replies that if he writes a whole line of zeroes, it is still—nothing. Kira stands before the official to get the Soviet passport. It is a citizen's permit to live. It is called Labour book, for labour and life are considered synonyms. The official holds a little book. On the clean page he writes the details of Kira. Her body is slender. Through any garment she wears, the unseen presence of her body makes her look undressed. It seems that the words she says are ruled by the will of her body so that her spirit seems physical and her body spiritual.

Kira is born in Petrograd on April 11, 1904 in the gray granite house on Kamenostrovsky. While her parents are visiting Nice and Vienna, she is left alone in the wild freedom of the rocky hill: "The first thing that Kira learned about life and the first thing that her elders learned, dismayed, about Kira, was the joy of being alone." (46) Kira has strange eyebrows. She can lift them in such a mocking smile while her lips remain motionless that the young men's intentions freeze at the very roots. The family shrugs at Kira's feelings. She has some feelings for eating soup without salt and discovering a snail on her bare leg and for young men who plead.

Kira has never been in love. The only hero she has known is a Viking whose story she has read as a child and who walks through life, breaking barriers and reaping victories. Kira seldom reads a newspaper and seldom laughs. Such has been Kira's entrance into life: "Kira Argounov entered it with the sword of a Viking pointing the way and an operetta tune for a battle march." (51) The official applies his rubber stamp on the last page. It bears a globe overshadowed by a crossed sickle and hammer. He hands her the book. Across the first page is printed the slogan, 'Proletarians of the world, unite!' Alexander opens a textile store. Kira has been admitted to the Technological Institute.

On the evening of October tenth, Victor takes Kira up to summer garden. There he tries to kiss her. But she gets herself free from him and starts walking alone. She sees a man taking a woman's hand and disappearing through a glass door. She understands where she is and starts hurriedly. Then she stops as she finds a tall man. His mouth is calm, severe and contemptuous, as that of an ancient chieftain who can order men to die. He greets her and takes her with him. They go to a little garden where he understands that she is not a street woman but a respectable girl. She comes to know that he is Leo, a fugitive and is going away at dawn. He says that he will meet her there again in a month on November tenth, if he can still enter the city.

In the evenings, Kira walks home from the Institute. The first question Galina asks is if she has got the bread as she is the only one in the family with a bread card. But Kira forgets to bring it. In the student's co-operative, Kira has waited for an hour to get the bread. A young woman next to Kira has a red kerchief tied over hair, eyes wide apart in a round face, thin lips drawn together with so obvious and fierce determination that they seem weak. She is Sonia who says: "We the new women who are ambitious to have a useful career, to take our place beside the men in the productive toil of the world—instead of the old kitchen drudgery—we must stick together." (69) An amphitheatre of crowded beeches rises like a dam. A young speaker gives his speech that sciences is a weapon of the class struggle and their sole aim in entering the Red Technological Institute is the vanguard of Proletarian Culture and Construction. The students call one another 'comrade'. Comrade Syerov is elected.

Kira remarks that when the traces of their republic are disinfected from history that will make a glorious funeral march. Then a man's hand grasps Kira's wrist and advises to be careful. She stares up into his gray eyes that look like the eyes of a tamed tiger, but she is not sure whether it is tamed or not. The first thing Kira hears when she rings Maria's door bell is her cough. It is because of the wood that does not burn. Vasili says that Europe is doing things and things will change soon. Maria sighs as she is used to listen to his words about the salvation coming for five years, but it never comes. He feels that the past is dead, but there is always a future. A girl's laughter is heard and Vasili says that she is Vava, Victor's friend. On November tenth, Kira meets Leo. She tells him about his future; about the steel skeletons she is going to build, about the glass skyscraper and aluminum bridge. He says that he is learning to desire something.

Then they depart with a promise to meet on December tenth. Kira is listening to a lecture at the Institute. A man enters the auditorium by mistake. Sonia asks her if she does not feel ashamed for walking with the reddest communist, Andrei Taganov. Kira replies that she is afraid that she may corrupt him. Andrei tells Kira that communists never do anything except what they have to do. But he is a very poor communist that he always does what he wants to do. Andrei has been in the Red Army; she frowns at his battles, but smiles with admiration at the scar on his forehead. He invites her to the opera, he holds her hand: "Their eyes held each other longer than their hands, in a silent, bewildering understanding." (91-92)

On December second, Kira suddenly finds Leo in a dark corner. As they walk down the steep, he tells her that he loves her. She does not know what he is saying, but she knows their union. In the room of the Communist Cell, Pavel asks Kira about the man at the gate with her. She says that she does not know him and he just asks the way to Sudovaia Street. In Soviet Russia it is very serious to protect counter revolutionaries. Andrei comes in and sends her away. In 1915, Andrei's name is in the list of a party. In October, 1917, when the party, whose membership cards Andrei and Pavel carry, seizes the power, they are both in the streets. Alexander's Navy soap is a failure. Their new patron suggests them to pack crystals and tablets. Maria visits them. She worries about Victor's bringing communists into the house.

Kira meets Leo. He tells her that he is going away to Germany. If they are caught, they may get death sentence. Kira goes with him. In his cabin, he says about his aunt in Berlin, who hates him. When Kira awakens in the morning, a sailor opens the door. Leo tells him that she has nothing to do with it and he has kidnapped her. Their leader, Timoshenko tells Kira to go away. Later when Kira goes to him, he asks her not to worry that Leo will be back. On the evening of the fourth day of her return, Leo takes Kira to his house. Leo also has a job. He translates books from English, German and French. It pays well, but after many deductions for the Red Air and so on. Kira meets Andrei at the Institute. He does not know about her relation with Leo. Communists awaken fear in her. It is not a fear of their guns, but she feels as if she were alone in the presence of a beast, its jaws gaping.

With Andrei she feels like a child appealing to a guiding hand. The first signs of spring in Petrograd are tears and smiles. The men smile, but the houses drop tears. England has treacherous designs on the republic workers and peasants. Kira comes to know that she is sick and nothing is left with them as the saccharine man gets arrested. Kira give that bread to Irina saying that they can get it from a private store. Vava invites Kira to a little party. Parties are rare in Petrograd in 1923. In the party, an anaemic girl says that abroad, they don't have co-operatives. The girl is afraid of the reduction of staffs. In the summer, Petrograd is a furnace. Whenever they can Kira and Leo go away for a day in the country. They walk hand in hand in the stripes of sun and pine shadows. Galina has made a bold decision and takes up the job of teaching in a school. Leo comes home earlier than usual. He tells Kira that he is fired for not being social-minded. She offers bread for dinner saying that she has eaten it already. Leo tears next week's coupon saying to Kira that he gets a two weeks' ration. So that Kira will eat that entire piece.

Leo gets a job for two days, cleaning the street and Kira for lettering cardboard inscriptions. They have one goal to remember:

to graduate. A girl comes with an order from the Gilotdel, giving "citizen Mania Lovrova" the right to occupy a room in their apartment. They have to forego their room. Mariana has continuous visitors. She is a student of the University Rabfac. Later, Marina tells Kira that she is pregnant by Aleshka Rilenko. Kira meets Andrei at the Institute. They take dinner. When he offers her some money, she thinks of Leo at home and takes it. Kira goes to the Marxist Club of the House of the Peasant and reads her thesis: "Leninism is Marxism adapted to Russian reality" (205) She walks home saying to herself that it is a war and she does not give up.

The notice board directs all students to receive questionnaires, fill them out and return them to the Purging Committee. If they are of bourgeois descent or if their parents have been wealthy, they are still a class enemy, though they are starving. Lately Leo has been drinking. She warns him to take care of his health. When Kira meets Vasili, she does not ask whether Irina and Victor have been expelled: "As after an earthquake, all were looking around cautiously, counting the victims, afraid to ask questions." (214) Irina tells Kira that Victor is such a talented young man that he is not expelled as he joins the All-Union Communist Party. Irina calls on Kira. As she opens the door without knocking, she finds Marisha and Victor together. Swallowing tears, she walks towards Kira's room. Kira is not at home, but Leo is.

As Kira comes home, she finds Vava clasped in Leo's arms. Kira does not ask anything. She comes to know from the doctor that Leo has tuberculosis. It is a fatal disease in Russia. She is convinced that the State sanatoriums are locked to Leo. She sees Andrei at the Institute. But he avoids her. On the first day of autumn, as Kira expects, when a reduction of staffs comes, she sees her name among those dismissed as antisocial element. It is Kira's last chance to send Leo to South and meets Andrei. He confesses his crime that he loves her and wants her. She whispers trembling that she has been in love with him too, but it should be kept very secret. Leo's place is reserved in a private sanatorium in Yalta. She explains she has got money from her uncle in Budapest. Leo is on train. When the train moves, something beyond terror which is not a human feeling seizes her.

The war makes St. Petersburg into Petrograd; the revolution makes it Leningrad. Petrograd is not born; it is created. It is the work of man. It is a coincidence that in the language of the Russians, Moscow is "she," while Petrograd has ever been "he." Andrei gives his salary to Kira and lives in District Club of the All-Union Communist Party which is given to him free of rent. She presents him a toy. It is a glass tube that ends in a bulb filled with a red liquid in which a little black figure floats, trembling. She says it is called American Resident. Kira's room has suddenly grown empty: "There had been nights when she buried her head under the blanket and her face in the pillow, as if trying to escape from her own body, a body with the touch of a stranger's hands—in the bed that had been Leo's." (251)

Irina introduces Kira to a tall husky young man, Sasha Charnov who has been thrown out of University for trying to think in a country of free thought. In the morning, Kira has to go to work. Andrei has found her job of lecturer. It is an hour later that Leo comes. He holds her and she leans back. The Kira who despises femininity smiles a tender smile. There is only one thing that matters: "I don't care what life is to be nor what it does to us. But it won't break us." (261) Three days later, a heavy woman, Antonina Pavlovna who is a neighbour in the sanatorium, comes to see Leo. She says to Leo that she is going to study. In the evenings, Kira tries to tell Leo that she has to go to Irina or to a meeting in order to meet Andrei. When Leo comes to her, she can think, with a cold wonder, of another man waiting for her.

When Kira goes to Andrei, he offers her his salary. But Kira rejects it. In her room she finds with Leo, Antonina and a man with drawling voice. Antonina introduces him as Karp Karpovitch Morozov. Kira learns that they are talking about a business deal. Morozov assures Leo that all he has to do is to see that the food shipment is pronounced worthless. Then the shipment goes to the basement and from there to their private dealers. There will be a clerk who sells half a pound of butter and that is all open and legal.

On the face of it Leo is the sole owner. Kira cries that it is a new way of committing suicide, but Leo wants to take chance on his life. She has to keep her job for the title of Soviet employee and she has to wear old clothes to protect her job.

Leo comes with a Royal vase. Kira objects to give it as gift on the wedding of Victor and Marina as they cannot be seen to afford it. Kira meets Vava in the street. She is married to Lolys Smiatkn working at Tobacco Club. Sonia forces Pavel that they have to get married as they are going to have a baby. On the following day, the secretary says that he goes far in the world with such a wife. Three days later, Pavel marries Sonia. Stepan Timoshenko who has served in Baltic Fleet warns Andrei that he is going to be kicked out because they do not lose their conscience when the Czar has lost his throne. Kira is returning from a political examination. She answers many questions except naming the latest amount of coal produced by the Don basin. Kira never knows what to expect of Leo at the end of the day. Sometimes she finds him drunk and sometimes all smiles.

Irina visits Kira, once in a while. Sasha is in a secret organization and they think they can overthrow the government. His friends have been arrested and so, he takes shelter in Irina's house. Galina comes to Kira and asks her hesitatingly if she can buy her wedding gown. Much of her salary is deducted for her membership in the Proletarian Society of Chemical defence. Kira is touched by her voice. Marina comes to Irina's room and tells her not to keep Sasha long. When Marina leaves, Irina takes for him a ticket for Baka and there are a few more hours to wait. But before that, Victor meets an official and reveals about Sasha. Marina and Sasha are arrested and are sentenced to ten years in a Siberian prison; Sasha for counter-revolutionary activity and Irina for giving shelter. Vasili tries in many ways to get them out, but fails.

Irina takes permission to marry Sasha, but after the marriage, they are kept in prisons, three hundred and fifty kilometres apart. Vasili obtains interviews to get Sasha and Irina sent to the same place, but he is refused. Even Andrei can do nothing to change Irina's sentence. Vasili leaves the house with Asia. Marina sobs silently. Kira sees Irina and says that she will wait for their coming back. Irina laughs saying that she knows the fate of Siberian prisoners. They die of cold or consumption and she is not afraid of it. Victor has been assigned a job on the Volkhovstory. He insists on Marina's remaining in the city: "She had developed a tendency to be too silent." (355) Andrei presents Kira a nightgown of black chiffon, so transparent. Kira comes home after midnight. Morozov calls her and asks to take Leo who is drunk from his house.

Kira pleads to Leo that they should apply for a foreign passport and run to the farthest place from that damned country, but he refuses. When he asks if she is afraid of losing him, she says she is afraid that he will lose himself: "He was smiling, his arrogant smile on a face that remains incredibly beautiful, a face that is like a drug to her." (365) Pavel goes to his house and leaves a note giving an ultimatum to pay what is due him. When Morozov goes to the European roof garden, Stepan who is drunk seizes the letter and goes away. Morozov reads the news that Stepan has shot himself through the mouth. Morozov does not know that Stephan has sent the letter to Andrei. Kira comes to know that Andrei has something to put before the G.P.U. She meets Leo at the theatre and tells him about it. An hour later, he transfers sacks and boxes in the store to a sleigh.

A few days later, Andrei's chief calls him and asks to forget about Pavel's letter and arrest Leo. Andrei searches Leo's house. In the wardrobe he finds a red dress, his gift to Kira. Leo says that it is his mistress's. He slowly turns to Leo to arrest. Andrei comes home and Kira enters. She bursts out that she does everything for the sake of a man she loves. Andrei says that if he had been in her place, he would have done the same. Andrei threatens Pavel that he should get Leo released within forty-eight hours, or else the photostat copies of his letter will be sent to Moscow. Leo cannot thank him from the bottom of his heart. He asks Andrei if he supposes Lazarus is grateful when Christ brings him back from the grave. Andrei walks out and commits suicide in his house. Kira wonders whether she has killed him, or revolution has, or both.

By calling her bitch, Leo says that Morozov has left Antonina leaving her a nice sum of money and she is going for a rest in the Caucasus. She asks Leo to come with her and Leo accepts it. The following morning, Kira fills an application for a foreign passport. Lydia works at night, but once in a while she plays piano for hours sobbing aloud. Galina takes it as just another one of her fits. Kira's passport is refused, but she learns that she has a better chance if she tries on foot across the Latvian border. She needs white clothes to crawl through the snow. Kira takes the white bear rug secretly to a tailor to be made into a coat. For the white dress she has Galina's wedding gown. She paints her boots white with lime. When everything is ready, she leaves the house.

It was dark when Kira reaches the village house. A man opens the door and she explains to him what she needs by slipping a bill into his hands. He tells her to walk as long as she can and to crawl when she sees a guard. On her way, her knees are hurt with the piercing pain of stretched sinews. Kira sees a six feet tall black figure. It is Ivan Ivanov guarding the border of the Union of Socialist Soviet Republic. He sees something moving in the snow, raises his rifle and fires. He goes away thinking it to be a rabbit. She lies still for a long time. Though she is shot, she walks. Suddenly her dry lips call softly one name, Leo. Then she looks down at the sky and smiles: "She knows she was dying. But it did not matter any longer. . . . She smiled, her last smile, to so much that had been possible." (464)

As Vivek Sharma states in an article: "The story takes place from 1922 to 1925 and explores the lives of primarily three individuals. One is Kira Argounova, the female protagonist who wants to be an engineer and is passionately in love with Leo. She is the younger daughter of a bourgeois capitalist. An independent spirit with a will to match, she rejects any attempt to cast her into a mould, by her family or the nascent Socialist State. She plans to storm the male bastion of engineers, and show her power by building strong structures and powerful machines." (http://www.wikipedia.com) It also proves that *We the Living* is a novel set after the revolution ended.

We the Living is a compiled and intriguing narrative that plays on the impressions of human will. It is the story of three characters—Kira, Adrei and Leo. The three characters represent three different attitudes to the oppression of communism. Kira represents the ideal woman who can withstand all obstacles. Andrei, a man of powerful character, is ruined because of his own choosing the wrong side of the communist party. Leo is an idealist who comes out of his illusion about the political system, and continues his struggle due to his uncompromising nature towards life.

Another critic, Rani Coloman concentrates on the publishing of the novel: "United States publishers were hesitant to publish *We the Living* because the book was anti-communist and anti-fascist and they were careful not to anger countries believing in those ideologies. After finally being published the tape was destroyed by the publisher because of the poor response. However, in England and in Italy, sales soared and the book achieved great success. Without Rand's consent, an Italian film company made a movie version, but the Nazis demanded Mussolini ban the movie and the book, realizing it was a protest against Mussolini's oppression. Twenty years later, after the success of *Atlas Shrugged*, the book was published in the United States and achieved great success." (http://www.ninetyandnine. com) This states that the book caused controversy from the beginning.

Two years after publication, word-of-mouth had pushed sales to 100,000 and became the bestseller. Ayn Rand had found her audience. Within three years, sales exceeded 400,000, and by 1949, the novel reappeared on bestseller lists and sold 50,000 copies within six months of the release of Warner Brothers' movie version. It was the movie which took Rand back to Hollywood: "The novel opens with the Argounova family scrambling for breathing space in a packed train. They are returning from the Crimea to Petrograd as the last of the White army is being destroyed—once at the top of the economic stratosphere." (http://www.everything2. com)

Rand describes the spirit of young Kira wonderfully as she steps off the train into the heart of Petrograd: "She had a calm mouth and slightly widened eyes with the defiant, enraptured, solemnly and fearfully expectant look of a warrior who is entering a strange city and is not quite sure whether he is entering it as a conqueror or as a captive." (19) The entire family is deeply affected by this abrupt change in socio-economic status, but Kira's mother Galina struggles to continue her past lavish lifestyle in a cramped bourgeoisie apartment, Kira's father Alexander vainly hopes for the return of the Russian monarchy, and her sister Lydia preens over petty romances and anything foreign. Kira is indifferent to it all. Kira says to Sonia: "Did it ever occur to you that I may be here for the unusual, unnatural reason of wanting to learn work I like only because I like it?" (70) Thus, Kira quickly stands out as an antagonist to Comrade Sonia, the obsequious Communist socialite of the Academy.

In the novel, Andrei is portrayed as the man with integrity, fighting until the end in the Crimea, while Pavel whiles away inside during the Revolution because of sickness and frailty. Robert Mayhew states in *Ayn Rand and Song of Russia:* "According to Rand, integrity is a virtue. It is morally wrong to betray your ideals, your values, your friends." (14) Thus, Andrei and Leo are seemingly contrastive, but both have mutual qualities and integrity that Kira is drawn to—an integrity that characterizes objectivism.

Critics say that Ayn Rand is at her story-telling best in this novel. She presents a powerful and emotional story, leaving a message to the reader. It is different from her other two novels *Atlas Shrugged* and *The Fountainhead*, where she is seen rendering a political philosophy in the thinly veiled direct voice. Also, the novel is seen more as rejection of a particular philosophy, while the other two novels advance an alternative. At various points in the story line, Kira's resolution to fulfil her dream is asserted again and again. In a society that has became characterless and anonymous, becoming an engineer would be Kira's answer to carve for herself a suitable role.

Kira's primary purpose in life has been reduced to subsistence, rather than excellence. Kira is a realist, who keeps her ideas and aspirations alive, but decides to go with the system anyway, until she feels powerful enough to challenge it. Kira's strong desire to be an engineer and her thoughts are very well reflected in this book. The second is Leo, the son of former Army General and third one is the unmistakable Andrei, who has risen from streets to become a formidable communist. Vivek Sharma rightly comments: "To complete the cast is Victor, Kira's cousin, who does the needful to shed his bourgeois past and rise through the ranks, Syerov and Sonia, who in their own way use communism to become richer and powerful, and other members of Kira's family." This is how Rand presents her characters.

The novel shows how revolution alters not the daily lives, morals, ambitions of its people, but also their basic human character. As a critic remarks, the novel is a tale of falsified hopes, broken dreams, corruption, love, and of the struggle of someone to survive a political system that is of utmost dislike to him or her. It results in his stooping to levels of moral depravity and Andrei, who is at constant conflict, because his deeds don't follow the voice of his inner conscience. But in reality, the novel is a powerful and passionate struggle of each of these *dramatis personae* with themselves, among each other's and against the state at the same time. When Kira furiously tells Andrei the whole truth, she does not love him, and she has done it all for Leo. Andrei is shattered at the realization of what he has done, and what Communism is. He decides to save Leo's life, and then shoots himself. Leo, however, cynically leaves Kira and chooses instead the prosperous life. The film ends here, but in the novel Kira is killed while trying to flee world.

The denouement shows Andrei as the nobler of the two men. Unlike Leo, he prefers death to dishonour and serves Communism only as long as he can believe in it. Except in his love for Kira, he serves communism sincerely. Leo, on the other hand, is willing to compromise himself. When Andrei sees the truth, he sacrifices himself for Kira as she has sacrificed herself for Leo. But Leo is as incapable of such love as he understands what Kira has done for him. Kira loves Leo, but not Andrei who deserves her love. When it comes to winning the maiden's affections, the smart money is still reckless virility rather than moral rectitude, and reckless virility happens to be Leo's long suit. He tells off Soviet officials including Andrei with courage that frightens Kira for him. But at the same time it makes her admire him all the more.

The sympathetic portrayal of the Communist, Andrei Taganov is one of the book's most interesting features. It is rightly said: "There is no remotely similar character in George Orwell's *Nineteen Eighty Four* and other books depicting life under a totalitarian regime, nor in any of Rand's own later books." (http://www.wikipedia.com) Indeed, Andrei's biography in Chapter 8 is replete with passages which could have come from the pen of an enthusiastic supporter of the October Revolution, such as: "In the year 1918, Andrei Taganov, in the uniform of the Red Army, marched with rows of other uniforms, from shops and factories, through the streets of Petrograd, to the tune of the International, to the depot, to the front of the civil war. He marched solemnly, with silent triumph, as a man walks to his wedding. Andrei's hand carried a bayonet as it had fashioned steel; it pulled a trigger as it had pushed a lever. His body was young, supple, as a wine ripe in the sun, on the voluptuous couch of a trench's mud. He smiled slowly and shot fast." (107)

All the above, however, takes place in flashbacks to the days of the civil war, the Monarchists have long been vanquished. Communist rule is unchallenged and is presented most negatively—especially when compared to the far-off Capitalist America as in other books. Rand's ideal is this. Andrei has his own courage, as his final Sydney Carton gesture shows. But as a GPU officer he's hardly in a position to display it; in executing its duties he simply appears ruthless: "The book's power lies in its depiction of the grim, grimy terror that prevailed even in the supposed golden age of Lenin. Everyone is reduced to a debasing dependence on the state, less because of the fear of arbitrary arrest, than because of the total absence of property rights and economic freedom. People can be suddenly deprived of anything—job, possessions, living quarters—that is coveted by some Party hack. The characters are driven to a dying, corruption, prostitution and treachery by the system that promised them liberation." (www.findarticle.com) Thus the novel makes the issue of property rights so vital that I haven't read it in any other novel.

"Miss Rand does for Lenin's Soviet Union something like what Bonfire of the Vanities does for New York—again ironically because she'd have had only scorn for Tom Wolfe's opinion that status information is the stuff of the novel." (www. findarticle.com) *We the Living* shows the formation of a malign status system in a society in which connections are given importance than talent. In movie version, though Communism appears as tyrannical, it was not in the fabric of the economy. It might because a Fascist-sponsored film would not tend to stress the dangers of central control as such. Leonard Peikoff aptly defines fascism in *The Ominous Parallels:* "For Liberalism (that is, individualism), the individual is the end and society the means; nor is it conceivable that the individual considered in the dignity of an ultimate finality, be lowered to mere instrumentality. For fascism, society is the end, individuals are the means, and its whole life consists in using individuals as instruments for its social ends." (17) Here, Peikoff distinguishes Liberalism from Fascism.

Randians like to say that the Italian public flocked to the film because they could perceive its relevance to Fascism itself, but I think they simply enjoyed the story and the stars. Fosco Giatti plays the role of Andrei with dignity and Rossano Brazzi as Leo looks young and handsome and in the later part of the movie, he slips from a passionate lover to a rogue nicely. But the best part of the movie is Alida Valli who plays the role of Kira. When she played the role she was twenty-one years old. The beautiful expressions over her pretty face are as clear as the waves on a wind-ruffled pond. Though the story is set against the background of the Red rule of the communists, it also depicts the story of Kira's endless struggle to live against all odds. She proves that life is not just to live, but to live with a purpose, to have an ultimate goal in life. The goal must not be of success, but of happiness. Rand proves through

Kira that happiness may not be a means to achieve anything or any specific goal, but is an end in itself. So, one must live not to be successful, but to be happy.

We can say Kira is an ideal fictional symbol of all the virtues, Rand holds to be ideal. She conflicts good and evil and she also idolizes political and economic freedom. She cannot accept contradictions in the man she loves. These three characters, Kira, Leo and Andrei, meant little to the totalitarian state and the communist party in Soviet Russia. But as individuals, living through that dark midnight that almost extinguished hope in their hearts are as alive as any of the classic characters found elsewhere in literature. When Kira enters the story, she is the daughter of an affluent Russian family that loses everything after the Bolsheviks came to power. Their lives changed dramatically after the Bolsheviks confiscated all their properties. Now, Kira loses her chance of continuing education and position as she will not confirm to the new Soviet ideal.

Later she meets a Russian aristocrat, Leo who seems to be unbowed before the Soviet justice. He does not recognize the hegemony of the new system over any aspect of his life. Kira loves him at first sight and later admires him for his spirit of individuality. She falls for him and comes to stand by his side. Andrei is the ultimate instrument of the Soviet state. He wears a leather jacket and carries all the authority of the new dictatorship. In past ages, he would have worn the helmet of a Roman Centurion or the armour of a crusading knight. But he would have been the symbol of governmental oppression always. He is a born secret policeman in a system that required men all-too-willing to torture and imprison their fellow men. More resonant are the struggles of all the young people in it against the heartless crushing bureaucracy. There is a small section dealing with a love story. One character, Sasha watches the love of his life, Marina disappearing on another train as they are separated and are sent to different parts of Siberia.

Vasili begs the officials to send them to the same place: "I'm not complaining, Comrade Commissar. It's ten years, you know, but that's all right. Only send them to the same place. What difference does it make to you? What difference does it make to the State? They're so young. They love each other. It's ten years, but you know and I know that they'll never come back—it's Siberia, and the cold and the hunger, and the conditions." (343) One cannot read it without tears. This section alone makes the novel worth it. Both Kira and Leo are the children of powerful families. They acquired great wealth through hard work and dedication under imperial rule. They struggle to free themselves of the oppressive regime. Andrei, on the other hand, is a high ranking party member with glorious combat record. He is just beginning to realize the high cost of his sacrifices. They hope to find salvation whether it is from within or without.

Rani Coloman rightly explains the three characters: "One character of this trio, Taganov will realize the truth and break, another, Leo will break under the pressure, and the third, Kira will leave to start over anew. At the end the character you vow to hate somehow turns into the one you love." (http://www.ninety andnine.com) Through these characters Rand began to formulate her ideas on the ultimate value of the individual and the worth of the reasoning human intellect. This is an indictment on the danger to mankind everywhere in any collective system. This is an unpardonable damnation of Communism as it was then and what it eventually became.

Rand shows no compassion or willingness to understand why men and women would give up themselves to be part of a system that denies basic rights and degrades the individual. After reading this book one will come to understand why Communism was ultimately destined to fail. Communism failed because it collapsed under the weight of its own inherent internal contradictions. In her early life, Rand saw all of this. Barbara Branden says in *The Passion of Ayn Rand*: ‘"Even at that age," Alice later said, "I could see what was wrong with communism. It meant living for the State. I realized they were saying that the illiterate and the poor had to be the rulers of the earth, because they were illiterate and poor." She was startled by the fact that while everyone complained bitterly about the physical hardships created by the communists, no one seemed equally indignant about their ideology.' (21)

Rand's predictions for the ultimate demise of Communist tyranny came true and that individual, political and economic freedom have taken root throughout countries that once denied even the slightest symptom of personal liberty. One must read the book to discover one of the most original minds in the twentieth century. Bathony writes about Rand' critics too: "There are lots of people who dislike Ayn Rand whether for the rather didactic and lengthy sermon. As Rand writes about the early Soviet system, it is obvious that this novel could have been set in any system that denied individual freedom. Rand chose to write about Soviet Russia because it was what she knew. Similar stories could have come out of fascist Italy or Nazi Germany. Rand chose Russia. (http://www.amazon.com) This shows that it is a story of what happens to people when freedom is lost. It is a moral allegory of just what happens to the human spirit when the individual is subjugated to the mind-numbing degrading indignities imposed from above by second-handers who created nothing but only denied everything.

Kira is shown as very young, emotional and sometimes impulsive woman. She loves the wrong man, Leo for wrong reasons. She sacrifices everything for him and learns that a life not lived as one wishes is not worth living. The tragic character of the novel, Andrei is unbelievably well done. The most poignant passage in the story is the confrontation between Andrei and Kira when Andrei knows about the relationship between Kira and Leo: "Andrei Taganov turned very slowly, his right shoulder drooping, every tendon of his body pulled to the effort of the motion, very cautiously, as if a knife had been thrust between his shoulder blades and he had to move carefully, not to disturb it. His left arm hung unnaturally, bent at the elbow, his fingers half-closed as if holding something they could not spill." (398-399) In the end, both Kira and Andrei realize what they have done to each other and how their passion and pretension have led them to the destruction of the reverence they achieved. The story ends in a tragedy for all the three. Andrei loses his position in the Party, and very soon thereafter, he commits suicide.

The only genuine mourner at Andrei's funeral, Kira wonders if she has killed him. Leo loses any moral sense that he may have left and as a perceptive Irina, Kira's cousin portrays him earlier, leaves Kira to begin a new life. After the departure of Leo, Kira makes another attempt to cross the border: "She knew she had been walking for hours, that which she had once called hours. There were no hours here; there were only steps, only legs rising and falling deep into the snow, and a snow that had no end. Or had it an end? That, real, did not matter. She did not have to think of that. She had to think only that she had to walk. She had walked west. That was the only problem that was the total of all the problems. Had she any problems? Had she any questions to be answered? If she had—they would be answered—there. She did not have to think. She had to get out. She would think—then—if there were thoughts to be faced. Only she had to get out. Only to get out." (456)

Till the end of her life, Kira remains loyal to her love for Leo. In her own words, when a person dies, one does not stop loving him. The love triangle of Andrei, Leo and Kira is a reminder of how some people try to lead a dual life hoping they can let two people be happily in love with them. Rand wishes to depict Kira as the martyr in her superhuman effort to be true to her individualistic ideals. Her character is the reason for calling this novel as primarily war of an individual against the state. Rand vividly shows on how and why communist Russia squandered the dreams of early revolutionaries. Vivek Sharma comments: "Apart from this Kira's love is flawed for it lacks the honesty and fidelity that one must show towards one she cherishes. Her ideals are made ridiculous by the manner which she sheds them for survival. Andrei is unlikely hero, who is victim of his own ideology, victim of treachery by both the women and the country that he tried to love and save. Leo is a failed ideal, and his character, throughout the novel does not show why Kira loved him so." I disagree with him here. Kira's love for Leo is pure. Her becoming the mistress of Andrei is only to save Leo's life. She has no other choice left. Even before going to die, she utters the name of Leo: 'She repeated, louder, without despair, as if the sound, that one sound in the world, were giving her life: "Leo! . . . Leo! . . . Leo!"' (463)

I cannot call Andrei as the unlikely hero. When his ideology is disillusioned, he is courageous enough to warn his comrades though he knows that by doing it, he is risking his own life. He says to Pavel: "get him out of bed if necessary. What you'll tell him and how you'll tell it, is none of my business. All I have to know is that Leo Kovalensky is released within forty-eight hours." (413) Vivek Sharma doubts why Kira loves Leo. For this my answer is that love is beyond reasoning. Moreover, she loves Leo at the first sight without knowing anything about him. She says to Leo: "Only because I like you, I don't care what you think of women, who like you—nor how many of them there have been." (82) There are other people in the novel. Rand portrays their state as the consequence of communism.

Rand believes the state that suppressed personal freedom and right to personal profit must have broken the spirit of one and many. In *The Ayn Rand Lexicon: Objectivism from A to Z,* edited by Harry Binswanger, Rand is quoted: "Altruism declares that any action taken for the benefit of others is good, and any action taken for one's own benefit is evil. Thus the beneficiary of an action is anybody other than oneself, anything goes." (5) That is what altruism preaches. As a grim reminder of how social catastrophes can alter family life, *We the Living* stands strong. Rand seems to be clear in her plot and loud in her characters, whether it is Comrade Pavel Syerov, Sonia, Sasha Cherov, Vasili, Irina, Vava, Kira, Andrei, Leo, Victor Dunaev, Maria, Stepan Timoshenko, Karp Morozov, Antonina, Acia, Galina, Marisha, Alexander or Lydia, the devout Christian and the piano player. All these characters are vividly drawn, clear and real like.

The repetition of the words like Citizen, Comrade, revolution, Proletariat and the misery of the Russian after revolution are all believable and they create an image on mind as happening or happened. Everyone here talks about rations and cooperative stores. Every character suffers from lack of food and reinforces the emotion which Rand intends to create in the reader's mind. I agree with the comments of Smisbahuddin who says that the snippets of dialogues in the funeral procession of Andrei are really fantastic and creative. It is better than watching scenes in a motion picture or a video program.

Smisbahuddin continues to say: "Kira will not be a hot and memorable character like Roark, she is very forward and subdued, emotional and cold, kind and obedient and rebel, it seems the author herself was hesitant and saw those days. Anyway Rand makes her central characters unbending and they do not surrender their inner heart chambers to any reason, pressure or emotions, this singular trait of the protagonist among the fallen human beings all around is a hallmark of this writer." (http:// www.wikipedia.com) These words prove that Rand gives a sense of being whole and full through her portrayal of heroes and heroines. Rand give these characters admirable qualities and also gives despicable attributes to many characters around to give her readers contrast and depth and that is her genius. Rand is admired by many a fundamentalist capitalist. *We the Living* shows evidence of a warm heart, and uncompromising intellect, and a fever for living well. It is an astonishingly first novel which should be kept for every serious book club and every list of great books.

Rand depicts her characters vividly and with complexity. As she is somewhat romantic, even her simpler characters, such as Victor, are developed in such a way that the reader must ask difficult questions about who he is, why he is in that way, and would we be different under the same conditions. Though Kira, the central figure, is sympathetic, tragic, heroic, and admirable, she is also a puzzle. So many people feel that of all of Rand's novels, *We the Living* is the most straightforward novel. The story is forwarded by narrative, rather than by the philosophy. Rand manages to encompass almost all of the dreariness and paranoia of Stalinist Russia by portraying the lives of three individuals involved in a triangle.

We the Living shows why Rand took such harsh stances in favour of Capitalism. An excerpt from the preface volumes has been written about the issue of Freedom versus Dictatorship, but in essence it comes down to a single question if we find it moral to treat men as sacrificial animals and to rule them by physical force. If as a citizen of a free country one can know what this actually means, then *We the Living* will help one to know. Rand describes the dreary grey skies, old buildings, dirty citizens waiting in queues of cooperative stores for millet. That millet may or may not be fresh or probably a loaf of stale bread which will be had with onions fried in rancid linseed oil to feed them for that day. This was the scene when Communism took over from Capitalism or Czarism. The price was paid not by the Capitalist or the wealthy who fled away to foreign lands, but by the traders who had to stay back. The affluent lives they lived were gone, their homes their assets, their bank accounts were all taken by the State.

All money was for the Proletarians, the one who worked, gained and the one who did not lose everything. One needs to be a member of any union to get a job and one need to have a job to be a member of the union. Kira and her family are caught in this vicious circle. The readers learn about Kira's exploits and of Leo and Andrei's. Many characters come in and go, but none of them are under-sketched by Rand. Clear links are provided for each character. As the story progresses the filth of communism is revealed. The novel reflects how the impact of the Russian revolution changes the common individuals on the street. There is a place for flowery endings but stark reality, confused minds as decisions are taken at the drop of the hat in the backdrop of the Russian revolution.

In the story, the disillusionment that seems to be both sweeping and seeping quietly among those are in the belief that there is a new and better tomorrow for Russia, which was under the rule of Lenin in 1922. Those who made up what were once deemed as the bourgeois, namely middle and upper class merchants and professionals are among the aims to balance the scales among the classes, the average and poor citizens, who are supposed to be the benefactors of government change, are finding themselves less able to afford the basic necessities of food, shelter and clothing. There is no clear solution before them and if they complain, then they will be promised, over and again, that progress will come and to be patient. If they condemn it, they will be considered the enemies of the state.

Kira wants to find her place in the world. She wants her own career, she wants the bond with the man of her choice, she wants to live in a home of her liking, and she wants to blaze her own trial, but not the one already prescribed or predetermined by others. She says: "Because I have less in common with you than the enemies who fight you, have. I don't want to fight for the people, I don't want to fight against the people."

At the beginning of the novel, personalities and perceptions seem diverse, ranging from youthful idealism present in those who anticipate positive changes in Russia's government reforms to cynicism among those who are pessimistic about the changes of the period. But later in the novel, the frequency and intensity of totalitarian tones set forth by the communist government increase and ultimately result in a unifying mindset among virtually everyone and that is fear. This regression to a primal state is gradual. It is one of the several elements that make *We the Living* seemingly realistic. It is not an engaging chapter-by-chapter sequence like Rand's non-fiction works, including *The Virtue of Selfishness*. However, this novel is a unique fictional, though nearly autobiographic expression of what happens when the wrong ideologies are institutionalized to set up and run a government or state.

As Rand repeatedly published in her myriad volumes, to constantly ignore personal pursuits in the name of perceived morals could lead to improperly placing our well-being in the hands of others, as in the case of totalitarian regimes. Even George Washington asserted that a good, effective government can only be established with the acknowledgement that men are more motivated by their self-interests than they are by seemingly virtuous ideals. Throughout man's history, theocracies were doomed to failure for trying to do it the other way around. *We the Living* has an amazing sense of the environment. It is always there but often not noticed in Rand's other works. One really feels like living in the worlds Rand creates. It is particularly seen in *We the Living*.

In the novel, apart from the result of communism which is evident, we can see the clear links to the cause, the absence of human rights. Above all *We the Living* has great characters that we get to observe as they change under the brutal regime. One can notice that Kira gets what she wants, though Lydia says she does not understand how Kira manages that. When Kira slips away from church and is returned home hours later by the police, she is never again sent to church. When her nanny buys a book Kira does not like, she throws it out of the window and her next books are those that Kira will approve. When her family returns to Petrograd, Kira announces that she plans to attend the Technological Institute to study engineering. Her cousin tells her that she is being selfish by choosing that route because there are other careers better suited to women.

Nathaniel Branden's explanation of John Galt's speech in *Atlas Shrugged* given in his *My Years with Ayn Rand* can be applied to the character of Kira: "accept the fact that in the realm of morality nothing less than perfection will do." By perfection, she meant an "unbound rationality"—that is, a commitment to use one's mind to the fullest of one's ability, a respect for facts, reality and a refusal to indulge wishes by evading knowledge or evidence. Ayn Rand says, "Live consciously. Try to be as rational as you can be. Don't make allegations you can't support. Be on the lookout for contradictions, and work to resolve them. Do your best to face the things that needed to be faced. When you act make every effort to know what you are doing, what the consequences are likely to be. Live responsibly. Accept that sometimes you will fail; don't collapse into guilt, because that serves no useful purpose. Pick yourself up, acknowledge your error, and try to do better in the future." (221) These words are proved by Kira.

Her philosophy was still incipient at this stage, but her dramatic sense had already formed. Rand manages to interweave her philosophy into her novel. Kira, though a frustrating heroine to admire, uses Andrei to give life to Leo, a fascinating but brutal hero.

The basic tenet of her philosophy is self-reliance, of holding no one higher than oneself. In reading *We the Living* again and again, one keeps thinking of how Rand was using Greta Garbo as her heroine. Though *We the Living* is a dark and brooding work, it is more realistic. The novel shows that there is no difference between Soviet Russia and Czar Russia because people lived in the exactly same conditions. There were secret anti-government societies, and people were forced to believe that the government is always right. In spite of all the slogans about Soviet Russia's bright future, people suffered just like they suffered under the Czar's rule. However, it is stated in an article that there are some serious problems with the plot. For instance, about one-third of the way through the book, we find that Kira, and Leo and Kira's family all make it on the Purge list and will be kicked out of Petrograd. And then absolutely nothing happens. It is never mentioned again.

Another problem, it is said, is the constant vacillation of Andrei. It seems he goes from bad to good and back again just to keep the plot moving. And Kira and Leo cannot stand Maurissa as their neighbour and then all of a sudden they become friends. I cannot agree with these remarks. Firstly, in the name of Purge, Kira and Leo lose their jobs. The following passage proves it: 'When a reduction of staff came to the "House of the Peasant" and she saw her name among those dismissed as "anti-social element," she was not surprised. It made no difference now.' (225) After losing job, Leo joins hands with Pavel. The character of Andrei is constant from the beginning. He has stood by his ideologies and deplores when other party members go against them. Lastly, Kira and Maurissa haven't become "best friends" as it is stated, but they just get adjusted themselves to each other.

Rand's view is that humanity is inherently free and that repressing freedom turns people into animals. From this premise she makes it clear that some moral systems are self-destructive and destructive to society. Since man exists as an end in himself, not as a means to the end of others, he must construct a hierarchy of values for himself to follow in order to achieve happiness. These values have to be rational and they must promote man's survival and make him feel that he has control over reality. He gets happiness by achieving his values, but that depends on how rational his values are and that is rational self-interest. This philosophy should not be taken as a refutation of ever helping others or as a license to act in an anti-social or even abusive manner. Helping and being good to other is a good thing, but it should not be by sacrificing oneself. If the people are rational and productive and have something to give, then we help them.

We give value for value or if we love them and if they have high position in our hierarchy of values, then we should be benevolent. This is all our own interest to do so. Therefore, helping others is bad if that help involves sacrifice of a higher value to a lesser value. Others have the capacity to hold the same values and the ultimate value is life. So, taking the life of another is not in our rational self-interest as it is going against our own values and against rational values in general. So, Rand's philosophy of Objectivism is not a license to act upon our own irrational whims. It is a philosophy for productive, independent, rational and voluntary human beings who value life and will be respectable to any human being, but will obviously gravitate to those who hold the same values.

Leonard Peikoff defines Rand's objectivism in his *Objectivism: The Philosophy of Ayn Rand*: "Objectivism begins by naming and validating its premises. Ayn Rand does not select questions at random; she does not plunge in by caprice. She begins deliberately at the beginning—at what she can prove in the beginning, and the root of all the rest." (4) Ayn Rand's view of the world is an oversimplified version of reality. She seems to believe in libertarian myth that all men have equal chances in life to pursue their ambitions. She says that one can achieve one's goals only through one's effort. One must never mind that some people like her fictional characters, Dagny and Readen are born wealthy while some people have to work full time just for their livelihood, not having much spare time to pursue their true ambitions. Rand is opposed to any form of altruism. This is another proof of her oversimplified worldview which leads me to the next point, how proudly she declares herself to be an extremist.

Many critics of Ayn Rand say that Rand gives more importance to her philosophy than storytelling and that she should have written her political and moral convictions in a non-fiction work, as other philosophical predecessors have done. *We the Living* successfully defies this criticism. It is a well-crafted novel and its romantic existence in post-revolutionary Petrograd is made into reality with often cynical characterization. Rand describes people waiting in bitter cold for food rations, the sickening propaganda that adorns the city's buildings and the plight of Leo and Kira who struggle to live in the heart of Petrograd. All this suffering of the masses is made tangible and the groundwork of Objective philosophy is laid without any lengthy sermons that annoy Rand's critics.

Rand repeatedly says in her works that constantly ignoring personal pursuits in the name of perceived morals will lead to improperly placing our fate in the hands of others, as in the case of totalitarian regimes. This is proved by Pavel's addressing his party comrades at the death of Andrei: "And in the years of peace and reconstruction that followed our victory, the years which are harder and perhaps, more heroic than any warfare, he did more than his share of the silent, self-sacrificing work which your party carries on for you, toilers of the U.S.S.R.! He falls, but the Collective lives forever. Under the guidance of the Soviets, under the leadership of the great All-Union-Communist-Party, we are marching into a radiant tomorrow when the honest toil of free toilers will rule the world! Then labour will no longer be slavery, as it is in capitalistic countries, but a free and happy duty to that which is greater than our petty concerns, greater than out petty sorrows, greater than our very lives—the eternal Collective of a Proletarian Society!" (435)

Rand makes a little fun of the workings of the new bureaucracy. But towards Kira, those little things like scent and lipstick which mean so much to a woman do not matter. *We the Living* is designed to promote greater awareness of the possible consequences of taking historical fiction to be entirely historically accurate. Some critics say that the conditions described in the novel are true to life, but fail to point out the positive effects of Soviet policy on conditions, because of the practical lack of contrast between pre-revolutionary and post-revolutionary conditions in Russia. Rand's conditions are aligned to a single viewpoint with an agenda to promote. But Rand was not writing history to present post- and pre-revolutionary conditions. She just wrote about the reality of her own hellish existence in Soviet Communist Russia and it motivated her to speak out and to write about philosophy.

Smisbahuddin states in an article: "Life is not a bed of roses is what the authoress seems to say. No overtly feminine sentiments, no broad shoulders, no sparkling eyes in her books. Her books reflect reality, stark reality in the 1920s. The proletarians of the world who loathe capitalists and preach one thing and practise another as parched throats and shrivelled bellies cry for help." (http://www.wikipedia.com) What he says is true. Life in those days was excruciatingly difficult. One of the novel's themes, such as the struggle between individualism and capitalism, is seen in Rand's later works, *The Fountainhead* and *Atlas Shrugged*. But *We the Living* is different as it was her first attempt at making it big in the sense of getting her message across and she accomplished it well. As Rani Coloman states, each of her books contains a very different plot, yet relates something so innate that one cannot help but feel passionately about it.

We may not accept every moral issue in the novel, but apart from it, if we see the underlying theme, the true meaning of the book is obvious. As Kira points out the great minds of the world will be turned into walking zombies and that is what turns off Objectivists about it. It is emotional and not serenely rational like her other novels. Apart from the ending, *We the Living* is more alive than her later novels as it is about the struggle of the characters to live their lives. They are not fighting for any ideas, but for the right to live and pursue their lives. Though Roark in *The Fountainhead* and Galt in *Atlas Shrugged* do the same thing, their fight is a philosophical struggle which makes their efforts to live more abstract and less direct than what is found in *We the Living*.

There is a scene with Kira and Andrei in which he says that they both believe in life, but that he is willing to fight for it and even die for it, but Kira says that all she wants is to live. She is living in the society that is disintegrating towards totalitarianism and is a-philosophical. She deplores this condition and says to Andrei: "What are your masses but millions of dull, shrivelled, stagnant souls that have no thoughts of their own, no dreams of their own, no will of their own, who eat and sleep and chew helplessly the words of others put into their brains? And for those you would sacrifice the few who know life? I loathe your ideas because I know no worse injustice than the giving to the undeserved. Because men are not equal in ability and one can't treat them as if they were. And because I loathe most of them." (90)

The Objectivists do not praise the novel as they do her later novels. *We the Living*, in its own way, is pre-Objectivist. But it is too early for the people to understand how to integrate these ideas into their lives. Nathaniel Branden says in *The Literary Method of Ayn Rand:* "As she has emphasized, her primary purpose for which these books were written was not the philosophical conversion of their readers. The primary purpose was to project and make real the characters who are the books' heroes. This is the motive that unites the artist and the moralist." (4) Thus, Rand's four novels have a major philosophical theme, yet they are not "propaganda-novels."

Rand calls herself a writing machine and does not cultivate the kind of balance that would have enabled her to be a happy person. What Gladstein says in his *The New Ayn Rand Companion* is right: "She was not interested in the same 'Mindless' activities that delighted her schoolmates. She formed her ideals of human potential early; her first hero was the protagonist of a children's serial adventure story. His name was Cyrus, and the character Kira in her first novel *We the Living*, bears the feminine equivalent of his name." (8) It proves that Rand was single-minded individualist even from early childhood.

When she was asked in an interview with *Playboy* if she is willing to die for Objectivism, she says: "I would. But what is more important, I am willing to live for it—which is much more difficult." (http://ellenspacent/ar-pboy.html) Thus, she is the founder of this philosophy of humanistic individualism effectively saying that the ideal is to live for the sake of Objectivism. *We the Living* provides an antidote to that kind of thinking. A contributing writer, Ryan Maloney says aptly: "Growing accustomed to Rand's aggressive writing style is a difficult task for someone who has not yet studied rational objectivist thought. Despite her talent for creative writing, Rand aims most of her novels at·die-hard followers and as a result, produces many complex works that teeter dangerously between philosophical fiction and philosophical dissertation." (http://www.vu.union. edu.com) But *We the Living*, however, captures the indomitable spirit of intellectual freedom and individuality without adding the objectivist ideals and beliefs.

Rand lived in Russia, but when things changed, she understood that the only way to live was to leave. When she comes to know about the horrible lives of the Russians, Rand is thankful as she lives in a democratic society, America and not under dictatorship. *We the Living* is an excellent story that has particular importance for all who fail to appreciate the level of intellectual freedom they enjoy. Even though the characters are fictional, all the events are based on reality. Rand puts forth her ideas in a forceful yet very convincing way in which the beauty of her works lies. Her themes are striking yet sublime, radical yet practical and thought-provoking. The same qualities are vividly seen in her *We the Living* to *The Fountainhead* to *Atlas Shrugged* which show her insatiable desire to live and lead a life for her own self. It is at once a philosophical and sociological question with much deeper connotations and far-reaching results for the way we all live our lives and our duties as a social being first and a human being later.

In all her works, Rand argues strongly that one is a human being first and a social being only after that, something which questions the very basis of societal existence. All of us, says Rand, have our duties to ourselves first and then to any entity whether it is family, society or state in that order. What makes *We the Living* a masterpiece is the way it has been written and the brilliance of Rand in portraying the pathos and struggle of the people trying to come to terms with life under the Communist regime which did not afford the luxuries of living for one's own betterment, but for the cause of the state and millions of depraved souls. When Andrei commits suicide, an editorial of the *Pravda* says: "Such is the sacrifice of a Party that rules, not for the sake of personal loot and fame, like the rulers of capitalistic countries, but for the sake of assuming the hardest work, the most pitiless tasks in the service of the Collective." (429)

Those were the times when no one was a free citizen, and everyone was just a Comrade. That is how they call each other. Sonia introduces herself to Kira: "Mine's Sonia. Just Comrade Sonia. That's what everybody calls me. You know, we're going to be great friends, I can feel it. There's nothing I enjoy more than helping smart young students like you." (69) These emotions have been captured by Rand with accuracy in the novel which makes it a compelling read. By the end of the novel, one does not know who is right and who is wrong, but one develops a detesting hatred for that way of life which says our life is nothing but a gift we have been given for not our cause but for the cause of others.

The let down of the book for some critics is Rand's shabby treatment of the leading lady, Kira. In all her works, the heroine is shown willing to be consumed by anyone and everyone without having the slightest of thought of her self-respect. Be it Dagny or Dominique or Kira, each of these ladies, say the critics, has a trait to fall into the abyss of self-depravity. But in the opinion of Rand, sex is not physical, but an intellectual union. They are willing to do anything and everything for the love of their lives, even if it means destroying themselves in the process. Rand is a master of philosophical story-telling. She blends philosophy into her stories so effortlessly that the readers do not realize that they are reading philosophy, until suddenly, they realize that the same applies to their lives too. The characters are perfectly drawn. Though Kira, Leo and Andrei can never be seen in real life, Rand brings them alive in this novel.

There are certain key themes in the novel which make it worthwhile. Firstly, except for the Communist Russia, there would not have been Rand's philosophical epistemology. People would be stuck with the forerunners of Locke and Nietzsche as references for trying to formulate a systematic and philosophical construct such as Rand's. The novel is written in third person from a semi-limited point of view because the story is about Kira and her life in Communist Russia and so this point of view is adequate. The reader can get some knowledge if the view were less limited, but the explanations and details of Kira's life are adequate to explain the story line. For instance, Kira learns that Leo plans to leave with Antonina only after she attends Andrei's funeral.

Leo tells her: "He's left Tonia—he wants no connections that could be investigated. But he's left her a nice little sum of money—oh, quite nice. She's going for a rest and vacation in the Caucasus. She has asked me to go with her. I've accepted the job. Leo Kovalensky, the great gigolo of the U.S.S.R.!" (441) He says that he has been tool of her relationship with Andrei and that knowledge makes it easy for him to tell her about his leaving Rand does not give direct information about Antonina's situation or the offer she makes Leo other than what Leo tells Kira. But this limited view is sufficient to understand the story line.

Rand must be credited for her colourful turn of phrase, several enrapturing descriptions and well-drawn characters. The way Rand built those amazing characters up to such high standards then tore each of them apart piece by piece fascinates the readers. The character of Leo is a great example of Ayn Rand's style of writing. The book is in broken English. But an interesting fact is that Rand learned English in six months before writing this book. Her flow of thoughts converted into words shows her stupendous command over the language. She portrays the young woman who must endure the turmoil of revolution and the imposition of a totalitarian state and who ultimately risks everything for freedom in an amazing way.

This novel was written before Rand stared her philosophical movement. Another Rand-like novel is *The Last Day* written by Glenn Kleier. In *The Last Day*, Kleier tackles the subject of authority in organized religion with startling and outrageous wit. It is a classic novel in the manner of *The Fountainhead* and *Atlas Shrugged*.

Rand lived what she wrote and that is what makes it one of the most reliable and interesting books. Robert Mayhew rightly says in *Ayn Rand and Song of Russia:* "The free countries of the West are natural enemies of the Soviet Union. Any country even practically devoted to the conviction that every individual has the right to life, liberty, property, and the pursuit of happiness is the natural enemy of a country devoted to the idea that these are 'bourgeois rights,' and that every person owes his life, his labour, and the product of his labour to society or the state" (122) This is proved by the novel.

We the Living was made into an Italian film. It runs over three hours and is amazingly truthful to the book. It is interesting to note that the film was made in Italy and not in Russia. The film was made when World War II was at its height and when the bombs were exploding all over the place. But Ayn Rand did not misunderstand socialism and communism. Director Gofferdo Alesandrini read it and thought it would make an excellent epic. But getting rights for the novel would be an obstacle as at that time Italy was at war with the United States. Alessandrini and screenwriter Anton Majano decided to base their screenplay on the novel.

As he was working on another film, the production company asked many other writers to rewrite scenes and dialogues from the existing screenplay. But when the final draft came, it was very much different from Alessandrini and Majano's original screenplay. So they both decided just to follow the book and start shooting the film without a script. They wrote all the scenes at night and handed them over to the actors in the morning. Weeks went by and it soon became clear that it would take longer than the customary three weeks of shooting to finish this film. Also the material was enough for two films. But it was not revealed to the actors because of the fear that they might request to be paid double. In spite of the fact that the novel is a criticism of the communist regime, the Ministry of Culture soon understood that Alessandrini was also using the film to criticize the Mussolini government.

The fascist officials interrupted the shooting many times and demanded to see the rushes. But Alessandrini kept two edited copies of the film, one that would be in line with the fascist ideology and another one which reflected his own vision of the story. As it was stated: "In September 1942, after nearly five months of shooting, the film was completed and presented at the Venice Film Festival where it received the highest accolades and was awarded the Volpe Cup. It went for general release in November of the same year as two separate films. "Noi Vivi" and "Adio Kira!" (1942) and proved to be a resounding success with the Italian public who regarded it as an indirect indictment of the Mussolini regime. But the authorities soon got the wind of this and the film was banned after five months, all copies seized and ordered to be destroyed but fortunately one negative was kept hidden. After the war, Scalera Film approached Ayn Rand to secure the literary rights to the film so it could be re-released, but she refused." (http://www.wikipedia.com) This shows how the film came out after facing many odds.

A few years later, Scalera Films went into receivership and as a part of the inventory of Scalera films, both *Noi Vivi and Addio Kira!* were turned over to a holding company and it relegated them to a vault. They remained there for over twenty-five years. After the war when Rand saw the film, she was pleased. It is faithful to the novel and the casting is superior to that of the Hollywood version of *The Fountainhead.* The post-war settlement gave her rights to the movie of *We the Living*. It was shown in two parts in Italy and it was a hit. Late in the 1960s, Rand could locate the original nitrate negatives. They were still in good condition in the vault in Rome. Both the films were restored and combined into one. When it was released with English subtitles in 1986 as *We the Living* at the Telluride Film festival in Colorado, it received rare reviews, over forty years after its original release.

In 1986, the film was distributed in the U.S. Though it was a success, the source print was not perfect. As a result the video version suffers from some distracting fuzziness, particularly towards the end. The film is necessarily heavy-going in nature, but the acting, featuring perhaps romantic idol Rossano Brazzi's finest performance are wonderful. As a whole, the narrative anticipates another troubled war time epic, Marcel Carne's masterpiece

Children of Paradise (1945), particularly in the way Valli is pursued by a number of suitors throughout the film but ends up alone by the end of it. In the end, with all the celebrated classics that have emerged from Italy, *We the Living* remains an important film and undeniably, one of the most impressive ever made in the country.

I agree with the comments: "I would never dare to recommend this book to anybody with a sane bent of mind. This book is to be read by only those people, who have a deep desire to live, and not just breathe. I recommend the book only for those people who have guts to think differently, those who have the guts to speak differently, and those who have guts to act differently. This book is for those people who have a consistency in their thoughts, words and action. If you think you can stomach it, go read it, right now. . . . If you can't; run, run as far as you can, because you aren't safe. . . . even from yourself." (http:// www.moutshut.com)

Theory of Human Nature
Anthem

Rand's portrait of the future, *Anthem*, was first released in 1983 in England and was re-edited for publication in the United States in 1946. This is the fiftieth anniversary edition which induces a scholarly introduction and a facsimile of the original British version. For its American debut, it bears Rand's handwritten alternative. *We the Living* was published in Britain by Cassell and Company in 1938, but it could not find an American publisher. Until 1946, it remained unknown in the country. When one of Rand's friends, Leonard E. Read, creator of the Foundation for Economic Education, arranged for it to be republished in a series of pamphlets advocating individualism, Rand took the occasion to edit the work. Though she did not change the essentials, she closely analyzed every sentence and eliminated the expressions she considered unnecessary. The theme of the novel and central conflict is the individual versus the collective and important element of her moral and political philosophy like her other novels.

The story of the novel takes place in an unnamed Communist or fascist like dictatorship of the future. Here an individual does not have any rights and exists only to serve the state. I think a clear picture of it is given in Cliffs Notes: "The citizens of this society are pawns without rights who exist as wards of the state. They are born in state-controlled hospitals, raised in state-controlled nurseries, educated in state-controlled schools, toil at state-assigned jobs, and sleep in massive barracks organized by the state." (4)

The novel starts with the words: "It is a sin to write this." (17) The name of the protagonist is Equality 7-2521. For the first time he has broken the laws. The laws say that men may not write unless the Council of Vocations did them so. Equality 7-2521 is six feet tall and that is a burden as there are a few who are six feet tall. The teachers and the leaders frown and say: "There is evil in your bones, Equality 7-2521, for your body has grown beyond the bodies of your brothers. But we cannot change our bones or our body. We were born with a curse. It has always driven us to thoughts which are forbidden." (18) He strives to be like all his brother men, as all men must be alike. When he is five years old he is sent to the Home of the Students, where men must learn till they reach their fifteenth year. Then they go to work. There they arise when the bell rings in the tower and they go to their beds when it rings again. They say all together with teachers: "We are nothing. Mankind is all. By the grace of our brothers are we allowed our lives? We exist through, by and for our brother who are the State. Amen." (21)

Equality 7-2521 is not happy there. It is not that the learning is too hard for him, but it is too easy. This is a great sin, to be born with a head which is too quick. It is not good for a man to be different from his brothers. The teachers tell him not to choose the work they like. They should do the work which the Council of Vocations prescribes for them. Equality is guilty of the great Transgression of Preference. He does not listen well to the history of all the Councils. But he loves the Science of things. He wishes to know about all the things which make the earth around him. He asks so many questions that the teachers forbid. He thinks there are mysteries in the sky and under the water. But the Council of Scholars says that there are no mysteries and they know all things. The questions give him no rest. He cannot resist it. It whispers to him that there are great things on the earth and that he can know them if he tries. So he wishes to be sent to the Home of Scholars.

The Council of Vocations comes on the first day of spring. The Council calls the Student's names and when the students step before them, one after another, the Council say, "Carpenter" or "Doctor" or "Cook" or "Leader." The students have to accept the work entrusted to them. Equality waits for his turn and the Council entrusts him with the job of "Street Sweeper." When the bell rings all of them walk in a straight column to one of the City Halls for the

Social Meeting and sign hymns of Brotherhood, Equality and of Collective spirit. Thus Equality 7-2521 has lived for four years. All forty men are sent to the Home of Useless, where the old ones live. They know that they are soon to die. Such would have been his life, if Equality 7-2521 had not committed the crime which has changed his life.

It is a day of spring. The Street Sweepers work in brigades of three and they are with Union 5-3992 who is of the half-brain and with International 4-8818 who is different. International 4-8818 is strong youth and there is laughter in his eyes. For this he is not liked in the Home of the students, as it is not proper to smile without reason. He is not liked also for he draws pictures upon the walls with coal. Only the men in the Home of the Artists are permitted to draw pictures. So International 4-8818 is sent to the Home of Street Sweepers. He and Equality 7-2521 are friends. On the day of spring, Union 5-3992 is stricken with convulsions. The Street Sweepers leave him to lie in the shade of Theatre and go to finish their work. Beyond the ravine there is a plain, and beyond the plain there lies the United Forest about which men must not think. When Equality 7-2521 is gathering the papers and the rags, he sees an iron bar among the weeds: "It was old and rusted by many rains. We pulled with all our strength, but we could not move it. So we called International 4-8818, and together we scraped the earth around the bar. Of a sudden the earth fell in before us, and we saw an old iron grill over a black hole." (31) Then he sees iron rings as steps leading down a shaft into darkness.

Equality 7-2521 hangs on the iron rings. He can see nothing, but he goes down. It is a great tunnel. Its walls are hard and smooth to touch. But he cannot follow as he is losing light. So he crawls back. He knows suddenly that the place is left from the unmentionable Times. International 4-8818 says that they have to report their find to the City Council. But Equality 7-2521 does not agree and says that the place belongs to him and no other man on the earth. When the Street Sweepers sit in the City Theatre, each night, Equality 7-2521 steals out and runs through the darkness to his place. He sits under the earth and reads the stolen scripts.

Equality 7-2521 has solved secrets of which the Scholars have no knowledge. There is no shame in them and no regret. The women who have been assigned to work the soil live in the Home of the Peasants beyond the city: "We wish to speak it, but we dare not speak it above a whisper; for men are forbidden to take notice of women, and women are forbidden to take notice of men. But we think of one among women whose name is Liberty 5-3000, and we think of no others." (38) Where the city ends there is a great road winding off to the north, and the Street Sweepers must keep this clean to the first mile post. There is a hedge along the road, and beyond the hedge the fields lie. Women work in the fields: "And there it was that we saw Liberty 5-3000 walking along the furrows. Their body was straight and thin as a blade of iron. Their eyes were dark and hard and glowing, with no fear in them, no kindness and no guilt." (38-39) Thereafter Equality 7-2521 looks at her each day. One day she suddenly turns to him. There is no smile on her face. But the following day she smiles.

Every morning thereafter, they greet each other with their eyes. It is his second Transgression of Preference. He has given the woman a name in his thoughts and it is the Golden One. Equality 7-2521 takes no heed at the Time of Mating: "This is the time each spring when all the men older than twenty and all the women older than eighteen are sent for one night to the City of Palace of Mating. And each of the men has one of the women assigned to them by the Council of Eugenics. Children are born each wither, but women never see their children and children never know their parents. Twice we have an ugly and shameful matter, of which we do not like to think." (41) One day Equality speaks to the Golden One.

There is a legend of the great fighting, in which many men fight on one side and a few, the Evil Ones on the other. The Evil ones are conquered and all the things including the scripts of them are burned; and with them all the words of them. Those words are not known. And yet, Equality 7-2521 feels, there is some word, one single word which is not in the language of men. That is the Unspeakable Word which no man may speak or hear. If they speak, they are put to death. Equality 7-2521 has discovered a new power of nature. When he is cutting open the body of a frog, he sees its leg jerking: "We could not understand it. Then, after many tests, we found the answer. The frog had been hanging on a wire of copper; and it had been the metal of our knife which had sent a strange power to the copper through the brine of the frog's body. We put a piece of copper and a piece of zinc into a jar of brine, we touched a wire to them, and there, under our fingers, was a miracle which had never occurred before, a new miracle and new power." (52-53)

Many days pass before Equality 7-2521 can speak to the Golden One again. He tells the woman the name he has given her. She has given him a name too and it is The Unconquered. She says that he has worked for many hours and he must be thirsty. She brings water and kneels by the moat. He gathers water in his two hands and holds the water out to his lips: "We do not know if we drank that water. We only knew suddenly that their hands were empty, but we were still holding our lips to their hands, and that they knew it, but did not move." (57) The Golden One steps back and looks upon her hands in wonder. Then she moves away. One night, after many days and trials Equality 7-2521 finishes building a strange thing, from the remains of the Unmentionable Times, a box of glass. It comes to life, turns red, and a circle of light lies on the stone before him.

Equality thinks of the meaning of that which lies before him. In a month, the World Council of Scholars is to meet in the city. It is a great council in which the wisest of all lands are elected. Equality wishes to confess everything to them. They will understand and forgive as his gift is greater than his transgression. For the first time he cares about his body. For thirty days he has not been in the tunnel. He has been in the glass which tells him when three hours have passed and it is the time to return to the City Theatre. Equality walks to the Home of Street Sweepers. When the Council of the Home questions him, he does not answer. So he is sent to Corrective Detention to be lashed until he tells.

When he opens his eyes, he is lying on the floor of a cell. Many judges come, but he does not speak. That night he thinks that he must escape. It is easy to escape as the locks are old and there are no guards. He steals through the dark streets and down his tunnel. The next day, he enters the great hall where the World Council of Scholars sits in solemn meeting. Equality displays the glass box. He puts wires to the box. Slowly as a flash of blood, a red flame trembles in the wire. Then it glows, but there is terror in the man of the council. They run from the table. Equality laughs and says: "Fear nothing our brothers. There is a great power in these wires, but this power is tamed. It is yours. We gave it to you." (70) But they say that what is not thought by all men cannot be true and what is not done collectively cannot be good. So the box must be destroyed. Equality seizes the box and runs to the window. He runs, but does not know, where he is going. Then he feels suddenly that he is lying on soft earth and he stops. His legs have brought him to Uncharted Forest against his will. Then he rises and walks on into the forest. Men will not follow him as they never enter the Forest.

Equality walks on with the box in his arms, his heart empty. But he cares for nothing on earth. Then a blow of pain struck them, their first and the only thought of the Golden One. It is best if the Golden One forgets him. It has been a day of wonder, his first day in the forest. When a ray of sunlight falls across his face, he wants to leap to his feet. But suddenly he remembers that no bell has rung and there will be no bell anywhere. He can lie as long as he wishes. He laughs at the thought.

On the second day in the forest, he hears the steps behind him. He hides in the bushes and sees a gleam of gold. He leaps forward and looks upon the Golden One. The Golden One raises her head. With a pride in her voice he says: "We have followed you and we shall follow you wherever you go. If danger threatens you, we shall face it also. If it be death, we shall die with you. You are damned, and we wish to share your damnation." (82) The man with the woman walks for many days. Each day adds to the chain of days between them and the city is like an added blessing. Equality makes a bow and many arrows to kill the birds. They find water and fruit in the forest. At night they choose a clearing and Equality builds a ring of fires around it. They sleep in the midst of that ring and the beasts do not dare to attack them.

One day, at sunrise, Equality and the Golden One see a white flame among the trees high on a peak. So they climb toward it through the rocks. The white fire comes from the sun on the glass of the windows of a house. The house has five storeys and a strange roof flat as a floor. There is more window than wall. That house must be left from Unmentionable Times. They step into the house. They need the days and years ahead, to look, to learn and to understand the things of this house. There are strange things which they have never seen and the use of which they do not know. There are globes of glass everywhere, in each room. They find the sleeping hall and they stand in awe upon its threshold. As it is a small room, there are only two beds in it. They find the garments and the Golden One gapes at them. There is a room with walls made of shelves, which hold rows of manuscripts. They have never seen such a number of them.

They have hard shells of cloth and leather. Their pages are so small that they wonder at the men who have such handwriting. They are written in their language, but many words are not known. When Equality has seen all the rooms of the house, he looks at the Golden One and they both know the thought in their minds: "We shall never leave the house nor let it be taken from us. This is our home and the end of our journey. This is your house, Golden One, and ours, and it belongs to no other men whatever as far as the earth many stretch. We shall not share it with others, as we share not our joy with them, or our love, or our hunger. So be it to the end of our days." (91-92) When the sun sinks, the Golden One falls asleep on the floor amidst jewels and flowers of silk. Then Equality lights a candle and starts reading the manuscripts. He thinks: "May knowledge come to us!" (93)

"I AM. I THINK. I WILL," this is the answer to the questions that rise in the individual's mind. Many words have been granted him, but only three are holy, "I will it!" Whatever road he takes, the guiding star is within him. He knows what happiness is possible for him on earth. His happiness is not the means to any end. It is the end. He is not a tool for the use of others: "I am a man. This miracle of me is mine to own and keep, and mine to guard, and mine to use, and mine to kneel before!" (95) Equality does not surrender his treasures, his thought, will and freedom. He is neither foe nor friend to his brothers. He will choose his friends among men. He will love and respect them, but neither command nor obey. They will join their hands when they wish, or walk alone when they desire. In the temple of his spirit, each man is alone: "For the word 'we' must never be spoken, save by one's choice and as a second thought. This word must never be placed first within man's soul, else it becomes a monster, the root of all the evils on earth, the root of man's torture by men, and of an unspeakable lie." (96-97)

Equality is done with the monster of "we," the word of plunder, misery and shame. Now he sees the face of god, the god, the one word. It is when he reads the first of the books, he finds the word, "I." When he understands the word, he weeps in deliverance and in pity for all mankind. Then he calls the Golden One and says: "My dearest one, it is not proper for men to be without names. There was a time when each man had a name of his own to distinguish him from all other men. So let us choose our names." (98-99) He wants to bear the name Prometheus. He gives the name, Gaea, the mother of the earth and of all the gods, to the Golden One. On the mountaintop, with the world below, Equality lives. Gaea is pregnant with his child. Their son will be raised as a man. He will be taught to say "I" and to bear the pride of it: "I shall call to me my friend who has no name save International 4-8818, and all those like him. Fraternity 2-5503, who cries without reason, and Solidarity 9-6347 who calls for help in the night, and a few others. I shall call to me all the men and the women whose spirit has not been killed within them and who suffer under the yoke of their brothers. They will follow me and I shall lead them to my fortress. And here, in this uncharted wilderness, I and they, my chosen friends, my fellow builders, shall write the first chapter in the new history of men." (100-1)

There on the mountain, he and his sons and his chosen friends will build their new land. It will become as the heart of the earth, lost and hidden, beating louder each day. The day will come when he will break all the chains of the earth, and raze the cities of the enslaved, and his home will become the capital of a world where each man will be free to exist for his own sake. For the coming of that day, he, his sons and his chosen friends fight. They fight for the freedom of Man: "And here, over the portals of my fort, I shall cut in the stone the word which is to be my beacon and my banner. The word which will not die, should we all perish in battle. The word which can never die on this earth, for it is the heart of it and the meaning and the glory. The sacred word: "EGO."" (104-5)

In the novel *Anthem*, Equality is the man who holds on to his own mind in a collectivist society that demands blind obedience to the group. Whenever they are tempted, they repeat to themselves:

> We are one in all in one.
> There are no men but only the great WE,
> One, indivisible and forever. (19)

From the beginning of time, men have always been curious about anything that cannot be explained. Men used to be attracted to anything that was not understood. This quality is wonderfully portrayed by Ayn Rand in her *Anthem*. No one is an individual and everyone is equal in every way. The protagonist dares to go past the boundaries so clearly laid out for him. For doing this, he is banished from society. But this banishment makes him gain a lot spiritually. He feels self-dependent for the first time in his life. He says: "And suddenly, for the first time this day, we remembered that we are the Damned. We remembered it, and we laughed." (80) Now, he is able to win man's most prized possession, freedom. Ego too comes to him with the freedom. In the story of Garden of Eden, Adam and Eve were punished for being disobedient. They were presented with a wonderful life, but there was only one rule. Adam and Eve broke the rule and were banished. Their natural instincts of curiousness and disobedience had got them in trouble.

Both these stories deal with the intrigue of untouchable: "Adam and Eve had everything, but both wanted just a bite of apple. They were both banished from the Garden of Eden. But they too gained from their exile. After they were banished, they both began to explore the nature of human begins. They started mating, and taking care of themselves, and so on. . . . When Adam and Eve got kicked out of the Garden of Eden, they created the world as we know today, or at least that's how the story goes. In *Anthem* too, there was a forbidden item. However, it was not a mere fruit. Prometheus' fruit was in fact knowledge. When he created light bulb all by himself, he thought he would be praised. Instead he was shunned for working by himself without authority to do so. In the story of Adam and Eve, we are told that they ate the forbidden fruit, and were banished. This story closely relates to *Anthem* in the fact that the characters in both stories had clear rules laid out for them, and the characters broke those rules due to their natural instincts." (http://www.collage tempapers.com) This proves that in the end, both the couples come out with something they did not have in their controlling world.

In spite of powerful pressure from the state to conform, Equality will not leave his values which are important to him. For him, scientific research gives meaning and joy to his life, so he does not leave it. Likewise, though it is forbidden, he loves the Golden One. Equality begins the story as an exceptional youth. He has barely realized that he may be different from his brothers around him. From the beginning, he describes himself as having a curse of being different from his brothers, being an individual. He writes: "We know that we are evil, but there is no will in us and no power to resist it. This is our wonder and our secret fear, that we know and do not resist." (18) Yet through the course of events he finally comes to the conclusion that the curse is a blessing, because it leads him out of captivity to the world of freedom.

Equality's relationship with International 4-8818, his only friend, demonstrates the half-hearted attempts he makes to eliminate all his preferences for individual people, to care for each brother equally, and to be identical to his brothers. Rand says in *The Romantic Manifesto:* "Consciously or subconsciously, explicitly or implicitly, man knows that he needs a comprehensive view of existence to integrate his values, to choose his goals, to plan his fortune, to maintain the unity and coherence of his life—and that his metaphysical value—judgments are involved in every moment of his life, in his every choice, decision and action." (19) However, at the discovery of the tunnel, Equality realizes that solitude pleases him and when he meets the Golden One, he cannot deny the fact that he prefers some of his equals to his brothers. As he wants to think about her all the time and that urge is so overwhelming, he decides to commit the sin. In doing so, he takes his first step down the road towards breaking with society.

Equality is attracted towards the Golden One because of her haughtiness and her strength. He also knows that she too likes the same qualities in him. Equality has become a complete rebellion with the discovery of the light bulb. He is ready to give his life for it. Equality has been thinking of his brothers and their welfare. He says: "We can light our tunnel, and the city, and all the cities of the world with nothing save metal and wires. We can give our brothers a new light, cleaner and brighter than any they have ever known." (60) But the moment the World Council threatens to destroy the light bulb, he changes his mind. He can tolerate his own destruction, but he cannot bear the light bulb destroyed. So he is forced into exile from his society.

Once Equality left the society, he adopts a vanity and pride that are unknown in his society. In doing so, he realizes his manhood. Equality feels the pride of killing his own food and the pleasure in eating it for the first time in the forest. The analysis in Spark Notes in true: "Upon discovering the 'I' while he is reading in the library in the house, Equality 7-2521suddenly becomes aware that he is the centre of his own universe, and the curse he has been fighting is actually a blessing to be embraced. . . . Rand intends Equality 7-2521's name to be ironic, since we know that Equality 7-2521 is far superior to his peer and does not believe in the doctrine of equality." Thus, the abandoned house in the forest symbolizes Equality's capacity to provide for himself.

Equality's actions form the earliest days of childhood are explained by his independence of thinking and of spirit. Equality yearns to be sent to the Home of Scholars, though in their society, youths are not permitted to desire a profession of their own choice. In the House of Scholars, he wants to pursue the research he loves.

In their culture, such thoughts never come to them. It is evident that Equality is a genius. Under the conditions where the powerful authorities have bitter antagonism towards him, he proceeds to the human kind's advanced knowledge. In Cliffs Notes point out Equality's commitment to his work: "Equality 7-2521 is a factious example of going despite the inherent difficulties of making intellectual break thoughts and of battling the conservative elements of society that oppose him. Equality 7-2521 will not surrender his creative work no matter the degree or variety of difficulties he encounters." (42) It shows that under the conditions where the powerful authorities have bitter antagonism towards him, he proceeds to the human kind's advanced knowledge.

Equality is an example of the kind of heroes responsible for the progress that the society has achieved. His integrity is displayed by his relationship with the Golden One. He clearly knows that she is different from all other women. When she asks him if he would look at her in a crowd of other women, he replies that he would look upon her if she were with all the women of the earth. Though he knows the power of the Councils, he decides that he will not permit them to ever take the Golden One to the Palace of Mating. When he flees the city under the threat of death, his only regret is that he cannot see the Golden One: "We thought of the Golden One whom we shall never see again. Then the pain passed. We are one of the Damned. It is best if the Golden One forget our name and the body which bore that name." (77)

Equality's greatest achievement is his realization that human beings are free individuals and they need political freedom to live happily. A perfect match for Equality is Liberty 5-3000, a beautiful peasant girl. She is Equality's companion, lover and soul mate. When Equality escapes to the Uncharted Forest, she too follows him. As she has a mind of her own, she does not blindly follow the authorities. She is more than a beautiful young woman. Her inner beauty can be recognized externally. Rand describes her: "Their hair was golden as the sun; their hair flew in the wind, shining and wild, as if it defied men to restrain it. They threw seeds from their hands as if they designed to fling a scornful gift, and the earth was a beggar under their feet." (39) Equality knows her virtues even before speaking to her. Equality gleans from her fearless eyes and her derisive mannerisms reveal that she is proud, with an inner reverence that comes only from an unbroken independence of spirit.

To pursue her goals, like Equality, the Golden One too violates the customs of the society. Later, she talks to him as fearlessly as he does. She tells him that he is different from his brothers and she does not wish him to be. Subsequently, she tells him that she has given him a name as he has given her. She thinks of him in her own mind as The Unconquered. She does not mind the social approval. Her personal values mean everything for her. She tells him in the forest: "Your eyes are as a flame, but our brothers have neither hope nor fire. Your mouth is cut of granite, but our brothers are soft and humble. Your head is high, but our brothers cringe. You walk, but our brothers crawl. We wish to be damned with you, rather than blessed with all our brothers. Do as you please with us, but do not send away from you." (83)

What Barbara Branden says about Rand in *The Passion of Ayn Rand* can be applied to her heroine: 'The human qualities she [Rand] cared about were, she believed, specifically masculine attributes, above all, purposefulness and strength. She would later insist that she had never regretted being a woman, but "it was hero worship from the first." And man, she would say, is defined by his relationship to reality; woman—by her relationship to man. Far into old age, she would comment about herself proudly, "I'm a hero worshipper."' (18) Thus like Rand, the Golden One is a hero-worshipper.

The character of the Golden one, like that of Equality, displays an important principle about Rand's theory of human nature. Rand thinks that independent persons form their own values. What is written about her in Cliffs Notes is true: "She recognizes that distinct persons are not equal in an absolute sense, and she loves Equality 7-2521 because his genius and proud independence cause him to stand out from the crowd. She chooses Equality 7-2521 for her reasons and in defiance of social regulations. She chooses to pursue him into the forest despite knowing that such a decision represents a literal point of no return: she will not be readmitted into the society. Her independence of evaluation is responsible for the vitality of her emotional life in contrast to the desiccated existence of her peers. Because other members of the society mindlessly conform, they have no passions of their own. Nothing means that much to the other members of the society because they have surrendered their minds to the state. Persons who do not think for themselves cannot value for themselves, and they end up with stunted emotional lives." (43) Thus, the society's beliefs are insufficient to shake her confidence in her own judgment, and this is what makes her a heroine.

Rand continues her theme of independent thinking and personal values in another form. The Golden One has been taught that the meaning of life is in selfless toil for her brothers and sisters. At a conscious level, she accepts it as they are the beliefs she ever heard. Yet inherently she cannot accept. She is attracted towards Equality because he has an unconquered soul. She refuses to leave her love, as she loves him for everything he stands for. She does not show any regard for what others believe. She thinks that she should be true in action, to her convictions in order to be happy. Through the characters of Equality and the Golden One, Rand shows that the meaning of life lies in personal values, but not in social values and in things and goals that are uniquely one's own.

The Golden One's name undergoes changes many times, but she herself is consistent throughout the novel. From the beginning, she is haughty and she rejects all the society except Equality. Almost immediately, she sees him, she becomes subservient to him and seeks to care for him as early as the third time they meet by offering water to cool himself. She says; "It is cooler in the fields and there is water to drink." (57) Though she is static in her character, the Golden One shows an extraordinary curiosity while discovering the "I" and when she finds her uncommon beauty. She is superior to her sisters because she at least doubts that there is more to the world than the collective equality enforces in her society. Apart from it, she stands out from the faceless and nameless masses as she is unbelievably beautiful. It is a sign from Rand because she regards physical beauty as the natural counterpart to intellectual and personal integrity. Rand idealizes physical beauty and this physical beauty sets her heroes apart from her villains.

The Golden One is originally proud, but her originality is at odds with her subservience to Equality. Her willingness to accept the new names that Equality gives her shows that she has broader willingness to accept the identity he gives her. Her underdevelopment is because of the fact that Rand presents her character as the only other example of goodness in a collective society. She is introduced by Rand, as the pinnacle of feminine power and wisdom. The Golden One feels the affection of Equality as a personal triumph. She is strong and unafraid like him.

Feminists often criticize Rand for her view of women. They argue that Rand dehumanizes and subjugates women to the will of men. I think it is apt to quote Barbara Branden who explains Rand's feeling about it in *The Passion of Ayn Rand:* 'In childhood, and all of their life, it appears that her most intense scorn was reserved for women. The scorn was evident in her recollections of childhood, and, equally, it is the impression of many of the people who knew her in later years. Even before adolescence, she was what she later called "an anti-feminist, I regarded men as a super value."' (17) However, Rand believes that the success of women is in their innate wisdom, an unspoken and intuitive kind of knowledge, and in their physical beauty. The relationship between men and women plays an important role in *Anthem*, like all her other novels. In *Anthem* she presents the City Palace of Mating as the ultimate evil in sexual relationship as it allows sex without choice. According to Rand, sex is not sex without choice. So the pure love felt by Equality for the Golden One cannot be compared to the City Palace of Mating.

A friend of Equality who possesses the same independent spirit as Equality and the Golden One is International 4-8818. Equality writes that he and International are friends. They do not speak of it, because they are not allowed to express such personal thoughts. But their relationship is understood by both of them: "We know when we look into each other's eyes." (30) The authorities want to discourage International's autonomy of spirit, so he is sent to the Home of the Street Sweepers, just as Equality. The state wants to break the spirits of these heroic men by taking from them the values they love. International 4-8818's role in the discovery of the abandoned subway tunnel reveals his true nature. It is the most important action in the story.

International says to Equality: "The will of our Council is above all things, for it is the will of our brothers, which is holy. But if you wish it so, we shall obey you. Rather shall we be evil with you than good with all of our brothers. May the Council have mercy upon both our hearts." (34) He is true to his friends and he does not reveal anyone through the years of Equality's research when his friend slips away from the City Theatre for hours every night. Like Equality and the Golden one, International has a mind and values of his own and he never betrays them. Because of this, Equality plans to steal back into the city and rescue International. International will be the first to defect from the global dictatorship and find freedom in the new society. He will escape to liberty just as many have find freedom in the new society. He will escape to liberty just as many have fled from such Communist States as Cuba, North Korea, Vietnam, China, and various nations of Eastern Europe.

Another important person in the story is the Saint of Pyre. His character appears only in the flashback. He is a young man whom Equality witnesses being burned at the stake. He is the one who had re-discovered and dared to state the Unspeakable Word 'I'. Equality sees him in his youth. He writes: "They walked to the pyre, and their step did not falter. And of all the faces on the square, of all the faces which shrieked and screamed and spat curses upon them, theirs, was the calmest and the happiest face." (50) Equality sees a thread of blood running from the Saint's mouth, yet his lips are curled in a smile. The transgressor recognizes his successor when he sees him and exhorts him with his eyes not to surrender the independence of spirit that is uniquely his. This episode, too, hints at what is to come.

In this aspect, Equality can be regarded as akin to the pioneers of the electric age as Thomas Edison, Nikola Tesla, and George Westinghouse. Edison invented the light bulb and also he created the world's first electric lighting system. He is the man who developed new ideas. But unlike those thinkers, Equality lives in a collectivist dictatorship that threatens his life for his crime of free thinking. The idea that comes to Equality is that the courageous man facing death calmly is like a Saint. His noble appearance is what one expects of a saint. In Rand's view, the willingness to die for an ideal makes a man or woman distinguished. Indeed when society makes a man hero, he feels nothing but joy at the discovery of his ideal. This is the reason why the Transgressor of the Unspeakable Word has no fear or pain when he is burned. There is only tremendous elation in his knowledge of the word that is forgotten by the rest of the society.

Equality writes: "There was no pain in their eyes and no knowledge of the agony of their body. There was only joy in them, and a pride, a pride holier than it is fit for human pride to be." (51) When the flames rise to engulf him, a strange thing happens. The Saint's eyes rove the crowd and stop on the youthful Equality 7-2521 the sound and the meaning of the Unspeakable Word—but the flames sweep over his body, leaving him no chance. It leaves Equality 7-2521 with an agonizing question regarding the Unspeakable Word, and a determination to discover its meaning, even if, as the Saint, he must burn at the pyre for it.

Rand seems to compose the novel in a lyrical fashion and the majority of the text embraces more faithfully poetry and prose. It does not affect the storytelling, but it makes the reader to view *Anthem* as an extended poem which detracts from the seriousness of the book. Through the struggle of Equality, Rand shows her own philosophy and her beliefs. In the society, all creativity is suppressed and the individual has been lost to assimilation. In this situation too, Equality has always been different. Rand wants to illustrate what happens if the state becomes too powerful. Her philosophy of Objectivism desires a limited government.

I agree with the comments in Cliffs Notes: 'Characters refer to themselves using the first person plural "we" and not the first person singular "I." The use of the plural rather than the singular self-reference, goes to the heart of the book's meaning. The collectivist society in which Equality 7-2521 lives is similar to the Nazi and Communist states of the twentieth century. . . . The rulers of Equality 7-2521's society seek to discourage even the realization of individuality; they attempt to inculcate an anti-colony mentality in which human beings emulate the self-sacrificial existence of insects serving the overall good of the whole. . . . No one has a personal name; instead each is tagged with generalized concepts of collectivism such as Equality, International, Solidarity, and so on. This attempt to extirpate all elements of individuality similarly explains why each person has a number attached to this collectivist label. Because the state considers individuality unreal, no person is unique or outstanding, human beings are interchangeable parts of a greater whole.' (46) This shows how human beings are subjugated.

The dictators of this society have succeeded in subjugating the people. Their ways are more terrible than the policies of such murderous tyrants as Hitler, Stalin, Mao and Pol Pot. In real life, these collectivist rulers forced millions of individuals to surrender their individuality in practice. The dictatorial regimes of Nazi Germany, Soviet Russia, Communist China, and Communist Cambodia forced their citizens to serve the state. Leonard Peikoff's writes it in his *The Ominous Parallels*: "Collectivism is the theory that the group [the collective] has the primacy over the individual. Collectivism holds that, in human affairs, the collective—the society, the community, the nation, the proletariat, the race etc.—is the unit of reality and the standard of value. On this view the individual has reality only as part of the group whenever it—or its representatives, the state—deems this desirable." (17)

Equality has two main accomplishments in the story. The first one is the discovery of "I" and the other is the rediscovery of electricity which he calls: "The power of the sky." (56) The light is the central symbol in the story. It symbolizes not only the enlightenment, but also the spirit and power of the individual. Rand has often been criticized for her work and how her philosophy excuses men's inhumanity to others, but she has an unbelievable vision to offer and it is in many ways a radiantly rational one. Rand's belief in individual human potential is shown by Equality's re-discovery of electricity. The box symbolizes the modern ideals of The Unconquered and The Golden One's individuality, the power of human reason, and the betterment of society through pure science instead of social planning. Rand defends the right of individuals to a life of their own by Equality's quest. It sounds a warning against modern society's relentless movement towards collectivism.

Another important thing found in the novel is that Rand makes her characters making choices. Her characters choose from alternatives available to them. They are significant and sometimes life-and-death issues. Equality refuses to bow to the Council's will. With his undaunted willingness to take control of his life, he stands as the most compelling example of the capacity to choose. Edward Wayne Younkins writes in *Philosophers of Capitalism:* "The proper values or ends for a human being are not open to choice, according to Rand. Choice is not the cause of the ultimate value of life, but life as the ultimate end is the cause—in the sense of creating the need for the activity of choice. It is only by choosing, which for Rand ultimately refers to attaining and maintaining a conceptual focus regarding the world, that the life which is proper to a man is attained." (178) Thus, Rand makes even the negative characters making choices too.

As is said in Cliffs Notes: "The most obvious example is the one made by the World Council of Scholars when Equality 7-2521 presents the electric light. After recovering from their fear, they realize the value the light possesses. They know the invention will put out of business the newly developed candle industry and will upset the plans of the World Councils, who will now have to incorporate the new invention into society. It is not that the Scholars do not see the light's value. The question is whether they want to take advantage of its value. The alternatives before them are strikingly clear: electricity, technological progress, and independent thought; or candles, technological backwardness, and thought control. They make their choice. They select more than candles over electric light; they choose suppression and dictatorship over independence and political freedom. They choose primitive stagnation over progress." 948) This proves that the World Council of Scholars represents one of the main evils of the collectivist society, that is, the collectivist government cannot come to a conclusion and take action on behalf of the society quickly.

The Spark Notes, unlike Cliffs Notes, puts the inability of the Council to accept the light bulb in a different and convincing way: "because the council members cannot all agree on technological advances, even a simple innovation such as the candle takes a huge amount of time and haggling to gain approval. Moreover, because consensus-building is difficult and dangerous in a society in which discard is viewed as a sin, the individuals in the council begin to fear any change as a threat to themselves." (http://www.sparknotes.com) For this reason, the council recoils from Equality 7-2521's lightbulb. Rand is arguing against a position that holds that socialism and collectivism are fundamentally useful and good propositions but were simply executed poorly in Russia. This position holds that Communism in Russia was a failure in large part because of the corruption, vanity, and cruelty of men like Josef Stalin, who lined their own pockets and carried out personal vendetta rather than truly pursue the good of the people. Rand, on the other hand, believes that collectivism is evil and doomed to fail no matter how it is executed, and the individual who fights for his own well-being over that of his brothers is the only effective solution to the problems inherent in collectivism.

Equality's friends also have free will. International makes a difficult decision when Equality says that they will not report about the tunnel. By deciding not to reveal it International is going against the orders of the Council and as a result he is risking his life. If he reveals it, Equality will be put to death. International's choice to support Equality is vital to the outcome of this conflict.

Rand portrays the totalitarian state of the future as a technologically backward society. The reason for this lies in her theory regarding the cause of production and wealth. Many examples for her theory are found in her novel. The electric light is the product of his mind and he discovers a new force of nature. His identification of this power, and his ability to harness it to create light, require his unswerving dedication to the laws of nature and the facts of reality. Society's beliefs are irrelevant to this creative process; in this case, they are mistaken. Equality, if he is to succeed in his endeavour, must allow himself to be ruled exclusively by the scientific facts of the case. Nature, not society, sets the terms in all such research and scientific investigations.

Equality regards the proud posture and haughty nature of the Golden One, as these outer characteristics show a spirit that refuses to obey. Equality is attracted to her by her independence of nature than by her physical beauty. The essence of her character is her free spirit. Indeed, part of her beauty that shines in her face and from her eyes is the outward reflection of it. Similarly, as she has an unbowed spirit, she likes the same in Equality. Equality likes the independent mind and he loves both Liberty 5-3000 and International 4-8818 as he finds the quality in both of them. Only men and women who hold personal values are capable of loving. The herd of conformists, who have relinquished their minds to the state, are incapable of experiencing this profoundly personal emotion.

The conditions while Equality is conducting his research are very difficult. He cannot find anyone with whom he can share his ideas. He does not have any support from his society, but he has the threat of punishment and death if caught. Equality passionately desires to understand nature's secrets. Equality is happy as his electric light will benefit society, but his primary motive is not the society's gain. Rather he is impelled by his own personal values and because of the importance he places on his creative work. Ayn Rand believes that creative work is personal, not social. When personal values are destroyed in any individual, he or she cannot engage in creative work. Equality prefers to be beaten to death than to reveal the light. After reaching the house, Equality and the

Golden One want to defend it even to the death. In all these incidents, Equality defends his work and property as extensions of himself as they spring from him.

A creator's recognition of achievement and of the value possessed by the one, who accomplishes I, fills him with a powerful experience of self-love. This sense of self-worth is why, for the first time, he desires to see his face and know what he looks like. The recognition of his inner beauty leads him to expect that his external demeanour will match it. After experimenting many nights, Equality succeeds in discovering the power of electricity, but he has to convince the Council of this new boon. Men never see their faces in this society, and are forbidden to ask their brothers. They have been taught that it is evil to have concern for their own faces and bodies. But now, for some reason he does not understand, he desires to see his face.

Equality's seeing his face for the first time is significant: "Appropriately, he recognizes his differences from the other members of society. He thinks and acts differently; therefore he looks differently. Where others have allowed their souls to be conquered and stand with bowed spine, he has maintained his independence and walks erect." (32) This shows that for the first time he knows about himself as he is surprised by seeing his face in the mirror for the first time. He has not yet discovered a literal mirror, the physical thing which shows his own form. This discovery comes later which is secondary. It is the result of his earlier discovery of the mirror of self-consciousness.

As a result of reaching of his own values, Equality for the first time feels a sensation of pride that is previously unknown. When he looks at the wires glowing in the dark, he is filled with a sense of accomplishment. He feels the wires to be veins in his own body. Now, he is ready to deny the tyranny of "we," and to discover the lost and sacred Unspeakable Word. In a Nazi or Communist society, the fundamental virtue is obedience. Individuals who act on their own thinking, like Equality, are considered dangerous to the system and so they are treated as criminals. The Councils have no danger from the mindless people who use their strong backs only for mutual labour. The freethinking mind is the only enemy for them. Equality is a danger for them as he has the brainpower to question the moral rectitude of their regime.

The actions performed by Equality are major violations of the conformity required by the society. Rand, here, wants to display the falsehood of the collectivists' claim to love mankind. The great thinkers should not have been punished, if the Communists were sincere. Equality's escape from prison so easily demonstrates two points. The first is at technological decline is so thorough that even the locks on the doors are rusted and aged, unable to withstand applied pressure. The state has no need to maintain systematic vigilance, for an independent thinker such as Equality 7-2521 has not appeared in anyone's memory.

Rand writes in *The Ayn Rand Lexicon: Objectivism from A to Z:* 'It is your mind that they want you to surrender—all those who preach the creed of sacrifice, whatever their tags or their motives, whether they demand it for the sake of your soul or your body, whether they promise you another life in heaven or a full stomach on this earth. Those who start by saying: "It is selfish to uphold your convictions, you must sacrifice them to the convictions of others." (5) This is the condition in any collectivist state. Equality's realization of this and a turning point in his talking occurs in his interview with the Scholars. He says to them: "Our brothers! We matter not, nor our transgression. It is only our brother men who matter. Give no thought to our, for we are nothing, but listen to our words, for we bring you a gift such as has never been brought to men. Listen to us, for we hold the future of mankind in our hands." (69-70)

The time Equality spends in the forest can be considered a voyage. He journeys physically from one place to another, but in a more profound way his journey is a long path of self-discovery and learning the fact is quick. In the society, his abilities are limited to sweeping the streets, but now, he learns his diverse abilities by engaging in hundreds of different activities. Rand portrays human beings with a heroic potential. The major theme in *Anthem* is fear. Rand believes that the only thing man has to fear is his fellows who will weigh him down and sap his strength, if they are given a chance. The Golden One is unafraid and so she appeals to Equality. By contrast, the persons in the Home of the Street Sweepers are so afraid that they cannot speak to each other at dinner or in the sleeping hall.

Equality writes: "The eyes of our brothers are dull, and never do they look one another in the eyes. The shoulders of our brothers are hunched, and their muscles are drawn, as if their bodies were shrinking and wished to shrink out of sight. And a word steals into our mind, as we look upon our brothers, and that word is fear. There is fear hanging in the air of the sleeping halls, and in the air of the streets. Fear walks through the city, fear without name, without shape. All men feel it and none dare to speak." (46) Generally, people in such a society characterized by fear can never make any progress.

Like fear, shapelessness in the novel symbolizes evil because it indicates the lack of ability to believe in something and to stand by it. Rand believes that the physical world mirrors the internal, personal world, and physical shapelessness goes hand in hand with fear and collectivity. That is why the entire world around Equality is shapeless and gray symbolizing stagnation and worthlessness. Equality describes: "There were five members of the Council, three of the male gender and two of the female. The hair was white and their faces were cracked as the clay of the Temple of the World Council. They sat before us and they did not move. And we saw no breath to stir the folds of their white togas. But we know that they were alive, for a finger of the hand of the oldest rose, pointed to us, and fell down again." (25-26) But the Golden One is hard, with sharply defined lines and an overwhelming physical beauty. Similarly, International 4-8818 stands out among his peers as he is taller and sharper than others.

In this context, Equality is compared to Adam in Spark Notes: "For this reason, Equality 7-2521 names the Golden One on two separate occasions, names himself, and searches relentlessly for the word 'I' Rand alludes to the power of naming granted to Adam in the Bible, where he is made master of the animals and they answer to the names he gives them. Likewise, Rand's heroes rename those things that are dear to them. By contrast, those in society are given numbers and social concepts as identifying tags, as yet another way of stealing their individuality from them." It shows that in *Anthem*, naming is a form of identifying one's possessions as one's own. Light in *Anthem* symbolizes truth. Thus, Liberty 5-3000 becomes the Golden One, and Equality 7-2521 becomes Prometheus, the bringer of light. Equality's contribution to the world is light and the house in the forest.

Equality and the Golden One find windows to let the light in: "Never had we seen rooms so full of light. The sunrays danced upon colours, more colours than we thought possible, we who had seen no houses save the white ones, the brown ones and the grey." (90) By contrast, the city is dingy and dark, and the only colours are gray, white, and brown. All the things are indistinct in the vast gray haze of that society. Those who have exceptional qualities can be differentiated from the crowd only when the light is brought. Therefore, Equality's lightbulb helps him see himself as the unique individual.

The forest is entirely different from city, an individual cannot claim anything his own, but the forest welcomes Equality and provides him what he needs. The forest is also a nexus between past and present. Manuscripts are sacred vessels of self-expression and they carry history. The manuscripts Equality steals from the Home of Scholars are very important for him as they are his only means of recording private thoughts. He says: "Manuscripts are precious, for our brothers in the Home of the Clerks spend one year to copy one single script in their clear handwriting." (36) The books he finds in the house of the forest are also important to him for they teach him the history of how the old world is destroyed and also it teaches him the word "I." The language and the theme of the novel contain many references to allegories from the lives of Christ, Moses and the story of genesis. Equality worships himself instead of worshipping any god. It seems that Equality is similar to other prophets in the sense that everything that came before is modified in the light of the message he bears. Though Ayn Rand makes many allusions to actual historical details about life in the Soviet Russia, *Anthem* does not refer to any particular historical setting. For example, the references to the councils and to the meetings at the City Theatre have close resemblance to the state of affairs in the Soviet Union in the early twentieth century, but the total regression of all technology is an exaggeration and it has no historical evidence.

Although *Anthem* certainly makes reference to the problems plaguing Russia at the time of its publication, the work is more than just an invective against Lenin, who inaugurated the communist era in Russia, or Stalin, who carried out horrifying purges against intellectual elite in the name of the good of the many. In the opening chapter, Rand sets up the images that occur throughout the novella to draw our attention to the values she is prompting. The most important element of this imagery is the contrasted pairs she sets up. These pairings point towards the characters and scenarios she believes are good or evil.

Equality prefers the dark and dingy tunnel, lit by a candle to the pristine white of the homes in which he has lied with his fellow infants, students and street sweepers. Apart from it, the villains of the novel are soft, featureless and seem dead, like the members of the Council of Vacations. In contrast, the hero and heroine are strong and vibrant. Indeed, in many cases, Rand turns the traditional images by making the dark and hard preferable to the light and gentle. For Rand, happiness is possible only with absolute freedom, and freedom allows all possibilities of fear. The Transgressor of the Unspeakable Word is another example of the impossibilities of fear in the face of freedom.

It is rightly pointed out in Spark Notes: "Rand does not explicitly say why the Transgressor is not afraid, but his bravery can be explained by the fact that Rand's philosophy holds that individualism brings great happiness and that is worth dying to experience one's own sense of self. Though the Transgressor's death mirrors the tales of Judeo-Christian saints and martyrs, thc nature of his martyrdom contrasts with nature of theirs. In Christian stories, the saints suffer on earth, even as they die, in the knowledge that they will be rewarded for their suffering in the heaven. They firmly hold the ideal for which they are martyred, but the martyrdom itself is torturous. For Rand, by contrast true happiness and ideals are possible on earth, and so death in the name of an ideal is its own reward. Her characters do not suffer from their faith; rather, their faith provides their happiness." It provides that a contrast that runs throughout *Anthem* is Equality's meditations on happiness involving fear and freedom.

Equality's breaking with the society manifests itself in explicit and structural ways. He is able to write with new fervour for his scientific exploration with the discovery of electricity. This shift signifies his increasing independence from the society. However, at this point, Equality still worries about the conventions of the society. *Anthem* consists entirely of musings about the state of natural and human world. This is the reason why it often bears resemblance to a scientific journal or a religious mediation. These musings gain even greater significance in their functions as expressions of individual will. In chapter I, the conversation between Equality and International shows Equality's willingness to break the law in pursuit of truth and his calling Golden One the dearest one indicates his willingness to break the law in pursuit of love. Equality writes about his conversation with the Golden One:

> For a long time we could not speak. Then we said: "Such thoughts as these are forbidden, Golden One."
>
> "But you think such thoughts as these and you wish us to think them." We looked into their eyes and we could not lie.
>
> "Yes," we whispered, and they smiled, and then we said: "Our dearest one, do not obey us." (56)

Naming, the original power of man in Genesis makes the Golden One and Equality more intimate with each other. It is interesting that Liberty 5-3000 is referred to throughout the novel as the Golden One, the name assigned by Equality to her, but her name for him does not appear again. Feminists argue that this disparity shows the fundamental inequality in Rand's view of men and women. But Rand might say that the issue is entirely stylistic. After all, Equality is writing the text, and so if he incorporates the name assigned by the Golden One to him, it would not appear meaningful. Another significant incident is the offering of water to Equality. This image is found very often in the Judeo-Christian Bible: "According to the New Testament, Jesus Christ often asked and received water from townspeople he met in his travel. Notably, Christ usually made followers of these who gave him water to drink. In this case, the Golden One's giving water to Equality 7-2521 accompanies her conversion into obedience of him." (http://www.sparknotes.com) It symbolizes the Golden One's taking the role of a caretaker and also it has biblical imagery.

The scene in the Palace of Corrective Detention in which Equality is flogged while bound naked to a post directly, resembles the Christian story about the scourging of Christ at the pillar. In the Christian story, Christ is stripped of his clothes and is beaten mercilessly at a pillar. He is mocked at by Roman soldiers before being crucified. This scene is used by Rand to heighten our sense that Equality is a new prophet and so he must suffer at the hands of the Councils in the interest of his Beliefs. By comparing Equality to Christ, she says that she is trying to reclaim religious language from religion to prove that it is possible to worship an ideal without having belief in the supernatural. Through the character, Collective 0-0009, Rand wants to expose the mastermind behind the demise of the old world.

Rand says that *Anthem* has no traditional structure and that it has no meaningful plot. According to her, the novel entirely revolves around the internal conflict inside Equality's mind. This conflict is resolved in the final chapter of the novel. Rand's belief that only other men can limit the freedom of a man and that in the state of nature man is completely free is reflected in Equality's return to nature to escape the evils of the society. This is a common theme in philosophy. For example, this is found in the work of the eighteenth-century Swiss philosopher Jean-Jacques Rousseau. In his *Confessions*, he suggests that man is a superior being before society. In *Anthem* Rand presents different ways of testing the world around us and finally she concludes that the best way to make determinations about the world is to test them against our own inner reactions. When Equality starts doubting his society for the first time, he engages in a kind of thought process previously unknown to him.

Anthem's extensive foreshadowing reveals many secrets of the story before Rand discloses them. For example, the Golden One's attempt to say "I love you" is one of the events that foreshadow the massive revelation, at the end of the story that the individual is the centre of the universe. The Transgressor of the Unspeakable Word's death before which he specifically seeks out Equality as he burns also indicates the coming realization that what Equality has been missing is the word, "I." Because of these clues, *Anthem* maintains little suspense. From the outset and at every step of the way it is clear that Rand is leading us to an ego-centred world.

The name Equality chooses for himself is Prometheus, a Greek man who crept up to Olympus, the home of the gods, and stole the fire from them: "Equality 7-2521 chooses the name Prometheus for himself in part as a reference to his inventing the light bulb and in part because he believes he will bring a new philosophy of individualism to the earth. Gaea, whose name Equality 7-2521 gives to the Golden One, was the Greek mother earth, who gave birth to the other gods and goddesses as well as to the sky and the sea. He chooses this name for her because she will, in his belief, give birth to a race of gods to rule the earth. Feminists object to the naming of the Golden One, who has now been named twice by her mate, and who apparently has no independent sense of self-worth. However, the Golden One is an active participant in the new world and that her part is to make the world beautiful and to endow her children with a sense of individualism." (http://www.sparknotes.com)

As *Anthem* was published in the United States on the heels of Nazi leader Adolf Hitler's defeat during World War II, critics of Rand's philosophy say that Rand's championing of a new race of men has particularly ominous connotations. Given that Hitler too advocated the founding of a superior race of men, specifically by killing off those he believed were weighing society down, *Anthem's* appearance was particularly ill-timed. Rand, however, is declaring the supremacy of human rights and that she believes each man is endowed with them. Rand sees her own time as the transition, from the glory of individualism, represented by the United States in the 1890s and 1920s, to the age of collectivism, represented by Russia starting around 1917, she wants both to warn those who believe in collectivism about its dangers and to bolster those who are still holding up the resistance in the name of the individual.

Taking new names is also significant for many reasons. Equality and the Golden One are rejecting the collectivist names imposed on them by the slave society. The name Equality 7-2521 stands for a particular aspect of collectivist thinking. For the collectivists, the term "equality" does not mean the individualistic principle that all individuals possess the same legal rights and are to be treated identically by the law. The collectivists mean that all individuals are equal in the real sense. I think it is rightly said in Cliffs Notes: "Believing themselves no more than a cog in a vast machine, they will seek no individuality and will be ready clay for their masters to mould. The hero rejects this philosophy of humanity." (40) It shows that no individual should be better than others, and no one should possess greater talent or intelligence than the crowd.

The numbers that follow every person's name are a means by which the rulers instil the same collectivist lesson. It indicates that each person is only one of the thousands having the same name and belonging to the same tribe and serving the same group. No one should be outstanding and unique. Further, even though the Golden One's given name is Liberty 5-3000, the word "liberty" is so corrupted by the collectivist culture, liberty means not the inalienable right of each person to subordinate to the group. George Orwell, in his famous book, *1984*, shows the collectivist dictators similarly corrupting the vocabulary of liberty by making such irrational claims as "Freedom is slavery."

Equality refers to the ideas of such seventeenth and eighteenth-century thinkers as John Locke and Voltaire. Those thinkers argued that rational human beings need not have blind obedience to church or state but they possess the right to direct the course of their own life. Equality also has in mind men such as Thomas Jefferson, James Madison and the other thinkers of America's founding period, who wrote the Declaration of Independence, the United States' Constitution, and the Bill of Rights. These men, who are responsible for the American republic, were individualists.

Equality realizes that as the collectivist doctrines spread around the globe, they eventually swallowed the free countries and turned them into totalitarian dictatorships as well. In this fictional universe, created by Rand in *Anthem*, there are no doctrines of individual rights in countries such as the United States as Human beings were gradually taught to worship the word "we" and leave the word "I." But Equality, like some Thomas Jefferson of the future, does not allow the spirit of freedom to die out on the earth. After centuries of absence he will bring the light of freedom back into human lives. He says: "Now I look ahead. My future is clear before me. The Saint of the pyre had seen the future when he chose me as his heir, as the heir of all the saints and all the martyrs who came before him and who died for the same cause, for the same word, no matter what name they gave to their cause and their truth." (99)

Equality is confident that ultimately, individualism wins over collectivism. Free minds like these do not confine their judgment to issues in the professional fields they choose; they think also on moral and political issues and recognize the grave injustices of the collectivist dictatorship. They think out on behalf of an individual's rights and in defence of political freedom. Thus, the authorities recognized the precociousness of Equality's intellect and confined him to the profession of Street Sweeper. In future, Equality's knowledge of electrical engineering will enable him to create new products that are useful to him and his friends. He will protect his mountaintop fortress by erecting a barrier of electrical wires. He is aware of the fact that in any conflict between mind and force, the mind will win.

Equality's individualism is not to pursue his own happiness but following his own mind. In *Hamlet*, Polonius says to Laertes: "To thine own self be true." Rand in Anthem proves that commitment to one's self is fundamentally commitment to one's own mind. A recurring point in the story is an innovator's struggle in collectivist society. It is rightly said in Cliffs Notes: "Equality 7-2521 is like many of the great thinkers and scientists of history who have met hostility from the leaders of their times. Socrates was put to death by Athenian society for the originality of his ideas. Galileo was threatened with torture by the inquisition for defending the heliocentric theory in astronomy—and his earlier colleague, Giordano Bruno, was burned at the stake for the same reason. In free societies such as the United States, inventive thinkers such as Robert Fulton, the Wright brothers, and innovative architect Frabj Lloyd Wright, merely face opposition from private citizens who follow tradition, but are not confronted with an all-powerful dictator who demands obedience. Such innovators are often mocked and ostracized, but not put to death. But Equality 7-2525 faces a collectivist state in which freethinking has been outlawed—much like an independent person in Nazi Germany or in Soviet Russia—and pursuit of new truths will result in his execution if apprehended" (12) This is the fate of an innovator in a Communist Society.

Rand agrees with the American principle that individuals should be equal before the law, but only in this sense they are equal. They differ from one another morally and psychologically. Some of them are better and some are worse. The thinkers in *Anthem* choose to have intimate relationships with one another than with passive followers. Their rejecting the egalitarian society indicates their refusal to allow personal values to perish from this earth. These personal values are critical to understanding why members of this society are unhappy. This is proved by the words of Equality: "All is not well with our brothers. There are Fraternity 2-5503, a quiet boy with wise, kind eyes, who cry suddenly, without reason in the midst of the day or night, and their body shakes with sobs they cannot explain." (47) Fraternity 2-5503 and Solidarity 9-6347 do not have the knowledge of individuality and personal values, but at emotional level, they experience the dreariness of a life without any meaning.

The idea of a planned society was there as far back as the militarist communism of ancient Sparta and the philosophical communism of Plato's *Republic*. It reappears in Thomas More's *Utopia* and in all succeeding visions of an ideal world. In the eighteenth century, Jean-Jacques Rousseau gives an important extension of collectivist thought when he argues that a society cannot be truly democratic unless its citizens possess substantially similar values, convictions, and degrees of wealth. Rousseau realized that people might not choose to make themselves politically free by making themselves materially and intellectually equal. So he predicted that it may be necessary to force a man to be free. His prediction would be fulfilled. As in the communist society of *Anthem*, so in every real-life collectivist state, freedom is regarded as inseparable from equality, and equality is enforced by government action.

Dr. Stephen Cox concentrates more on economic system. He writes that Rousseau believed that democracy cannot exist without an equalization of property; later collectivists insisted that the problem was private property itself. They saw capitalist system as "heartless," "wasteful" and "undisciplined" because it allows people to compete for and acquire private property. Most political movements of the twentieth century, whether communist or non-communist, called for a system of "social" planning, either to keep capitalism in check or to abolish it completely. This is the intellectual tendency to which Rand refers in her Foreword to novel. She was working from a different premise. She saw progress as dependent on the freedom of the individual mind. She knew that it is individuals, not social forces, who learn, create, discover.

In *Anthem*, the collectivist society, in spite of all the talk about equality and brotherhood, is ruled by a small section of people. Rand gives the reason for this. If "equality" means equal obedience to a social plan, then, as Rousseau says, the plan has to be implemented by force. This enforcement is done by certain people and they will constitute a separate class, superior to all others. Such a class will have not the best, but the worst elements of the society. They will enslave, torture, and kill their brothers in order to maintain a lie, the lie of their view of equality. These people will say things like: "Take your brother Equality 7-2521 to the Palace of Corrective Detention. Lash them until they tell." (64). *Anthem* is like a house of mirrors where the words, equality and brotherhood are parodied by the distorted image of equality and brotherhood as they appear in a collectivist society. *Anthem* is more than that because here the mirrors appear to come alive and a society devoted to the repression of the self is finally confronted by Equality who manages to reflect upon himself.

Since childhood, Equality has been taught to refer to himself as "we" as the self were a mere reflection of the group. He says: 'The word "We" is as lime poured over men, which sets and hardens to stone, and crushes all beneath it, and that which is white and that which is black are lost equally in the grey of it. It is the word by which the depraved steal the virtue of the good, by which the weak steal the might of the strong, by which the fools steal the wisdom of the sages.' (97) For the collectivists, the primary lies on the outside—society and physical labour, but for Rand, an individualist, everything starts from the inside, with a thought in the mind of the individual. Equality's discoveries are all made possible by his prior discovery of himself. As Stephen Cox says, this discovery does not come without error and pain. Rand knows that no story exists without conflict, and that conflict brings pain. Equality 7-2521 is in conflict with society; before that he is in conflict with himself, a self that he does not yet completely realize he possesses. Later, his assessment of collectivism will change, but his pride in himself will endure.

Words are mirrors of the self. For Rand, a woman who left her homeland, learned a new language and suffered years of privation in order to write her thoughts freely, words are always the primary means of understanding both the world and the self. Similarly, in *Anthem*, the story of self-discovery starts and ends with the written word. In the beginning, Equality has to write: "We wish to speak for once to no ears but our own." (18) He speaks to himself by means of the written word and finds the proof that he has a self, a self that he can analyze, and name, that he can make fully his own property. His quest for himself comes to an end when he discovers the ancient word, for the self as single, independent and the sacred word, Ego.

In Latin, ego simply means "I." In English, it has extensive associations, it is the root of such words as "egoism" and "egotism." "Egoism" suggests the idea that the self is, indeed, primary, that everything starts from the self. Rand, like here hero, was a proud egoist, but she knew that egoism is often confused with what is sometimes called "egotism"—the arrogant desire to dominate others. That is why her hero emphasizes the idea that respect for the self and its freedom requires a similar respect for the freedom of other selves.

Every culture has mythic stories that identify its values and dramatize its idea of the way things happen in the world. One of the famous stories of Western culture is the myth of Prometheus. The other story is the Bible's account of the world as the creation of God who works his will by means of words: "And God said, Let there be light: and there was light." Rand combines the two stories, Greek and Judeo-Christian and makes her hero a Promethean scientist and a worker with words. An anthem is a solemn hymn to God. Though Rand does not believe in God, her title suggests that she tries to project the secular correlative of intense religious feeling. Like the Greek poets, she feels free to remake traditional stories to suit her own philosophy. The new in *Anthem* is created by a human being, but not by a literal god.

Stephen Cox affirms the same point when he writes that America has its myths, and Rand exploits them, too; but here, nothing essential has to be changed. Myths are sometimes based on fact; American myths are often nearly identical to American realities. Thus, Equality 7-2521 is a creator in the same way as Franklin and Edison and the Wright brothers were creators. The American parallels run still farther. Like Franklin, who "snatched the lightning from the heavens and the sceptre from the tyrant," Rand's hero is a revolutionary as well as a scientist. Like millions of Americans who journeyed to new lands and created a new civilization, he is both explorer and pioneer.

Anthem can be called a crystallized epic. Though the values at stake are of the central character, they are the professed values of an entire civilization—our own. Cox is apt in saying that in the epic poetry of Homer, Virgil, and Milton, in the epic novels of the past centuries, in America's epic histories of its own development, the central story is a complex union of many stories. Usually, it is a union of apparent opposites—a myth of both separation and unification, discovery and recovery, adventure and return. Homer's *Odyssey* is the story of a man who leaves his home and then returns to it with newly assured self-mastery and power. Virgil's *Aeneid* is the story of a man who flees his home, then recreates it in a distant country. The history of America's pioneers and inventors is the story of men and women who set themselves apart from other people and, in so doing, create the means to a better life for everyone. So it is in *Anthem*.

By separating himself from his "brothers," Equality 7-2521 becomes their greatest benefactor. As Equality 7-2521 is driven by his "sin" from the purported paradise of collectivism and regains the true paradise of individualism, one hears a distinct echo of the Christian story of redemption. In *Anthem* the original paradise is false, and the sin is in fact a virtue, but the outlines of the story remain. It makes sense for Rand to use this story, because she, like the writers of the Bible, or Milton in *Paradise Lost*, is trying to grasp the largest and loftiest of all literary themes—the theme of the eternal things.

The martyrs of individualism may die, but their cause can never be defeated. This seems paradoxical that a battle is lost but not lost. It means that humanity transcends individual failures because of the spirit that manifests itself in individual attempts. Rand's myth does what myths should do; it offers a change of perspective and allows the reader to make sharp distinction between the things that appear to be superficially the same. It demonstrates that man is at the opposite end of the spectrum from men in their collective groups, the crow or the council. It shows that the spirit of individualism which spontaneously regenerating itself can be lost any number of times without being truly lost.

In order to move her readers to her point, Rand uses the plain standard language which is suitable to a certain intellectual accent. She shows the action simple and rarely uses description. She uses the first person narration, not only to emphasize the importance of "I" but also because a person writing for and to himself feels no need to provide long descriptions of familiar objects. Equality does not know history, philosophy, politics, or economics, and no one expects him to start with a comprehensive explanation of the world. Nothing will stand between the reader and the intense crystallization of the story. Rand provides the imagery traditionally associated with epic and myth to sharpen the focus still further. Her imagery concentrates on the contrast between the two competing views of life, collectivist and individualist.

In the collective world, the space is confined and every object is cheap and clumsy. It is a world of security. By contrast, the individualist world is a world of choices and risks, a world of tunnels and stars. To his imagery, Rand adds the images that connect two worlds and emphasize their conflict. One of the most vivid images is the execution of the Saint of the Unspeakable Word who is punished for his pride and it is the symbol of Equality's spirit. Rand's argument in the image is that the slave society lives by exploiting Equality's own attributes, pride, energy and intellect, and turning them against him. Rand poetically personifies natural forces like the ancient epic writers. Electricity is a like a friend who will grant us anything we ask.

As Equality sees, the sky is not threatening but welcoming, blue and glowing. As he is a scientist, it also appears to him as rational and orderly. It rises before him as the sun rises every day. It is obscured by the collectivist intellectuals. They are about to betray and persecute the man who has come to grant them more than they expect. But they cannot block the sky. The sky remains as the aspirations of Equality. In the forest Equality feels: "And now we look upon the earth and sky. This spread of naked rock and peaks and moonlight is like a world ready to be born, a world that waits. It seems to us it asks a sign from us, a spark, a first commandment.

We cannot know what word we are to give, nor what great deed this earth expects to witness. We know it waits." (92-93)

Rand chooses to write an epic story and she writes it in few words to achieve the intensity to effect. This is what Cox stresses when he writes: "Looking back on her life, she might have said what Equality 7-2521 says near the beginning of his story: 'We have come to see how great is the unexplored, and many lifetimes will not bring us to the end of our quest. But we wish no end.' And she might have remembered those moments, many years before, when she watched while the insight of Equality 7-2521 grew "sharper than the hawk's and clearer than rock crystal." *Anthem* is the crystalline product of that crystalline vision." When *Anthem* appeared for the second time, it could not be ignored. Rand's *The Fountainhead* had achieved great success. Its success was followed by her next novel, *Atlas Shrugged*. These two novels repeated and enormously extended them.

Ayn Rand's work is popular for the same reason Equality had been popular. Any major company will list Rand as a major influence. She influenced the Hollywood stars, ranging from Brad Pitts to Angelina Jolie to Vince Vaughn and directors like Oliver Stone, who is fond of Castro, says that Rand is one of the most important figures in his intellectual life. Rand was a novelist who became a systematic philosopher and her philosophy is repeated in *Anthem*: "Love her or hate her, Ayn Rand was never dull. Her words were clear, challenging, and memorable. Her ideas were boldly expressed. For the most part, the writing in *Essays on Ayn Rand's Anthem* is far below the standard if original, but there is still enough in the collection to provoke healthy curiosity about Rand's superbly individual." (http://www.geo cities.com) The reader at first feels it difficult to understand the "we" speaking as one person. It is a part of Rand's philosophy.

Even now people often strive for the communal good and what is good for society. But Americans have a sense of individuality and the importance of freedom. Rand proves through *Anthem* what happens if the sense is lost. *Anthem* makes them think and makes them want to be selfish. Though the novel is short, it gives the message forcefully. *Anthem* is not like *Atlas Shrugged* about a deteriorating society. It is already in deteriorated condition. As Thomas Jefferson wrote in the *Declaration of Independence*, every individual has right to life, liberty and the purity of happiness. Rand's message appears as important as it was fifty years ago. Human progress requires that the State has to stand back and allow the individual to act in his own interest. *Anthem* is an excellent introduction to her emotional polemical style and also of her passionate political philosophy.

Liberation as Idealism
The Fountainhead

According to Ayn Rand, the goal of her writing is the presentation of an ideal man. Howard Roark in *The Fountainhead* is the first such figure in her novels. She holds that man's creative mind is sacred, and consequently admires the great original thinkers of mankind—the artists, scientists, and inventors, such as Michelangelo, Newton, and Edison. *The Fountainhead* was first rejected by twelve publishers. Finally, Bobbs-Meril accepted it when a young editor threatened to quit if it were not published. His confidence proved to be just. *The Fountainhead* has sold some six million copies and continues to sell over 100,000 copies each year.

Mimi Reisel Gladstein is right when he says in *The New Ayn Rand Companion:* "It was positively reviewed in both the *Saturday Review of Literature* and *The New York Times Book Review* which compared it to Arrowsmith and called Rand's novel a work of remarkable vigour and interest." (12) At the time of its publication, Lorine Pruette wrote in the *New York Times* that it was the only novel of ideas written by an American woman that he can recall, with characters that are amazingly literate, romanticized as larger-than-life representatives of good and evil. Gladstein aptly says in *the New Ayn Rand Companion*: "Although *The Fountainhead* has become a marvel of the publishing world, it was not an instant bestseller. Like *One Flew over the Cuckoo's Nest*, another underground classic, it grew by word-of-mouth: developing a popularity that asserted itself slowly on the bestseller lists." (12) Thus he wrote about the way the novel became popular.

The novel opens with the laugh of Howard Roark: "That morning he has been expelled from the Architectural School of Stanton Institution of Technology." (16) As the Dean phones for him, he goes to him in his casual wear. The Dean speaks of his attitude towards the subject of architectural design. But Roark replies: "And I can find the joy only if I do my work in the best way possible to me. But the best is a matter of standards—and I set my own standards. I inherit nothing. I stand at the end of no tradition. I may perhaps, stand at the beginning of one." (24-25) The Dean realizes that Roark is a man not to be encouraged.

Guy Francon, the vice president of architects in Francon and Heyer, from New York addresses the architect in Stanton Institute of Technology. Then Peter Keating, the classmate of Roark, addresses as the president of the student body. When he thinks of Roark, he makes a determined effort to feel sorry: "But the secret glow came back, whenever he thought of the expulsion." (30) Keating takes the job offered by Francon and Roark goes to New York to work for Henry Cameron though he is not getting any important buildings. On his way back, Keating comes across the Dana Building designed by Cameron: "He chose what he wished to build. When he built, a client kept his mouth shut. He demanded of all people the one thing he had never granted anybody: obedience." (44) Roark enters Cameron's office and he accepts Roark.

Keating learns that Francon's wife has died leaving her fortune to their only daughter, Dominique, now nineteen, away at the college. At office, Keating makes friends as he knows how to become part of any place he enters. He offers help to Tim Davis to finish his work. He suddenly feels lonely and sends a wire to Catherin who lives with her uncle, Ellsworth Toohey. After helping Tim, Keating starts doing his daily assignments as well as making Francon realize that Tim is the least needed in the office. Tim loses his job and Keating arranges for him a new job. Keating feels a warm pleasure that he has influenced the course of a human being. His next target is Stengel who plans to open his own office. Keating encourages him to do it and achieves the position of chief designer. Keating meets Roark to make plans from Roark's sketches. He shows them to Francon saying that he has studied Francon's buildings and knows how to catch his ideas.

Sermons in Stone by Toohey is published in January of the year 1925. It is subtitled *Architecture for Everybody* and its success is sensational. Toohey states further: "Architects are servants, not leaders. They are not to assert their little egos, but to exercise the soul of their country and the rhythm of their time" (78) One day in February, Cameron collapses suddenly. A sister of him appears from somewhere and takes him to her home in New Jersey. It is the third year for Keating. His clients will accept anything he gives them: "Keating did not care so long as his clients were impressed, the clients did not care so long as their guests were impressed, and the guests did not care anyway" (81)

Roark joins the firm in engineer's department. He has no friends and he is there like a piece of furniture, as useful and as impersonal. Early in May when Keating is away, Francon says that a client wishes his office buildings to look like the Dana building. Roark agrees to design for him but he does not want to copy that building. For this he is again expelled from the firm and he starts searching for a new job. John Eric Snyte looks through Roark's sketches and gives him opportunity to sketch for a department store. Roark meets his fellow designers and learns that they are nicknamed as Classic, Gothic, Renaissance and Miscellaneous and Roark is addressed as Modernistic.

Keating hears the latest story about Toohey that he has been signed to write 'One Small Voice,' a daily syndicated column for Wynand papers. When Keating goes to a meeting to meet Catherine, he sees Austen Heller, the star columnist of the *Chronicle*, a brilliant newspaper, speaking. On a Sunday afternoon in March, Keating drives to the mansion of Ralstone Holcombe, the president of the Architects' Guild of America. There in a library he meets Dominique. Once Snyte gives the work of building a house and gives five hundred dollars to Roark to get himself an office.

On the advice of Francon, Keating invites Dominique to lunch to bring them closer. At lunch she speaks to Keating as to an old friend and he starts to meet her frequently. Suddenly Catherine comes to Keating and asks him to marry her as soon as possible as something dreadful is happening to her. Keating consoles and sends her home. His mother says that Catherine is a girl who is obedient to her mother-in-law. On the other hand she suggests that Miss Francon is a more suitable match to him though she never cares for an uneducated woman like her. In March Heller sends Mr. Robot L. Mundi to Roark. He wants not just a house but a symbol. He listens to Roark in polite astonishment: "It's a monument you want to build, but not to yourself. Not to your own life or your own achievement, to other people, to their supremacy over you. . . . Will you steel yourself for the rest of your life in the borrowed shape?" (163) Mundi agrees with him but does not change his mind. Roark asks him to select another architect. Late in May Roark receives another commission.

Mr. Whit Ford Sanborn decides to have a new country residence. On the suggestion of Cameron, he signs Roark. Lucius N. Heyer recovers from the stroke and returns to office which Keating does not like. Cosmo-Stonic Pictures of Hollywood has decided to erect a stupendous office and Keating applies. He gets the alternations in his sketches from Roark. Throughout winter Roark finds no other work. In the last week of April he is asked to submit the drawing for the new building of Manhattan Company. Suddenly Cameron calls for Roark and after three days he dies. When Keating threatens Heyer to retire, and the frightened Heyer dies. Keating comes to office, but the thought follows him that he is a murderer. He learns that Heyer has left everything to Keating. He also wins the competition of Cosmo-Slotnick building.

Dominique goes to Connecticut to take over her father's place for the summer. He goes to Roark and advises him: "'Howard, think of it! You'll be rich. You'll be famous. You'll be respected. You'll be presided. You'll be admired—you'll be one of us!" (192) Roark vacates the room and asks Mike Donnigan for a job. He sends Roark to a quarry in Connecticut where Dominique sees Roark. He too stands looking at her. She makes a long scratch across the marble in her bedroom and asks him to repair it. But he sends another one to do it. Later when she is sits at the dressing table Roark enters. They become closer and in the next minute they close on the world. Weeks pass and Roark is called by Roger

Enright. Half-an-hour later he is on the train. Dominique too gets a letter from her father and goes to New York.

Keating has to select a sculptor for the Cosmo-Slotnick Building. Mr. Slotnick awards it to Steven Mallory whom Keating does not like. He sends Mallory's model to Slotnick and he asks him to select another architect. Later he comes to know that Mallory fires at Toohey. He creates a sensation when he appears in Mallory's defence. Enright hires Roark at the end of their first interview. Roark again reopens his office. On an evening in December, Heller takes him to a party given by Mrs. Rolston Holcombe. There he meets Dominique. Toohey looks at Roark for a long time: "He looked at the man as he looked occasionally at the pavement from a window on the thirteenth floor wondering about his own body were it to be hurried down and what would happen when he struck against the pavement." (262)

Dominique suggests to Joel Sulton to choose Keating instead of Roark and he is convinced. He sees Roark laughing without sound. Later Dominique goes to Roark's room and says: "I'm going to pray that you can't be destroyed—I will tell this too—even though I believe in nothing and have nothing to pray to. But I will fight to block accept self-torture as an endurance test. Toohey does not care for material things. His sonorous voice is in his puny frame. His memory is like a spread of liquid cement. It holds anything that falls upon it. At school he uses to talk about God and the spirit. He starts writing a daily column in Wynand's *Banner*. He is a great success and the public is suddenly interested in architecture. He is now forty-one years old.

The Enright house is open in June of 1928. That winter Roark's office has grown to four rooms and his staff loves him. He spends the nights with Dominique. She never demonstrate her power over him: "She felt no thrill of conquest; she felt herself owned more than ever, by a man who could say these things, know of them to be true, and still remained controlled and controlling—as she wanted him to remain." (311) Late in June, a man, Kent Lancing chooses Roark to build a hotel, Aquitania. That evening, Toohey meets Hopton Stoddard who has a dream of building a temple. He suggests Hopton to take Roark as architect. Roark agrees and he wants to take Mallory. His secretary gets him Mallory's address. When Roark meets him and says that he wants him for his own sake, Mallory sobs.

Roark listens for hours while Mallory speaks of his thoughts. He comes to Roark's office and faces him as his equal. Roark shows him a figure, the statue of a naked woman and suggests to him a model that is Dominique. Toohey writes in his column that Stoddard Temple is not a house of God, but the cell of megalomaniac. On November 3, Hopton files a suit against Roark for breach of contract. The case opens in February of 1931. The plaintiff's attorney states that the building in question cannot be considered a temple by any known standards. When her turn comes, Dominique says that exaltation means joy and that joy is man's birthright. At the end Roark is instructed to pay the costs of the Temple's alterations. Dominique comes to Keating suddenly and asks him in the same impersonal voice if he marries her. He thinks he is paralyzed and agrees. They get married at Greenwich.

In the evening, Dominique tells Roark about her marriage and explains: "They'll destroy you, but I won't be there to see it happen. I will have destroyed myself first. That's the only gesture of protest open to me." (275) He tells her to learn not to be afraid of the world. When she does, she will come back to him. Next day at noon, Dominique comes to Keating. She wants to fit herself into his life as it is. The temple is rebuilt and Catherine moves into the House as a permanent resident. Dominique's statue has been sold, but no one knows that it is bought by Toohey. Roark's office has shrunk back to one room. He pays Mallory's rent and for most of their frequent meals together though Malory objects to it. Heller says it is amusing to see Roark in the role of an altruist.

Gail Wynand raises his appearance. He looks like the decadent of the long line of exquisite breeding, and everybody knows that he comes from the gutter. Late in the afternoon, Toohey meets Wynand and says that there is no other architect for Stonebridge who can equal Keating and he can confirm that by meeting his wife. He asks Wynand to see his gift and telephone him later. He is sixteen when his father dies. A man from the city calls him to run an errand. In two years he is an associate editor. At twenty-one he falls in love. He says to her: "My darling, anything you wish, anything I am, anything I can ever be. That's what I want to offer you." (406) The girl asks him if she is prettier than Maggy Kelly. He says nothing and walks out of the house. He does not fall in love again. Two years later, he smashes a political gang and remains as sole owner of the *Gazette*.

No one can say whether Wynand has a private life. He keeps the details of his secret by making it glaringly public as a whole. At forty-five Wynand loses interest and does not care any longer about the delicate sign of effect on circulation. When he goes to his study to have drink, he sees Toohey gift the statue of Dominique. He telephones Toohey. Dominique meets him half way across his office. Wynand takes her to his art gallery and she remembers that it is the place no outsider ever enters. Then they get into his yacht. She sees the golden letters, 'I Do.' Suddenly when he asks her if she will marry him, she cannot hide the shock. She agrees to it and Wynand informs Keating. Wynand wars Alvah not to mention her name in his papers. Dominique meets Roark and says that she is going to marry Wynand. She has brought him at last to a shock she had never expected.

In the past ten years, the principle of Cameron has won the field of commercial structures and many steal his form. Francon announces his retirement and the firm becomes Peter Keating & Cornelius Dumont. A week later on Tuesday, Dominique and Wynand get married. Roark is chosen to build the summer resort at Monadnock valley. He enters Wynand's office. There has been a moment when both forget the purpose of their meeting. Wynand wants a residence for two people. Dominique and Roark behave like strangers. The great depression has hit all the architects. Now at thirty-nine Keating hears himself described as old fashioned. Keating wants to get the government housing project, Cortlandt Homes and asks Roark to design it for him. Roark does not ask for any fee, but the guarantee that it will be built exactly as he designs it. They sign a contract.

On seeing the design Toohey exclaims that Keating is a genius. Wynand knows that the *Banner* is losing some of its popularity. In this paper, he is giving Roark the fame he deserves. Late one afternoon in the fall Wynand takes Roark to Hell's kitchen. He shows Roark from there the first piece of property he ever bought; he wants to erect a building there for Roark. Wynand is miserly about two things on earth, Dominique and Roark. He is a millionaire who has never owned anything. Toohey appoints Prescott and Webb associate designers. Gradually, the changes come in the drawings. Roark asks Dominique for a help to dynamite the Cortlandt. She follows his instructions and in the process she is seriously injured. It has become like another Stoddard trial. It is Wynand who gets him released on bail. On a morning late in May, appears in 'One Small Voice' that in the person of Roark, one must crush the forces of selfishness. Wynand reads it and fires Harding, Allen, Falk and Toohey for publishing it. The city room of the *Banner* walks out on strike. He tries to hire new men, but none responds.

Roark stands at the window of his house in Monadnock Valley. He feels no astonishment to see Dominique coming. Next morning she wears his pyjamas and reports to the police that she has lost her ring presented by Roark. It is published in newspapers. Alvah shows the newspaper and says that Wynand can divorce her. He calls Wynand's lawyer. The courtroom is crowded to witness the trial of Roark. Roark puts before them his own argument: "Throughout the centuries there were men who took first steps down new roads armed with nothing but their own vision. . . . Every great new thought was opposed. Every great new invention was denounced . . . they fought, they suffered and they paid. But they won." (678)

The parasite needs others. He preaches altruism as a weapon of exploitation. Lastly he gives the reason why he dynamites Cortlandt: "I designed Cortlandt: I gave it to you. I destroyed it because I did not choose to let it exist." (683) There is an odd silence in the room. Roark feels certain that he has won his case already. Late in August, Wynand is granted divorce. Toohey wins the case and Wynand is ordered to reinstate him, but Wynand closes the *Banner*. Later many newspapers bid for the service of Toohey. He selects that Courier. On a spring day, eighteen months late, Dominique walks to the construction site of the Wynand Building. The skeleton of the building rises completed, to the sky. The novel ends when she sees Roark standing above her, on the top platform of the Wynand building.

Leonard Peikoff rightly remarks in the introduction of his *The Early Ayn Rand:* "In 1926, Ayn Rand was twenty-one-year-old Russian Immigrant to America struggling with her first short story in English. She was barely able to speak the language, let alone handle complex ideas or project a convincing hero. In 1938, a mere twelve years later, she was writing *The Fountainhead*, in full command of her distinctive philosophy, aesthetic approach, and a literary style. A profession such as this represents an astonishing intellectual and artistic growth." (ix) This shows how Rand has established as a reputed writer over the years. David E. Levine says in his "Brilliant Despite Stilted Dialogue" that the book is full of passion, including a flaming, complex romantic affair between individualist architect Howard Roark and socialite Dominique Francon.

Their relationship develops from one in which they each seek to assert power over the other while achieving sexual release of true love between genuine soul mates: "It was an act that could be performed in tenderness, as a seal of love, or in contempt, as a symbol of humiliation and conquest. It could be the act of a lover or the act of a soldier violating an enemy woman. He did it as an act of scorn. Not as love, but as defilement. And this made her lie still and submit." (217) *The Fountainhead* is a tribute to a creative thinker, Roark. He is an innovative architect whose brilliant and radically new designs are not understood and are rejected by the majority of society. Like many other thinkers of history, Roark has to struggle to get acceptance for his ideas against the tradition-bound masses, who follow established norms and are fearful of change.

The theme of the novel, as Rand states, is individualism versus collectivism in men's souls. It is the conflict between those who think for themselves and those who follow others blindly. As Nathaniel Branden writes in *My Years with Ayn Rand:* "The man passionately committed to becoming an architect, he has just been expelled from school designing buildings that represent a bold break with tradition. Unmoved by the expulsion, he knows he will not be stopped. His direction comes not from the opinion or values of others but from his own inner vision and convictions." (8) His name contains the words "hard" and "roar." Both of them describe accurately his tough and determined character. Even his buildings suggest his personality as they are like Roark, innovative and austere.

Rand holds up as everything that man can and should be. I feel what is said in Spark Notes is true: "Consequently, Roark does not develop over the course of the novel—the ideal man does not need to change. Although Rand despised religion, she often describes Roark as if he is a religious figure." In this way like all Christ figures in literature, Roark's enemies persecute him. Though Roark's character is not based on the specific events of Frank Lloyd Wright's (1869-1959) life, Roark possesses many of the qualities and faces many of the obstacles that the great real life American modernist did. During the historical period of the 1920s and 1940s, architects are expected to emulate the designs from the past in their own buildings, using Roman, Gothic, or Renaissance styles, Roark, on the other hand, designs buildings to be useful, and stresses substance over useless ornamentation. Roark is fiercely independent like Wright. He is courageous enough to stand for them in the face of an antagonistic society.

Rand believes that a man's thinking and values are not controlled by God or the fates or society or any external factor, but only by his own choice. Mimi Reisel Gladstein describes how Rand worked on the subject *The New Ayn Rand Companion:* "Once [Rand] had decided that Howard Roarks, her main character in *The Fountainhead* would be an architect, she immersed herself in the study of that subject. She read voraciously throughout 1936 and

1937 and, by late 1937, was ready to gain some practical experience. In order to facilitate her exploration of the world of contemporary architecture, she worked, without pay, as a typist in the office of Eli Jacques Kahn, a famous New York architect." (11) Rand's description of Roark's Monadnock Valley development in *The Fountainhead* seems to be framed after Wright's Como Orchards Summer Colony in Darby, Montana.

Ayn Rand tries to answer an important moral question concerning the relationship between the moral and the practical. Like Wynand and Dominique, many people in real life believe that a betrayal of moral principles is needed to get practical success. But Rand builds in *The Fountainhead* a convincing argument and proves that this cynical view is false. Roark is shown to be both a moral and practical man. He takes a labourer's job rather than compromise on the smallest detail of his building. He excels at every aspect of building from design to construction. By the end of the novel, he achieves a significant commercial success too. Rand proves that Roark is practical because he is moral and that these qualities exist in a casual relationship. Roark believes that mind is the attribute of the individual. Just as there is no group stomach to digest for men collectively, so there is no group mind for collective thinking.

A perfect compliment to Roark is Dominique Francon, Roark's lover and later his wife. She is an ardent idealist. She observes Greek Sculpture, Roark's buildings, the music of Tchaikovsky and Rachmaninoff, and she understands the human potential. She is filled with despair when she sees manipulative Keating, power-hungry Toohey and the masses who prefer Keating's work to Roark's. She believes that this unthinking herd wields the power in society. She is a major example in Rand's writing of what the author terms the malevolent universe premise, the belief that the world is closed to the aspirations of men. Dominique has the belief that Roark has no chance to succeed in this world. Dominique by the experience with various men, struggles to humiliate herself in order to experience some of the pain Roark feels.

I think Paul Deane rightly quotes Ayn Rand's opinion in *Neurotic Personalities of Our Times* (1970): "The obtaining of satisfaction by submersion in misery is an expression of the general principle of finding satisfaction by losing the self in something greater, by dissolving the individuality, by getting rid of the self with its doubts, conflicts, pains, limitations, and isolation." (125-99) It shows that sex for her is a degrading experience when it is carried on with inferior men. Only after she recognizes the good succeeding on its own terms. Then she frees herself and takes his side. Though she has a mistaken pessimistic philosophy, Dominique is independent in using her mind. This is proved by her evaluations of architecture. The evidence supporting Dominique's first-handedness is her assessment of Toohey.

Dominique says to Wynand: "He's a corrosive gas. The kind that eats lungs out. I think there really is a secret to the core of evil and he has it. I don't know what it is. I know how he uses it and what he's after." (500) The charismatic and aristocratic Wynand straddles the line between mainstream society and Roark's world, and this division makes him the novel's tragic figure. He is a publisher of vulgar tabloids that oppose everything Roark stands for. But like Dominique, he too loves man's noblest achievements which is known by his owning of a private gallery of great artworks. His error is to hold the opinion that in this world, a man either rules or is ruled, either conquers or is conquered. Wynand is self-centred and egoistical and unlike Dominique, he is full of self-doubt.

Paul Deane's comment is true: 'Wynand's ideas have merit, but they are offered with such a narcissistic attitude, his bosses are insulted. He talks down to his bosses as if they are inferior, and when they refuse to listen he gets angry and loses his job. 'He has more or less contempt for all persons who agree with him or give in to his wishes."' (125-99) In essence, Dominique and Wynand are neurotic opposites. They are motivated by different goals as they have contrasting approaches to life. As Mimi Reisel Gladstein remarks in his *The New Ayn Rand Companion:* "The problem as she [Rand] saw it, was the most ambitious man of the times achieved success by pandering to the masses and in doing so negate the self, thus becoming, in her words selfless." The character of Gail Wynand is the personification of the man who becomes a slave to those he thinks he controls." (11) But, Roark befriends him because he recognizes Wynand's uncompromising desire for purity. Though Wynand knows what is good, he hides it away like his art collection.

Wynand uses his power and empire as vehicle for power over others. When he asks Roark if he has ever held power over a single human being, Roark answers that he would take it if it were offered to him. This proves that Roark is averted to power structure inherent in the dependent versus independent. It is a lesson learnt too late for Wynand. Like Roark, he has extraordinary capabilities, but unlike Roark he lets the world corrupt him. He eventually feels he cannot escape the ugliness he has created. Tragically Wynand compromises the last minute and loses his last chance at salvation. Another contrast to Roark is Peter Keating, a conformist. He surrenders his judgment and allows others to dominate his life. He prefers the career of a painter, but becomes an architect, because his mother selects it.

Though Keating loves Catherine, he marries Dominique because Dominique's beauty and grace impress other people. He attempts to rise to the position of partner in the country's most prestigious firm. For that he uses any means necessary to attain this end, including flattery, deceit, and in the case of Lucius Heyer, near murder. He is conventionally treated as selfish. But Ayn Rand presents a revolutionary analysis of such a status-seeker's nature. Peter Keating, she says, is selfless. He sacrifices the things that he wants in order to place others. Rand has little sympathy for the rise and fall of Keating. She shows the contrast between Roark and Keating to illustrate what Rand would later call the virtue of selfishness.

A perfect antidote to Roark's creative genius is Ellsworth Toohey. He is a power-seeker and he attempts to gain control over the lives of other people. At personal level, he is a type of cult leader like Jim Jones, David Koresh and Sun Myung Moon. He maintains a private army of unquestioning followers such as Hopton Stoddard and Mitchell Layton: "Hopton Stoddard felt safe whenever he followed Toohey's advice." (315) Toohey like virus gains survival only through his victims. Apart from his cult activities, Toohey seeks to establish dictatorship in America. As he is a Marxist intellectual, preaching communism to the masses, he desires to control editorial policy of the Wynand papers. Toohey makes *The Banner* his platform and he hopes to spread the ideas necessary to establish a totalitarian state in America.

Toohey's motive can be proved by his reaction to the famous Biblical question that what profits a man, if he shall gain the whole world, and lose his own soul. Toohey asks in response that in order to be truly wealthy, if a man should collect souls. His whole life has been devoted to that end. Toohey knows that in order to establish a dictatorship, a majority of individuals must be willing to give up personal autonomy and to surrender their minds to a leader. Roark's employer, architectural teacher and mentor, is Henry Cameron. He is the godfather of Roark. As a fictional example of an early modern designer who is among first to build skyscrapers, he is similar to the real life American architect, Louis Sullivan (1856-1924).

Cameron is a great architect rejected by society as Roark. Cameron is a benevolent figure in Roark's life. He continues to be his mentor. Even at his death bed, he continues to preach Roark. Although Cameron is a failure commercially, he is more than a moral and artistic success. With the triumph of his symbolically adopted son, Roark, he helps ensure the final victory for his architectural principle. A brilliant young sculptor who becomes a close friend of Roark is Steven Mallory. Roark believes him to be the best sculptor and tells him: "I think you are the best sculptor we've got. I think it, because your figures are not what men are, but what men could be—and should be. . . . Because you have a magnificent respect for the human being. Because your figures are the heroic in man." (328)

One of the most psychologically revealing scenes in the novel is Roark's summing up of Mallory's plight and his own with the sentence that the one who brings joy of life to the world and suffers rejection and alienation as the reward. It makes Mallory's characterization so psychologically interesting, especially in regard to the plight of the artist. Though he loves his work, the power of his love is not strong enough to overcome the fears. He drinks and womanizes, yet his intentions are all good. The first meeting of Roark with Mallory is in Mallory's Greenwich Village. Roark's treatment of Mallory in this scene is overwhelmingly benevolent like the beginning of David Kelley's *Unrugged Individualism* (1996). Just like Cameron, Mallory is loyal to his ideas and will not compromise. But also like Cameron and unlike Roark, he is affected by rejection. Roark's character is an inspiration to Mallory. It helps him realize that a man's values and ideals are the most important element in life, not the beliefs of others.

Like Roark, Mallory is very much the bohemian individualist, in loving his life and his work and in fearless pursuit of those values. Yet, unlike Roark, he is fearful of the people. In a conversation with Roark, Mallory refers to himself as a weaker version of Roark, one who knows the disease and sickness that infects the world. To be an artist or writer is an act of courage in any society, but the road ahead for the objectivist artist is more difficult. The objectivist artist starts from fundamental view of the world that is much at odds with others of artistic bent, a view that often sets him apart in a vacuum of isolation. Then, again, there is one other area of much importance to the objectivist artist. The creative persons like writer, actor, artist, etc., must experience, explore, and be open to difficult ways of seeing the world, in a free and spontaneous manner. Mallory does not ask Roark's approval for his work on the nude statue of Dominique, any more than Roark sought his approval for the creation of the Enright House.

A free and open objectivism is the main tool in the act of creation. A minor figure in the novel that dramatizes a significant point in Rand's philosophy is Mike Donnigan. He both admires competence and recognizes Roark's. The bond that unites them is their mutual love of construction. A consistent supporter of independence and, for its reason, a friend and ally of Roark is

Heller. His character is demonstrated by means of several important details. Firstly, he does not give a penny to charity. Secondly, he gives more money than he can afford to help political prisoners around the globe. Heller does not contribute to charity as he believes that it merely furthers financial dependence and so it is not in the self-interest of the recipient. His helping the political prisoners is inconsistent with this.

The political prisoners are freethinking individuals with the courage to stand up for their ideals. The man who recognizes Roark's extraordinary talent is Kent Lancing. He has a rare appreciation of artistic genius and has the willingness to fight for it. When the construction of the hotel is stopped due to certain lawsuits, Lancing vows to win legal control of the project, and retain Roark to complete it. He proves that independence and integrity are not the exclusive prerogative of the creative artist, but are sometimes possessed by middleman too. Another self-made millionaire is Roger Enright. But he is more than that. His way of conducting business is innovative. He branches out into many fields. Though many succeed, some of his ventures fail. But he continues to run them all with ferocious energy, working twelve hours a day.

In the group of second-handers, the least antagonistic to Roark is Guy Francon. His success is based on two factors. He copies from the classical designers, and he impresses customers with urbanity. But despite these flaws, he possesses good qualities that enable him to attain the level of happiness in the end. Francon's redeeming quality is his genuine love for his daughter's best qualities. Among the few women characters in the novel, Catherine Halsey is a victim of Toohey. The only passion of her life is her love for Keating. The remark made in Cliffs Notes is true: "Her sweetness, innocence, and good nature are inadequate to protect her from Toohey's evil. A lack of independent thinking is what dooms Katie's attempt to gain love and happiness." (59) Thus, Katie serves to illustrate an important aspect of Ayn Rand's philosophy.

An outstanding example of the meaning of nonconformity is Lois Cook. She defies social belief in beauty, attractive houses and even personal hygiene. In this attitude she is far worse than Francon because Francon uncritically follows the best of society's norms and Cook rebels against them. She says her house should be magnificently ugly: "Keating where's your courage? Aren't you capable of a sublime gesture on occasion? They all work so hard and struggle and suffer, trying to achieve beauty, trying to surpass one another in beauty. Let's surpass them all! Let's throw their seat in their face. Let's destroy them at one stroke. Let's be gods. Let's be ugly." (241) It shows that he is an example of nihilism, a desire to destroy the best that human society has to offer. Another of Toohey's followers and an avant-garde architect is Gus Webb. Like Cook, he is a nihilist, a rebel against the best of other men's values.

Webb is a fictional forerunner of the New Left of the 1960s whereas the Old Left of the 1930s, represented by Toohey, was a movement of cultured, highly educated intellectuals opting for political activism. Cliffs Notes point out: "At a political level, Webb's character represents a prediction by Rand. Because Marxism stands for totalitarian dictatorship and suppression of the freethinking mind; it must necessarily lose all vestiges of cultured intellectuality." (61) In the character of Webb, Ayn Rand predicted the existence and nature of the New Left, twenty-five years before it appeared on the America cultural scene in the late 1960s. *The Fountainhead* answers the question who shall rule the soul. Toohey's attempts to dominate Roark and Keating and the reactions of each dramatize the confrontation between collectivism and individualism in man's soul.

As Barbara Branden writes in *The Passion of Ayn Rand*: "'My concept of good and evil," she [Rand] would later comment, "already in the process of being formed, saw its vindication everywhere"—as if reality had become the sort of fiction she later would create: a conflict written larger than life, between two opposing views of human society, two opposing views of morality.' (19) As Roark is a man of self-sufficient ego, he does not want a demagogue to dictate his thoughts and actions. So Toohey cannot break his will. Peikoff is right in saying: "Roark's unflinching resistance and ultimate triumph over Toohey and his followers demonstrate the power of the self-contained individual over the forces of collectivism. Roark's victory foreshadows the ultimate, inevitable prevalence of the first-hander. His victory foreshadows a world of egoists, a world in which each person exists for himself—and asks no other person to live for him." (681) This is the philosophy of Rand.

It is a world of people who are all first-handers and innovators. It is a world in which all recognize the human ego as the fountainhead of progress. In several important passages of the novel, one finds a concise summation of Rand's philosophy, especially during the conversation between Roark and the other characters. In a conversation with Wynand, Roark sums up the dilemma of altruism: "What else can one do if one must serve the people? If one must live for others? Either pander to everybody's good. Can you think of any other way?" (632) Roark is the epitome of independence, rationalism and love for fellow men. He demonstrates this through example. He lives to serve fellow men by serving himself first and foremost.

Unlike *Atlas Shrugged*, *The Fountainhead* deals with important issues on a personal level. Other issue of significance is Roark's violence. The theme of *The Fountainhead* is the contrasts and conflict between persons of independent functioning and those of dependent functioning. *The Fountainhead*'s plot is an ideal vehicle by which it presents its theme. These men are aptly classified into three types in Cliffs Notes and each is a variation on the theme of psychological dependence: "The first type is the traditionalists—those who are blindly wedded to the thinking of the past that they cannot see the truth of any new ideas. History abounds with examples of traditionalists: those who rejected Copernicus' heliocentric theory because of their commitment to the order of geocentric view; those who could not see the truth of Darwin's theory of evaluation because of their Fundamentalist religious beliefs; those who rejected futon's steamboat because their prior experience was limited to sail." (62) Thus, the plot and theme are intertwined together that they seem to analyze the specific men who reject Roark.

The second type of men those who reject Roark are the conformists, those who blindly accept the ideas of their peers. Many people who hold religious convictions, Catholics, Protestants, Jews or Muslims, do not study comparative religion. The third type is the people like Mrs. Wayne Wilmot of Long Island.: "There was no such person as Mrs. Wayne Wilmot; there was only a shell containing the opinions of her friends, the picture of post cards she had seen, the novels of country squires she had read; it was this that he [Roark] had to address, this immateriality which could not hear him or answer, deaf and impersonal like a wad of cotton." (162) One can understand the subtlety of Rand's style by examining a scene near the end of Part One. Roark is offered the commission to design the Manhattan Bank Building. He is in need of it and it is a major commission. But when the board wishes to alter his design, he refuses.

Rand's presentation of the scene is revealing. Roark concentrates on the effort of standing. It makes the rest easier. He leans on the table with his right hand. When he answers, the board of members cannot tell whether he is too calm or too emotional. But because his word moves forward evenly, with neither anger nor excitement, they conclude he is calm. She does not tell the reader the emotions Roark feels. Instead, she gives the observational details that the reader would get, if he were sitting in the room with the board members.

Cliffs Notes point out: "They believe that, because Roark speaks softly and rationally, he is clam. But the factual evidence indicates otherwise. Roark leans on his right arm, he refuses to move it, he turns pages with his left hand, looking like a man with one arm paralyzed. Clearly, Roark experiences powerful emotion in this scene. His disappointment, the pain, the anger at their stubborn, blind refusal to see and hear the truth so compellingly obvious to Roark is overwhelming. Roark struggles with the intensity of his feeling, struggles to keep his mind and his voice calm so that he can reason with the men, so that he can show them the brilliant lucidity of his ideas—and, perhaps, he clutches the table to keep from clutching the throats of men before him" (67). It shows that

Rand presents mere facts of Roark's appearance, his posture and the sound of his voice.

Rand leaves out many other facts that can also be observed in that room like the clothes of Roark, the length of his hair, his rosy complexion from the clod of the streets, the wallpaper and other details. She chooses not to present these details, but the reader is provided all the observational evidence he requires and he must himself infer the conclusion. In any literary work, themes are fundamental. *The Fountainhead* revolves around the struggle of Roark to retain his individuality. This struggle is not confined to Roark. All the sympathetic characters struggle to act independently from society. The novel ends triumphantly not because Roark has won the right to act according to his own principles. Dominique thinks: "They say the heart of the earth is made of fire. It is held imprisoned and silent. But at times it breaks through the clay, the iron, the granite, and shoots out to freedom. Then it becomes a thing like this." (692)

The theme at the heart of the novel is that society has a herd mentality, and individuals must act selfishly in order to be free. The novel disapproves of sentimentalism and asserts that everything worth thinking or feeling should be the product of reason and logic but not emotion. In the novel it is proved that love, like integrity and invention, is a principle worthy fighting for. The main characters constantly improve their relationships. Even Roark and Dominique forego some of their fierce devotion to independence and eventually allow themselves to surrender to one another. The emotion of love appears to contradict the novel's devotion to reason, but the characters demand relationships so perfect that they come to seem logical and mathematical. While Dominique marries Keating and when Wynand, Roark stands by as if he is watching her enacting an algebraic equation.

Roark and Dominique refuse to yield to emotion even in their passionate encounters. Instead, they make love with a violent and calculating fury in the sense that Rand writes in prose more technical than romantic. In *The Fountainhead*, technical progress indicates the forward movement of society. As it is said: "The novel measures the progress of mankind by the number of buildings and scientific innovations it produces, rather than by its art and philosophy." (http://www. sparknotes. com) Roark, Dominique and Wynand all gaze admiringly at the skyline, which serves as a reminder of their ambitions and goals. Roark tells Dominique: "I like to see a man standing at the foot of a skyscraper. It makes him no bigger than an ant—isn't that the correct bromide for the occasion? The god damn fools! It's man who made it—the whole incredible mass of stone and steel. It doesn't dwarf him; it makes him greater than the structure. It reveals his true dimensions to the world. What we love about these buildings, Dominique, is the creative faculty, the heroic in man." (498) This means that the skyscrapers represent human conquest over nature and symbolize modernity.

The novel shows architecture as an ideal art form and journalism as corrupt. As a manipulative journalist, Toohey works his ill will. When Wynand tries to use his paper for supporting Roark, he fails. He says: "Howard, the *Banner* is not helping you. It's ruining you." (653) According to Rand, newspapers are fundamentally weak as they have to cater to the public taste. In her novel, she shows physical labour as a pure and productive activity and so something admirable. But labour needs unions and the novel condemns groups. Rand sees socialism as the greatest threat to the United States as it grows out of the labour movement. The novel admires labourers as individuals, but it fears and mistrusts them as a group.

In the novel, Rand makes symbolism interpret her characters. Rand associates granite with Roark's character. Like the rock, Roark's face, body and mind are hard, rare, unchanging and beautiful. Roark, however, is stronger than the rock. In many of the scenes, Roark is shown while he is breaking granite or using it for his designs. When Dominique first sees Roark at a granite quarry: "She liked to think of the granite being broken by his hands." (207) She wishes the drilling would hurt and destroy Roark, but by the end of the novel, Roark's ability to shape the granite according to his desires pleases her. In the novel, ice symbolizes Dominique's character. Rand describes Dominique's body as fragile and angular: "Her slender body seemed out of all scale in relation to normal human body; its lines were so long, so fragile, so exaggerated that she looked like a stylized drawing of a woman and made the correct proportions of a normal being appear heavy and awkward beside her." (111)

The cloths that Dominique wears either glitter like ice or shine like glass or they are of the colour of water. The diamond necklace, Wynand presents Dominique looks like loose pieces of ice shattered on her cool skin. Ice also reflects her personality at the beginning of the novel, blank and frig. Once Roark warms Dominique's spirit the associations between her and ice grow infrequent and eventually disappear. Spark Notes point out: "Ayn Rand intentionally crafts simplistic prose and characters in order to avoid distraction and keep the focus on her philosophy. She writes simple sentences, and does not use figures of speech that most writers use. This stark style makes her sentences sound didactic or instructional rather than entertaining. Like the novel's protagonist, Roark, the language of *The Fountainhead* is absolute and unwavering." The main characters of the novel—Peter Keating, Ellsworth Toohey, Gail Wynand and Howard Roark—are the four men whose names serve as the titles for the four parts of the novel. The superficial similarities between Roark and the other three men serve to emphasize the fundamental differences between him and them. Each of the characters represents one value or belief.

Rand makes it clear that different personalities like Roark and Keating start at exactly the same point. Roark is first shown as standing naked among granite cliffs. This suggests that he is as clean and pure as the elements that surround him: "He stood naked at the edge of a cliff. The lake lay far below him. A frozen explosion of granite burst in flight to the sky over motionless water. The water seemed immovable, the stone flowing. The stone had the stillness of one brief moment in battle when thrust meets thrust and the currents are held in a pause more dynamic than motion. The stone glowed, wet with sunrays." (15) Rand presents Keating, in contrast, as self-absorbed and unable to think for himself. Rand uses the employers of Roark and Keating to suggest what her main characters will become. Francon, like Keating, is a fake who takes credit for the work of others and enjoys great economic and social success. But Cameron, like Roark, is strong, stubborn and idealistic.

The readers easily get the impression that Francon and Cameron are the older counterparts of Keating and Roark. Rand labels each character strong or weak by measuring each against the epitome of Roark. Every new character's initial reaction to Roark in the novel indicates how Rand values that character. Toohey presents a friendly surface compared to Roark's cold genius, but Toohey uses his charm for evil. The perspective of Spark Notes about Toohey somewhat differs from that of Cliffs Notes: "His speech about cooperation and unity should appeal to us, but instead it feels manipulative and oppressive. The people come together to hear their leader speak, but Rand presents their unity as slavery, not cooperation, as if the people are prisoners of Toohey's voice." But, Dominique is different. She is stern and masculine like the severe architectural designs of Roark.

However, unlike Roark, Dominique has no great passion or mission. She recognizes beauty and genius, and writes about it, but she does not create it as Roark does. Roark's frigidity and indifference come from his firm conviction, but Dominique's come from neuroses. Roark's work on the house for Austen Heller epitomizes the difference between the pureness of his architectural designs and the forced nature of the architectural designs of those in the corporate world. These corporate architects work from a purely technical point of view, and the principles they apply so rigidly to their designs constrain expression and emotion. Thus they prevent the buildings from being truly beautiful. Roark, on the other hand, goes into a design without any preconceived notions as to how a particular building should look.

Roark takes into account the function of the building and the environment around the proposed building site, for example, in the case of Heller's house, the granite cliff. He says to Heller: "Your house is made by its own needs. Those others are made by the need to impress. The determining motive of your house is in the house. The determining motive of others is in the audience." (136) Both Roark and Keating face a number of choices in their careers. Rand uses such choices or trials to fine-tune her characters and reveal their true nature. She illustrates and proves his strength step-by-step by showing us how he interacts with his circumstances.

However, it is an expression of Rand's carefully designed plot, in which every detail has a purpose and each trivial incident points to the future events. Catherine's sudden panic about her uncle points to the events that will be revealed only much later in the novel. Rand wants the readers to understand that the bad things will happen because Keating the coward refuses to heed Catherine's cry for help. Though punishment does not always happen immediately, Rand leaves certain hints that it will come eventually. With each decision they make, Roark and Keating solidify their personalities and walk farther down the paths they have selected. Rand sets up a sharp contrast between the two men by putting them in identical situations. Roark rushes to the dying man he respects. In complete contrast, Keating rushes to the bed of a dying man in order to threaten him with humiliation. Their love affair demonstrates the novel's premise that real passion involves struggle and submission.

Rand contrasts the harsh and violent love of Dominique and Roark with the tender love of Keating and Catherine. Spark Notes point out: "Both Katie and Keating feel that they could make each other happy; Keating could protect Katie from Toohey and Katie could make Keating feel honest and pure. Yet Keating is too weak and greedy to know what is good for him. Dominique and Keating marry not to find happiness, but because Dominique wants to punish herself." It shows that they always treat each other with consideration and consequently their love falls flat. The marriage does not give Keating any happiness. He enjoys the congratulations of his friends, but he is afraid of Dominique's cold indifference. He says to her: "But it's . . . it's like death. You're not real. You're only a body. Look, Dominique, you don't know it, I'll try to explain. You understand what earth is? When a body can't move any more, when it has no . . . no will, no meaning. You understand? Nothing. The absolute nothing." (425)

Their relationship lacks the understanding of each other as that of Dominique and Roark. In *The Fountainhead*, the only character who does not fit into any category is Wynand. He is the tragic character who resembles Roark. Both of them are self-made, dynamic and gifted. Because of this dual nature, Dominique has a mixed reaction to Wynand. She does not like Wynand's contempt for beauty, but she is attracted to his strength. Rand introduces Wynand's character into her narrative to maximize his importance to the characters and events of the novel. Keating's conversation with Dominique demonstrates his ability of thinking honestly and purely: "I loved you. There were two people—you and another person, a man, who always made me feel the same thing—not fear exactly, but like a wall, a steep wall to climb." (426)

Though Keating does not get rid of his flaws, his knowledge of his crimes and his grudging admiration of Roark make him less despicable than the other characters who remain happily ignorant of their shortcomings. Rand likens Toohey's machinations to events following the Russian Revolution of 1917. Toohey starts growing more powerful in a series of moves just like the men in the lowly positions in the communist party. At the time of elections, Stalin's opponent Trotsky was ousted by a party of Stalin's loyalists. When Stalin came to power, he eliminated many of able and distinguished men so that no one could challenge him. The compassion in Spark Notes is right: "Similarly, Toohey tries to create a world where men like Roark and Mallory are not only ignored but actively destroyed."

Keating always draws his strength from the praise and loyalty of others. Wynand, on the other hand, regains the beliefs of his youth and as Dominique's influence begins to chip away at his disillusionment, he becomes stronger. Rand stresses that men themselves shape their personalities, but not the circumstances. She gives the men the same background to argue that if Roark could transcend his early years, then Wynand could have done the same. Like Dominique, Wynand first tests Roark by trying to corrupt him.

He offers him work, but on a condition: "But the house you've designed for me shall be erected as you designed it. It will be the last Roark building to rise on earth. Nobody will have one after mine. . . . You've a simple choice: if you refuse, you'll never build anything again: if you accept, you'll build this house which you want so much to see erected and a great may of other houses which you won't like, but which will make money for both of us." (532)

When Roark refuses the offer and passes the test, Wynand understands that Roark truly stands by his principles. Now, Wynand changes his worldview. Wynand welcomes the change, but he feels it difficult to enact, because it needs to dismantle the ugliness he has created throughout his life. As Toohey's influence goes on spreading, Roark's work intensifies. This reflects Rand's belief that art can combat evil. *The Fountainhead* can be treated as an anthem for the indestructible spirit of mankind. Roark is the embodiment of this spirit and his works stand as a proof that perfection is possible in this untidy world. Rand gives extensive personal histories of Roark, Keating and Wynand, but she does not mention how Roark grows up though the fourth part of the novel that is named after him. The readers understand that he comes from a poor family, but no details are given about his parents or upbringing. Rand says: "Roark's father had been street peddler somewhere in Ohio and had died long ago. The boy's entrance papers showed no record of nearest relatives." (25)

Because of Roark's mysterious past, his story can be applied to any one. Rand wishes to suggest that a man's background has nothing to do with his personal genius or principle. It also makes him a perfect man. He has no history as he does not change. He does not have a family which makes him more independent and free from the influence of others. Everything that is important in his past, present or future resides in his buildings. Roark bombs the Cortlandt building in the climax of the novel as the opposing forces in the novel come into conflict. The bombing is the first gesture of defiance by the few talented people against the mediocre people.

Though Roark is the person who bombs the building, all the major characters are involved. It is officially designed by Keating,

Toohey alters it, and Dominique helps Roark in destroying it. Spark Notes comment: "He does not care what the world does with his finished buildings but insists on finishing his buildings as he wishes. The Cortlandt complex perverts Roark's ideas before they have been implemented. Unable to tolerate this kind of compromise, Roark must destroy the mediocrity to maintain his integrity." Thus, Roark's reaction to the Cortlandt building is different from that of the Stoddard temple as the temple is constructed according to his design and changed later.

Dominique has always been provoked by violence. Her lifelessness after the explosion is a part of her rebirth. With the destruction of the building comes the destruction of her resistance to the world. The reader can understand later that Dominique's cutting herself in the car is her final act of machismo. The violence in the destruction of the building heals her and consoles her with Roark, the man she loves. Rand sums up the ideology of the novel by the two lengthy philosophical monologues of Roark and Toohey. These two monologues serve the same role as closing arguments in a courtroom, a last chance for each side to make its point. Rand employs setting and tone to indicate that we should prefer Roark's monologue. Roark discusses his beliefs on the importance of the ego in the serene setting of a luxury yacht trip. He expresses his philosophy of selfishness as he terrorizes the pathetic, beaten down Keating.

When the time comes to choose between his paper and his principles, he faces the same situation Roark has faced many times. Both of them must choose between closing their offices and compromising their principles. While Roark chooses to be physical labourer than losing his principles, Wynand chooses to save his paper though his decision makes his life meaningless. After meeting Roark, Wynand gets an opportunity for redemption. Wynand's fall seems to be a tragic one because it comes when he stands on the verge of redemption. Wynand does not even get any fame or fortune at the expense of his self-respect, as in the end he closes his paper down rather than taking Toohey again. Wynand commits emotional suicide for the sake of a paper he destroys.

The final images of the novel evoke the first scene in the novel. When Dominique climbs the unfinished building of Wynand to see Roark, she rises up past a cityscape full of the same hard, beautiful and natural elements that surround Roark when he stands naked over the cliffs in the first chapter. In the last chapter, Roark's standing on a skyscraper he has created, appears as if he has seized the elements in the first chapter and made them even more beautiful with his genius. Roark stands laughing at the beginning of the novel, scoring the convention and enjoying his independence. In the climax of the novel again he stands apart from the mediocrity of the world below him. The novel closes with the words: "The line of ocean cut the sky. The ocean mounted as the city descended. She rose above the spires of churches. Then there was only the ocean and the sky and the figure of Howard Roark." (694) By comparing Roark to such profound bodies as the ocean and sky, Rand elevates him. It is a virtual deification of Roark, a declaration that his spirit alone matters.

To illustrate the characters' personalities, Rand uses physical characteristics. The following quotation from the third part of *The Fountainhead* shows a physical symbol of Wynand's redemption. When Wynand is sitting on his yacht, Dominique sees him and thinks that his gestures reveal his true self. At first she knows him as an evil publisher, but now understands that he has become an idealized aristocrat: "He was an aristocrat aboard a yacht. He looked, she thought, like what one believes aristocracy to be when one is young: a brilliant kind of gaiety without guilt." (495) In the physical appearance, Wynand is like Roark, tall and carries himself with confidence. He moves quickly, showing his vibrancy. He is on a yacht and is surrounded by luxury that would overwhelm most people, but his brilliant kind of gaiety overwhelms his surroundings. Wynand, who has attempted suicide once, has changed his worldview. He has become optimistic and his new personality is so forceful that it overwhelms the facts. Though he is still a corrupt publisher, his good intentions show that Wynand is not corrupt.

According to Roark, the people like Keating are second-handlers as they do not create original work, but steal the work of others. After many years of chasing fame and money, Keating can finally look into his soul and realize the pointlessness of his existence. But it is too late when he tries to save himself by admitting his failure. He humbly requests Roark for help: "Howard, I'm a parasite. I've been a parasite all my life. . . . I have fed on you and all the men like you who lived before we were born. . . . I have taken that which was not mine and given nothing in return." (578) Now, Keating has become exhausted and bares his soul in this monologue as Roark and Toohey do in their own monologues. Rand's worldview is voiced through the three men.

Toohey says to Keating: "Tell men that altruism is the ideal. Not a single one of them has ever achieved it and not a single one ever will. His every living instinct screams against it. But don't you see what you accomplish? Man realizes that he is incapable of what he's accepted as the noblest virtues—and it gives him a sense of guilt, of sin, of his own basic unworthiness. Since the supreme ideal is beyond his grasp, he gives up eventually all ideals, all aspiration, all sense of his personal value. He feels himself obliged to preach what he can't practice. But one can't be good halfway or honest approximately. To preserve one's integrity is a hard battle. Why preserve that which one knows to be corrupt already? His soul gives up its self-respect. You've got him. He'll be glad to obey—because he can't trust himself, he feels uncertain, he feels unclear." (635) Thus, he makes a speech to terrified Keating.

Only here Toohey for the first time reveals his true nature. Everything else he says is intentionally devoid of true meaning. So only here one can see the sinister inner workings of Toohey's mind. Rand wants her readers to condemn the concepts that Toohey supports. Toohey uses the religious words "Divine Purpose," "Paradise," and "Universal Harmony," suggesting Rand's low opinion of organized religions like Christianity and Buddhism. The phrases like "Racial Supremacy" and "The Dictatorship of Proletariat" refer to and condemn respectively, Nazism and Communism. Rand believes that almost all kinds of social engineering restrict individual liberty. She stresses this point in her novel by having her villain Toohey referring to these catchphrases as his tools.

Nathaniel Branden remarks in *My Years with Ayn Rand:* "The writing had the most marvellous purposefulness and clarity. I had the sense that every word was chosen with excruciating care; the book seemed absolutely devoid of the accidental. This was the stylization I had never seen before, and it was maintained to the smallest detail. The author's ability to provide an experience of visual reality was instantly evident, and it was visual reality of the highest level of luminosity and precision." (8) And also in *The Fountainhead*, one can find her brand of conservative treatise. Her views are expressed through a series of characters. One gets a vivid picture of her philosophical view by comparing and constructing the approach to life and basic motivations of the characters Roark and Cameron, Keating and Toohey, Wynand and Dominique.

Roark rejects the neurosis of her various characters and offers an alternative in Roark. Through the character of Wynand, Rand rejects narcissism and through Keating she rejects socialism and its idea of human conformity. It is the idea that all men have equal worth regardless of their abilities or willingness to work. Through Dominique, she rejects self-doubt and through Cameron, she rejects fear and timid personality. Rand proves that a person should be without the arrogance of Wynand, but he needs to be confident like Roark. Roark represents the type of person Rand believes society should eliminate. Roark does not accept shoddy work. Rand believes that what is wrong with society is the shoddy work. People have to take pride in their work. And for this attitude they will be rewarded. A good society should not seek greed and wealth as goals. Wealth is important, but it comes from the production of good work. Rand here offers her view of an altruistic utopian society, a society that is best for all.

Though Rand promotes rank differences and wealth, she is not materialistic. Her characters are in fact very influential persons who are the leaders of society mostly. Rand's critics mock at her that her philosophy is unrealistic and appears to be the things that occur in fairy tales. However, Rand's belief is different. In using her characters as great achievers, she shows the power of philosophy and the potential of those followers who strive to attain their goals with the best of their abilities. Symbolically, her characters represent the highest potential that exists within each individual. For Rand, the colour green maintains two polarities. For most of the people, this colour glorifies the power of money and to others it resembles the pale sickness that originates from greed. In fact, there is a correlation between these similar opposites.

According to the mechanics of time, one event leads to another in a chronological order. In matters of money and greed, the old phrase, "There is no smoke without the fire," holds true. Ayn Rand promotes such a character in her novel, honouring greatness, then includes in the package, a terrible flaw. By introducing her character, Wynand, Rand mocks at the world for its imperfection. His power is very concrete and true to life, but only to the extent the public permits. When he plays the role of dictator who denies his dictatorship, the readers of his newspaper pretend to fear him. His business etiquette involves sacrificing himself and dedicating his newspaper, his whole life's work as a service to the people and for the people. The pain Wynand suffers is internal and the pain is unbearable due to the disappointment and a sour appointment with reality.

Some reviewers say that her dialogues are stilted, but I do not agree with them. There are long passages where the characters appear to preach instead of talking. But they are the vehicles for Rand's ideas. Apart from that her dialogues are mostly dynamic and quite believable. As an example we can take the first meeting between Wynand and Dominique. Rand has a beautiful descriptive style. For example, Rand describes the aftermath of rain as: "The lake below was only a thin steel ring that cut the rocks in half. The rocks went on into the depth, unchanged. They began and ended in the sky. So that the world seemed suspended in space, an island floating on nothing, anchored to the feet of the man on the cliff." (15) There are also memorable lines like: "All love is exception making." (496)

As some critics of Rand say, Roark is not inhuman. He feels pain too. It is not only the pain of his struggle with society, but also the pain for Cameron and his friend, Mallory. As Rand says, the pain goes down to a certain point because it cannot touch the core of his independent soul. One must consider the passage in which Dominique says to Roark that she has married Keating: "It would have been easy, if she had seen a man distorting his mouth to bite off sound, closing his fists and twisting them in defence against himself. But it was too easy, because she did not see him doing this, yet knew that this was being one, without the relief of a physical gesture." (374) We can believe that he is the man who feels and suffers. Rand makes us feel sympathy even for the characters who are not perfect. Keating is a despicable man in many ways, but he is sympathetic to some extent. His love failure with Catherine, whom he loves truly, is very poignant. The scene near the end, where he meets her years after, is really touching. Wynand is a fascinating and tragic character and his relationship with Dominique is more interesting than the romance of Roark and Dominique.

Ayn Rand refuses to tolerate imperfection and despises power gained through self-derivational and unjust sacrifices. Thus she can be treated as a towering deity who rules with an iron fist. She mimics the qualities of collective society in Keating. Keating is not a man, but a representation of the collective. Rand speaks of the society as a whole when she refers to Keating. Keating voices the thoughts of millions when he speaks of himself. He deceives others while deceiving his own self. But that deceit has its limits. According to Rand's version, progress is measurement of power and a solution to the process of self-sustaining actions. Man as an individual exists not to triumph over other men, but in the conquest of nature. Nature is a formidable enemy which can tremble the heart of the weak, but to great men, its dangers are an inspiration.

Wynand says to Dominique: "I like to see a man standing at the foot of a skyscraper. It makes him look bigger than an ant—isn't that the correct bromide for the occasion? The god-damn fools! It's the man who made it—the whole incredible mass of stone and steel. It doesn't dwarf him; it makes him greater than the structure. It reveals his true dimensions to the world." (498) By creating the character of Roark, a symbol of strength, Rand humbly honours man. Roark is not an image of merely a man, but he is a hologram that is not affected by outside interference. Inside every individual, individualism is the power lock. Our responsibility as an individual on this earth is to tap that incredible source of energy and utilizing this feud to propel humanity into the depth of the future. The followers of Rand's philosophy will never forget this lesson.

The comparison between Rand's literary method and legal method is highlighted by the trials of Roark. In *The Fountainhead*, as in all of Rand's other fictional works, the law figures prominently, especially in one or more trial scenes. Trial scenes are essential elements for the development of the plot in her works. Alan D. Hornstein concentrates on the legal trials in Rand's fiction: "First, trials to Rand have often advanced the position that ethical and political change follows intellectual change, that it is on the intellectual battlefield that the fight for a culture is waged. The courtroom is the modern-day intellectual equivalent of the battlefield or the tournament, and so it is an appropriate setting for the clash of ideas presented in Rand's work. Second, what is necessary to prevail on the courtroom battlefield are certain methodologies of persuasion and understanding—methodologies shared by Rand's literary presentations and the working out of the law through judicial opinions." (432) This proves that these trials are an illustration of philosophical principles, though her work is distinctive in its use of the trial.

The Fountainhead has two trial scenes which are critical to the development of the story. Roark is the defiant in both the scenes. In the two trials, his behaviour is quite different. This difference says much about the development of his character. The second trial is at the end of the novel and it brings together all the other subplots. As Alan D. Hornstein says: Roark's testimony and closing argument constitute the dramatic and philosophical centrepiece of the novel. In a long speech Roark justifies his action, defending not just himself, but the creative impulse and the discipline of reason that permits its productive exercise." (433) Finally, Roark is acquitted by the jury.

The Stoddard trial is a civil action apparently tried without a jury. The publicity of Toohey ensures a full courtroom. The plaintiff claims that the building designed by Roark cannot be a temple. The dispute is not about the journalistic facts of what happened and who did what to whom, but as Hornstein says: "Instead, the question concerned the meaning to be ascribed to the concept of temple. By centring the trial on the notion of a temple, Rand is able to reveal differences in what is viewed as holy, and thus what sort of souls these differences reveal." (436) Roark's design is described as scaled to human height in such a manner that it does not dwarf man, but stands as a setting that makes its figure the only absolute. It is a joyous place where the joy of exaltation must be quiet. One will come to this place to feel sinless and strong and finds that the peace of spirit is never granted except by one's own glory. What Roark builds is a temple to the human spirit. According to him, a place built as a setting for man is a sacred place. But for Toohey it is a monument to a profound hatred of humanity.

As one can imagine, Roark loses the case and is found liable. Roark's innocence is revealed in his refusal to offer a defence. I agree with Alan D. Hornstein's view: 'There is some support for such a view: Roark hires a sculptor, Steven Mallory, for a statue to be erected in the Temple as its only ornament. Mallory, Roark's philosophical soul mate, has been beaten down by the same sort of cultural miasma that Roark has been resisting. In a conversation between them, Roark explains that he sought out Mallory "for a simple selfish reason—the same reason that makes a man choose the cleanest food he can find. It's a law of survival, isn't it?—to seek the best. Dequacy—within the culture he finds himself—of simply presenting his work.'" (438) Here, his innocence is not in the legal sense, but in the sense of a fundamental inability to understand the existence or nature of evil.

Hornstein rightly says that in a number of respects the Cortland trial is similar to the Stoddard trial: "In both there is a torrent of pre-trial publicity orchestrated by Toohey; Peter Keating appears as a witness against Roark and is broken by the experience; and Roark refuses a lawyer and appears on his own behalf. The Cortland trial also differs from the Stoddard trial in that Cortland is criminal case. Similarly, and unlike the judge presiding at the Stoddard trial, who was preoccupied with the appearance of female witness, the judge presiding over the Cortland trial is described as erect on the tall bench. He had grey hair and the stern face of an army office, a man worthy of respect." (44) At the Cortland trial, Roark offers a verbal defence and it is not so in the Stoddard trial.

Roark tells the jury: "Man cannot survive except through his mind. He comes on earth unarmed. Hs brain is his only weapon. Animals obtain food by force. Man has no claws, no fangs, no horns, no great strength of muscle. . . . We can divide a meal among many men. We cannot digest it in a collective stomach. No man can use his brain to think for another. All the functions of body and spirit are private. They cannot be shared or transferred." (679) It is aptly said by Hornstein that Roark explains that the motive of the creator is not primarily the welfare of others but, it is the realization of his own vision. His truth was his only motive . . . a symphony, a book, an engine, a philosophy, an airplane or a building—that was his goal and his life . . . the creation, not its users. The creation, not the benefits of others derived from it." (434) And this vision, this creative impulse is, for Roark, a creation of the self.

Roark reminds his audience that his precise for Cortland is to see it built exactly as he designs it and that he is not paid. It is persuasive to the jury and Roark is acquitted. As Hornstein says: "Earlier in the history of the United States, Alexis De Tocqueville, perhaps the most acute observer of American ways and mores, declared that all issues of public importance find their way into the courtroom: 'Scarcely any political question arises in the United States that is not resolved, sooner or later, into a judicial question.' That is no less true in Rand's fiction where trials play so prominent a role. Her novels comprise battles between good and evil. But the confrontations are not the physical contests of pulp fiction. The battles are essentially intellectual. And the modern battlefield for intellectual contests of this sort is the courtroom." (445) One can understand that these trials say little about law, but they are a setting for a philosophical battle.

However, the differences between the trials show that the good is self-evident. It needs rational argument. But, as the novel itself shows, the argument is more likely to be appreciated in the context of particular events. I believe in the argument of Hornstein: "Unquestionably Rand's position is both more understandable and more persuasive for being explicated not merely through a philosophical treatise, but through the events of a story with the philosophical discourse integrated into that story." (446) In short, the integrate of the abstract and the particular is what provides the power of Rand's argument.

Like Pruette, Rand sees her characters as ideal types and embodied principles. Here I would like to quote Mimi Reisel Gladstein who says in *The New Ayn Rand Companion:* "Rand credited her husband, Frank O'Connor, with providing her the necessary emotional sustenance to complete the book. In her introduction to the twenty-fifth anniversary edition of *The Fountainhead*, she recalls him "the fuel for her spirit." The book is dedicated to him, and a reproduction of his painting 'Man Also Rises' adorns the cover." (1) The book's surprising success led to the production of a 1949 movie version with the stars, Gary Cooper and Patricia Neal. I was directed by King Vidor. The screenplay was written by Ayn Rand. King Vidor turned Rand's preposterous novel into one of his finest and most personal films.

The images have dynamism, a spatial tension that comes partly from Frank Lloyd Wright and partly from Eisenstein. Yet the pattern of their deployment is Vidor's own. The title character is played by Gary Cooper. His wooden and stock personality suits ideally into the theme and structure of the film. As Cooper is so beautiful in his performance, it plays right into his character. Patricia Neal is the ideal counterpart to Cooper. Raymond Massey does his best in the film as an opportunistic newspaper publisher that owes to Welles' Charles Foster Kane. The film also makes use of wonderful shadows, architecture and sets. Interestingly, the film first excites the audience, captivates with its wonderful photography and then backs off to allow the subject matter to become the principal focus.

It is apt to quote Gladstein who writes about Rand's experience in *The New Ayn Rand Companion:* "By Rand's account, her experience with the filming of *The Fountainhead* was in many ways a repetition of her trials during the production of *Night of January 16th.* When a novelist sells movie rights, she loses control of her work. Even though Rand had been hired to write the screenplay, the studio could and did demand certain changes. Rand argued with all concerned to try to maintain the integrity of her vision, and she was satisfied with the result. The movie's script preserves the original theme and meaning." (13) It is really a remarkable technique and a lesson in filmmaking that many modern directors can draw upon.

I feel reading the novel is the need of the hour for the young Americans as they face the rise of becoming second-handlers who cannot think for themselves. They are in dire need of a strong sense of self-worth which was Roark's greatest asset. They must learn from Roark how to value themselves as they are. Then only, Roark's prophesy and Ayn Rand's vision of the future will be fulfilled. As for the philosophy, the occasional super-individualist like Howard Roark is wonderful. Many of the great genius, including Leonard da Vinci, did not have the gene of the people. But we can hope if all the people behave like that, it will be such a great world to live in.

Creating a Different Utopia
Atlas Shrugged

Rand's third novel, *Atlas Shrugged* has many layers and sub-plots. In her writing on the art of fiction, Rand says that it needs such multiple perspectives and that they must be coherent and this quality differentiates her from other writers. It is rightly said: "The novel's title is an allusion to the Greek Titan Atlas who was described as literally holding the world on his shoulders as per Atlas, discussing what might happen if those holding up civilization suddenly decided to stop doing so." (http://www. wikipedia.com) In the novel, the mythological analogy comes during a conversation of Francisco and Rearden. Francisco says to Rearden that if he could suggest to Atlas that he should do one thing, it would be to shrug. As the independent productive achievers begin to be socially demonized, society stagnates in the world of *Atlas Shrugged*. Independence and personal happiness flourish only when the people are free and achievement is rewarded to the extent that individual ownership of private property is strictly respected.

What Nathaniel Branden writes about Rand's words in *My Years with Ayn Rand* seems true: "To Barbara and me she said, 'I know I am challenging the cultural tradition of two and a half hundred years.' She said it to the whole Collective and to Bennett Cerf and Donald Klopfer. She warned them that they should not expect—should not count on—any favourable reviews." (199) These words came true later. Harod Leiendecker is right when he says: "Rand's working title was *On Strike*. Her husband's view that the title be changed to *Atlas Shrugged* was a valuable contribution. (It reminds me of another great title change, when Victor Frank's book *From Death Camp to Existentialism* was renamed *Man's Search for Meaning*.) Atlas can be read as a mystery story, as science fiction, as a feminist tale, or an Arthurian quest and romance, as well as a novel of philosophy, politics, and economics." (http://www.wikipedia. com)

When the novel first appeared in 1957, it was controversial. The productive businessmen honestly absorb this view of their profession, while experiencing unearned guilt over their work and so they are unable to morally challenge the ever increasing rules and regulations foisted on them in the name of public good. *Atlas Shrugged* moves their world. The American economy is gradually collapsing and the industrial production is in steady decline. The stores are closed and the workers become unemployed. A general gloominess appears pervading the culture. The theme of Atlas shrugged is the role of mind in man's existence.

Rand expresses it in *For the New Intellectual:* "A country without intellectuals is like body without a head. And that is precisely the position of America today. Our present state of cultural disintegration is not maintained and prolonged by intellectuals as such, but by the fact that we haven't any." (12) The novel proves the morality of rational self-interest. The main conflict of the book is about the desiccation of the men of minds to go on strike. They refuse to contribute their inventions, art, business, scientific research and other new ideas of any kind to the world. They believe that society hampers them by interfering with their work. By confiscating the profits and the dignity they have earned rightfully, they are underpaid. Without these individuals, the peaceful cohesiveness of the world disintegrates.

The novel opens with the question, "Who is John Galt?" (11) It is asked by a bum on the streets of New York. Eddie Willers, special assistant to the vice president in charge of the Taggart Transcontinental Railroad, does not like the question. This phrase is uttered as a sign of despair and hopelessness. Its use in everyday language is a sign that people believe that answers don't exist to the problems that plague American society. Eddie tells James Taggart about the wreck of the Rio Norte Line that serves Colorado. He reminds him that Colorado—the home of Ellis Wyatt, whose discovery of a new method of extracting oil from shale rock led to the boom—is vital to the country's survival.

When Eddie is going to say about Rearden Metal, he says that Orren Boyle is his friend and he will deliver that rail. James' sister, Dagny says that she has cancelled Orren's contract as Rearden Metal has been their chief supplier for ten years. He says that she is lucky as others cannot do it: "Other people are human. They are sensitive. They can't devote their whole life to metals and engines. You're lucky—you've never had any feelings." (30) When Rearden approaches his house, his mother, his brother Philip and Paul, their old friend, turn to him. He apologizes to them for being late. He presents his wife, Lillian a bracelet made of Reardent Metal. His mother says that his intention is plain selfishness.

Rearden does not understand what they all seek from him. In the most expensive Burrough in New York, four men—Orren, James, Paul and Wesley Mouch—gather. Orren says that nobody can get the iron ore any longer because of the natural exhaustion of the mines. They feel that the use of Rearden Metal is a public hazard. James has brought in the construction of the San Sebastian Line. Dagny fights against its building. But the Board approves it and steel rail is laid across the Mexican desert. Dagny stops at the news stand. Its owner is an old man with a hobby of gathering cigarettes from all over the world. He says: "I like cigarettes, Miss Taggart. I like to think of fire held in a man's hand. Fire, a dangerous force, tamed at his fingertips." (64)

Upon taking over the San Sebastian Mines, the government of Mexico has discovered they are worthless. Dagny asks Eddie to take the appointment of Francisco. Francisco's parents are old friends of the Taggart family. Once he comes to Dagny suddenly. They walk to a clearing and they come closer. He always comes to her unexpectedly which she likes. Later she does not see him for three years. It is Rearden's wedding anniversary. Dagny hears the words of Lillian that she is ready to exchange her bracelet of Rearden Metal for a diamond bracelet. Dagny takes it. For the rest of the evening, Rearden remains by the side of his wife. By spring, Dagny thinks, the track will meet the Rio Norte Line. Rearden proposes a bridge made of Rearden Metal to replace the old one and Dagny agrees to build it.

Dr. Potter comes from the Science Institute to Rearden. He wishes to take all the rights of Rearden Metal. Rearden asks him to get out. Dagny makes a proposal to James that she will form a company in her own name and she completes the construction of the Rio Norte Line. After they have seen how the Rearden Metal rails can take it, she will transfer the line back to Taggart Transcontinental and James agrees. Dagny names her company, the John Galt Line. Outside her window, Dagny sees the shadow of a man. She runs to know his identity, but the alley is empty. The first run on the John Galt line is a success. As they step down at the Wyatt junction, Wyatt takes them with him. There Rearden takes Dagny to his room. For the first time they become intimate.

Rearden says: "Now I have broken an oath I give for life. I had never committed an act that had to be hidden. Now I am to lie, to sneak, to hide." (238) He holds it as his guilt and she her pride. John Galt Line is the Rio Norte Line again. Dagny likes to go to the Twentieth Century Motor Company in Wisconsin. She goes with Rearden. Dagny finds the remnant of the motor and shows it to Rearden. He says it becomes the greatest revolution in power motors. They should find the inventor of the motor. Dagny gets the address of an engineer working in a diner. He is philosopher Hugh Akston. On her return Dagny notices a strange taste in the cigarettes offered by him. Wyatt has set fire to his wells and disappeared. One by one the men, who have built new towns in Colorado, have departed.

The monthly report from Quentin Daniels, appointed for the invention of Motor, lies on Dagny's desk. She asks him to remain in Utach. She has to attend the marriage of Jim with Cheryl. The old man at the cigar stand says that the cigarette she gives is not made anywhere on earth. Rearden supplies his metal to Ken Danagger secretly. It is late and the lights of the underground cafeteria are low. Eddie says to the unnamed worker that Dagny says that she should arm Ken before the destroyer comes. When Dagny enters his office, Ken says that he is going to retire. When

Rearden reaches his office, Francisco has been waiting for him. Francisco says: "You're guilty of a great sin, Mr. Rearden, much guiltier than they tell you, but not the way they preach. The worst guilt is to accept an undeserved guilt—and that is what you have been doing all your life. Your have been paying blackmail, not for your vices, but for your virtues." (422)

In a Thanksgiving dinner, Philip comments that businessmen pursue an antisocial policy based on selfish greed. Rearden warns him that if he says it again he will find himself in the street. Rearden, the victim, now withdraws his sanction. Rearden hears that three ships of d'Anconia copper have been attacked by Ragnar. The sailors whisper the story that Rangnar always seizes the cargoes of relief vessels, but never touches the copper. Dagny hears the declaration that the John Galt Line will be closed in six weeks. Lillian comes to know that Dagny is Rearden's mistress. In a conference, Wesley says that stringent controls are to be taken to meet the deteriorating economic condition of the country. Dagny resigns the job and asks Eddie not to tell anyone about where she is. Ferris asks Rearden to transfer to the nation all rights to Rearden Metal or his affair with Dagny will be made public.

Dagny's honour is used as a tool of blackmail. So with no second thought he signed. Rearden asks his attorney to get him divorce. He walks towards his house: "he had once built his fortune, starting out with empty hands, now he had to rebuild his life, starting out with an empty spirit." (528) Suddenly a stranger approaches Rearden. He says that Rearden has a large bank account waiting for him. Then he reveals that he is Ragnar. Rearden tells him that he will not accept the help of a criminal. But when two policemen come there, Rearden protects him. Kip Charlmers bullies the railroad employees into bringing the coal-burning engine through the tunnel despite the risks involved: "As the train went into the tunnel, the flame of Wyatt's Torch was the last thing they saw on earth." (560)

When Dagny knows about the disaster of the Taggart Tunnel, she returns to her office and telephones Rearden to supply Rearden Metal or steel. When Rearden learns that Francisco is the man whom Dagny loved once, he slaps Francisco's face. The scream comes from Dagny. Francisco leaves. When Rearden throws Dagny against him: "She felt Francisco's presence through Rearden's mind, she felt as if she were surrendering to both men, to that which she had worshipped in both of them, that which they held in common, that essence of character which had made of her love for each an act of loyalty to both." (591) Dagny receives a letter from Quentin, It reads that he cannot work under the terms of Directive 10-289 designed to enslave productive men. She requests him to stay in Utah until she goes. Dagny sits at the window of the train.

Dagny finds an aging tramp who previously works in the Twentieth Century Motor Company. He explains about a plan brought out in the company. If anyone works hard, the more is demanded of him for his neighbour's supper. In four years the company ends in bankruptcy. John Galt is the only man who does not accept the moral law of the factory. The train suddenly comes to a stop, and Dagny learns that the crew members have deserted it. She rents a plane and flies to Utach. She learns that Quentin is going with a stranger. Their plane vanishes behind the rock. She follows it, but her motor is dead.

When Dagny opens her eyes, she sees the man who kneels by her side. He is John Galt. Dagny discovers that all the great minds, who have vanished from society, now live and work in this remote Colorado valley. It is not a town, only a cluster of houses scattered at random. When they reach Galt's house, the doctor who arrives is Thomas Hendricks who has vanished six years ago. Galt shows her the power house. There stands an inscription: "I swear by my life and my love of it that I will never live for the sake of another man nor ask another man to live for mine." (670-71) It is the oath that is taken by every person in that valley. Galt raises his face to the words carved and repeats them slowly and evenly. At the end of the last sound, the door opens slowly.

Galt takes Dagny to meet some of her lost friends—Mulligan, Akston, Halley and others. He leaves her in the guest room. When she sits at the table, a man hurries up to the house and waits there for Galt. When Galt comes, he introduces that man as Ragnar

Danneskjold. Ragnar tells her even she has got an account in Mulligan's bank. Dagny says that she earns her room and board by working in the capacity of his cook and housemaid. She sees him take the shock of the unexpected. From Kellogg, Dagny comes to know that everybody in the outside world is thinking that she has died in a plane crash. Next morning, she hears the voice of Francisco. Galt takes him to Dagny. The first moment that Dagny grasps is when she sees him on his knees, holding onto her, his face pressed to her legs. He reveals her about himself that he has never touched the women he chases.

Dagny realizes that all these four days he has been looking for the wreckage of her plane over the Rockies. He continues to say about their relationship: "I am still what I was, and you'll always see it, and you'll always grant me the same response, even if there's a greater one that you grant to another man. No matter what you feel for him, it will not change what you feel for me, and it won't be treason to either, because it comes from the same root, it's the same payment in answer to the same values." (704) Dagny feels a special pleasure in watching Galt eat the food she prepares. It is the pleasure of knowing that she has provided him with a sensual enjoyment that one form of his body's satisfaction has come from her.

Dagny thinks there is reason why a woman wishes to cook for a man: "The castrated performance of a sickening drudgery was held to be a woman's proper virtue—while that which gave it meaning and sanction was held as a shameful sin." (710-11) Rearden is searching for the wreck of her plane. Galt tells her that he will remain as her last key, before the door of the valley closes altogether. Dagny leaves the valley. Dr. Ferris call Stadler to a conference. He explains Project X in his speech. It is a sonic weapon, capable of destroying everything in a 300-mile radius. Ferris explains that it is an instrument of public security. Dagny telephones her secretary and goes to her office. About the Unification Plan, James says that it is a policy of national survival.

The railroads of the country have been unified into a single team. All of their gross revenue is turned over to the Railroad Pool

Board which divides the total income among the various railroads. Jim asks Dagny to appear on Bertram Scudder's radio program. There, she reveals that Rearden's signing the Gift Certificate is blackmail by their government and rules. When she reaches her apartment, Rearden stands across the room: "And suddenly, broken by the whole of this day and of that month, she was sobbing in his arms, slumped against him, sobbing as she had never done in her life, as a woman, in surrender to pain and in a last, futile protest against it." (783)

Rearden's achievement of his life serves the worst of his enemies. But as to the only two persons he ever loves, she and Francisco, he has brought a deadly insult to one and public disgrace to the other. James feels irritation at Cherry's unastonished manner. Her eyes disturb him, as they are watchful ad questioning. It is Eddie who tells her the truth that Dagny runs Taggart Transcontinental and that glory belongs to her. What she feels is not shock, but worse. Cherryl meets Dagny and apologizes to her for what she speaks on her wedding. Dagny consoles her. Lillian meets James at his house to ask to stop her divorce and they become closer unexpectedly.

When Cherryl returns, she hears two voices behind the door of James. She runs out of the apartment, to escape from him. She throws herself into the river and drowns. Dagny knows who is getting money out of railroad business. Meigs is selling trains and it cannot be discovered. James wants her to protect him from Meigs. He says that it is her moral failure if he suffers as he is her brother: "She wondered whether people accepted the doctrine of sacrifice provided its recipients did not identify the nature of their own claims and actions." (840). The Unification Board is controlling Rearden's sales. On September 7, Dagny stares at a news item that an Emergency State Tax has been passed in California. He feels a sense of detached unconcern when he is granted divorce.

Dagny receives a phone call that the freight cars intended for the wheat of Minnesota have been sent to carry soya beans. In Minnesota, farmers are setting fire to their own farms and are dying. The harvest of soya beans has been reaped prematurely and is unfit for consumption. She gets a call from assistance manager that the interlocker system is out and the trains are held up. She starts rapidly, forgetting what she wears. She asks him to call all their unskilled labourers with any sort of lantern they get. They are going back to where there was no electricity and the train signals were the men holding lanterns. Dagny slips away from the crowd followed by Galt.

The next span of moments is like flashes of light in stretches of blinded unconsciousness except the sensations of her body as they come closer: "it contained her pride in herself and that it should be she whom he had chosen as his mirror, that it should be her body which was now giving him the sum of his existence, as his body which was giving her the sum of hers." (876) She comes to know that it was he whom she had seen, that night. He has been a track labourer there for twelve years. That is why he laughs when she offers to work for him as his cook. He tells her to chalk a dollar sign on the pedestal of Nat Taggart's statue if she is ready to quit. Rearden receives a call from Tinky Holloway pleading to him to attend a conference on November fourth. Rearden knows that it is a trap.

Rearden's mother expresses her doubt that if he vanishes like those men, they are lost. They want to keep him as sacrificial flame. As he tries to go, Lillian reveals that she has been unfaithful to him with James. He stands listening like a scientist studying a subject of no personal relevance. Then he leaves for the conference. The heads of the looters inform Rearden that they will put a new Steel Unification Plan into effect. Rearden points out that, under the plan, he will go bankrupt regardless of his output, while Orren's Associated Steel will receive the bulk of his earnings. Then Rearden offers to take over his mills and be done with it. The jolt that shakes them is genuine terror. When James tells Dagny that Rearden has vanished, she bursts out laughing. It is a sound of triumph.

Rumours spread through the country in whispers of cynical terror. An announcement appears that Mr. Thompson will give the people a report on the world crisis on radio and television.

Thompson wishes to meet Dagny. When she comes to broadcasting studio, the station's chief engineer comes rushing. He says that the station is dead. It looks like a wall of radio waves jamming the air and they cannot get through it. Then they hear a voice addressing them, ladies and gentlemen. It is John Galt. He says all the men who have vanished are the men they hate, yet dread to lose. They, the men of mind are on strike.

Twelve years ago, Galt was an inventor of a motor. Then one night, at a factory meeting, he hears three parasites asserting that his brain and his life are their property and the purpose of his ability is to serve the needs of those who are less able. Then he realized that the parasites around him are expecting him voluntarily to accept slavery: "I quit that factory, I quit your world. I made it my job to warn your victims and to give them the method and the weapon to fight you. The weapon was justice." (960) He gives a call to people to trust their mind. If they are afraid because they know so little, he asks them to live and act within the limit of their knowledge and to keep expanding it to the limit of their life by redeeming their mind from the hockshops of authority.

Neither he nor the rest of them will return until the road is clear to rebuild this country. What all they need, says Galt, is nothing but freedom to earn their profits and to make their own fortunes. As the speech is over, no one moves through span of silence. Sadler asks Thompson to find him by watching every move Dagny makes. Eddie says to Dagny that he knows Galt and has been talking to him in the cafeteria. Dagny searches for Galt through the tunnels. She sees the words, "John Galt, 5th, rear" and presses the doorbell. Suddenly Galt seizes her inside the room. He tells her that the looters' agents who follow her, will be there to arrest and she must take their side and act as his worst enemy.

Then four men enter the room. When they ask about Galt, Dagny screams that he is Galt and she will report the proof. They ask Galt to open the laboratory, but he does not agree. They break down the door. The soldier jumps back. They do not find anything except the heavy drifts of dust on the floor. Dagny understands why Galt tells her not to use force to open the door in the valley. If the door is opened forcibly, the machinery inside will collapse. At Wayne Falkland Hotel, Thompson offers Galt that they will turn the production of the country over to him. He will be the economic director of nation. But Galt does not agree to it as he cannot do this at the point of a gun. When Galt asks to abolish all income taxes, Thompson screams that without them, they cannot pay government employees. Thompson tells him to think it over and relax.

Next evening, Dagny notices an envelope, when she comes to her apartment. There is a note written by a hand she knows. It says: "Dagny: sit tight. Watch them. When he'll need our help, call me at OR 6-593." (1017). Dagny extends her hand to Eddie saying good-bye. Next morning Dr. Stadler is asked to talk to Galt. He tries to convince Galt, but fails. Early on the evening of the fourth day, a muscular man holds Galt's arm pressing an invisible gun against his ribs. They enter the grand ballroom where the sound is the applause of five hundred people. The announcer says that they are to bring them the inauguration of the John Galt Plan, but facing cameras Galt says to get the hell out of his way.

Dagny informs Francisco about it and they move away. In the cellar room, under the ground, Ferris, Mouch and James sit in armchairs. There is a machine, Project F, originated by Ferris. Galt lies strapped to the matters nakedly. They ask him to tell them measures to save their system. As he does not answer, the mechanic presses a button under one of the dials. A long shudder runs through Galt's body. Then the shocks come at irregular intervals, but he does not answer. Suddenly the motor ceases and Galt bursts out laughing. Dagny walks straight towards the guard standing at the door of "Project F," but he does not allow her in. Calmly, she, who would have hesitated to fire at an animal, fires at the heart of that man. Francisco is first to join her from a corner, then Rearden, then Ragnar. In a moment it is Rearden who goes up swiftly.

Ragnar smashes the lock and Francisco enters. He sees Galt's glance of greeting. Dagny kneels by the side of the mattress. Rearden and Dagnar are cutting his bonds. As Galt is not fully steady, he encircles Rearden's shoulder and holds Dagny's shoulder to gain support and to give it. They enter Francisco's airplane hidden in the bush. It runs fast: "Galt leaned silently over and pressed his lips to Dagny's hand: he was leaving the outer world with the one value he had wanted to win from it." (1058) The Comet breaks down in the middle of a desert in Arizona. Eddie sees a train of covered wagons. A man from the engine offers to give him a lift. But Eddie cries that he cannot abandon comet and collapses across the rail and lays sobbing at the foot of the engine. Galt is now to pronounce that they are going back to the world: "He raised his hand and over the desolate earth he traced in space the sign of the dollar." (1069)

In *The Art of Fiction*, Rand writes about the book: "I can give the reason for every word and every punctuation mark in *Atlas Shrugged*—and there are 645,000 words in it by the printer's count. I did not have to calculate it all consciously when I was writing. But what I did was follow a conscious intention in relation to the novel's theme and to every element involved in that theme. I was conscious of my purpose throughout the job—the general purpose of the novel and the particular purpose of every chapter, paragraph and sentence." (4) This is proved in every page of her novel. The heroes are all great achievers, mostly businessmen. They are like the businessmen of today who live patently in a world that always damns, shackles, and drains them. But these productive men fight back by going on a strike.

They refuse to work for the society that depends on their achievements and still brands them immoral. They want to show the world what happens if their immorality is removed: "We are evil, according to your morality, the leader of the strike, John Galt tells the world in a radio address, "We have chosen not to harm you any longer. We are useless according to your economics. We have chosen not to exploit you any longer. We are dangerous and to be shackled, according to your politics. We have chosen not to endanger you, nor to wear the shackles any longer." (925)

A world without the great achievers and businessmen is a world that quickly spirals downward into poverty and destruction. Rearden makes his appearance when he is at the triumphant moment of his ten years' work to revolutionize the industrial world with his Rearden Metal. It is an alloy far lighter, stronger and cheaper than steel. After his success, naturally he expects to profit from the sales to the customers who want to buy his new product. But, he is punished by the government for his hard work by the nationalization of his product. The essence of what human life requires, Rand believes, is the selfish pursuit of his own well-being by his own thought, production and trade. Therefore it is the highest moral virtue.

Galt says that they have known of Rearden and of other strikers that theirs is the power: "We have granted you everything you demanded of us, we who had always been the givers, but have only now understood it. We have no demands to present to you, no terms to bargain about, no compromise to reach. You have nothing to offer us. We do not need you." (925) As a response to the charge that he is working for nothing but his own profit, Rearden responds: "I work for nothing but my own profit—which I make by selling a product they need to men who are willing and able to buy it. I do not produce it for their benefit at the expense of mine, and they do not buy it for my benefit at the expense of theirs. . . . I refuse to apologize for my ability—I refuse to apologize for my success—I refuse to apologize for my money." (444-45)

I think it is apt to quote Edward Wayne Younkins who writes in *Philosophers of Capitalism:* "Under Randian capitalism, which historically has never existed, there is a complete separation of State and economics. Men deal with each other voluntarily by individual choice and free trade for their mutual benefit. The profit motive is just and moral. Profit is made through moral virtue and measure the creation of wealth by the profit earner." (107) Rand proved this through *Atlas Shrugged.* The main character is sketched out in Spark Notes: "The worker Eddie dines within the Taggart cafeteria is a key figure in the story, but still we know nothing about him. In a novel filled with dialogue, he himself has no lines. Everything he says is inferred from Eddie's responses." But the action and the conflict of the story are driven by his principles.

One of interesting things in the novel is that its dominant character works behind the sense and his existence is not known to the reader for the first two-thirds of the novel. The question relating to his name adds a legendary quality to his character as if he were a mythological character. From the choices he makes results in the mystery around the story's unfolding conflict. The strike itself is kept secret, so the disappearance of the world's great thinkers one by one is a mystery to all the characters outside the Galt's circle. Nathaniel Branden says about the question of Rand in *My Years with Ayn Rand*: "'Galt doesn't sound like he's arguing or debating, Does he?" She had asked this before, "His speech must never convey that, and yet I have to provide the reasons and proofs for all of his statements."' (152) As she says, the novel provides the proofs.

During the implementation of communist principles at the Twentieth Century Motor Company, Galt realizes that the only way of ending the exploitation of the mind is by means of a strike. His insight has the potential to usher in a new historical period to be epoch making. Galt is a man of prodigious intellectual gifts—a physicist who brings about a revolution in man's understanding of energy, a philosopher who defines a rational view of existence, and a statesman who leads a strike that transfigures the social systems of the world. The enormity of his intellectual achievements is made possible by two characteristics. One is his unique genius and the other is a trait that men can replicate: his unswerving rationality. In a moving scene, Galt says to Dagny about his love for her and how he has felt when he knows that she is Rearden's mistress.

His description of the scene to Dagny is the key to understand Galt's character: "And for one instant, I did what I had never done before, what most men wreck their lives on doing—I saw that moment out of context. I saw the world as he [Rearden] made it look, as if it matched him, as if he were its symbol—I saw a world of achievement, of unslaved energy, of unobstructed drive through purposeful years to the enjoyment of one's reward—I saw, as I stood in the rain in a crowd of vagrants, what my years would have brought me, if the image of everything I should have been and he had everything that should have been mine. But it was only a moment." (878) Galt emotionally suffers when he experiences loss, but he does not allow his emotions to interfere with his grasp of reality.

Galt knows that the strike is right and whatever the pain resulting from it can defile the purity of his conviction. He is a hero as he represents the best of modern civilization with its science, medical research, technological progress and its application of intellect in serving human life. He embodies the novel's essential theme, that is, by means of mind only human beings can achieve prosperity on earth. It is easy to overlook the other aspects of Galt's life: his light way moving, his passionate love for Dagny, the tenderness and concern he shows for his friends, Francisco, Ragnar, and his respect for his teacher and spiritual father, Hugh Akston because of his towering achievements of his intellect. Though ruled by reason, Galt is able to express and experience is emotions as well. Just as Rand uses Dagny to shatter the mind-body dichotomy that separates physical pleasure from higher thought, she employs Galt to reject the split between reason and emotion. The special bond that Galt has with these four persons shows Rand's rejection of the conventional belief that an individual can be either rational or emotional, but he cannot be both.

Dagny is the female protagonist and primary narrator of the story. I feel that her character is rightly estimated in Cliffs Notes: "Her knowledge of engineering and industry enables her to expertly run a transcontinental railroad. Her understanding of physics allows her to identify the virtues of Rearden Metal. The independence of her judgement lets her stand by the metal and her railroad in the face of virtually unanimous social opposition. Her dauntless determination drives her to build the John Galt Line. The qualities that make Dagny a towering character are the same qualities that make real-life individuals such as the scientist Marie Curie and the innovative educator Maria Montessori great heroines." (89) It shows that her great stature is the outcome of the combination of characteristics she possesses.

Galt too possesses the same qualities as does Dagny and they make him also great like Aristotle, Michelangelo, Leonardo da Vinci, and Isaac Newton. Rand dramatizes a crucial point in Dagny's character that human greatness equals rational achievement irrespective of gender. Instead of projecting Dagny as a great writer, composer or artist, Rand depicts her as a genius specifically in the field of heavy industry. It is because in addition to the relevant plot considerations, Dagny's career makes a philosophical point and it is that if intellect is more life-giving than physical strength, then women can create new physical products, look after heavy industry, raise the material standard of living, and so on. Dagny's emotional life is as intense as that of Galt.

The men of mind give value to man's life and they love industry, technology and science that promote life. They have great attraction and admiration for the giants among mankind. Because of this admiration, Dagny falls on her hands and knees while shaking with excitement when she realizes the nature of the left over scrap of the motor: "Her sudden grasp was not a sound, but a jolt that threw her at the junk pile. She was on her hands and knees, crawling over the wreckage, seizing every piece of paper in sight, flinging it away, searching further. Her hands were shaking." (269) This is the reason why she runs desperately back to New York when she hears the news of the Taggart Tunnel disaster. Dagny has committed mind, body and soul to man's life on earth.

Rand's Objectivist philosophy stresses the virtue of productivity. She shows Rearden as the embodiment of this virtue. Among all the other industrial giants in the valley, Rearden's productivity is legendary. Andrew Stockton, the owner of the country's best foundry, says that Rearden would put him out of business if he ever comes to valley by joining their strike. I agree with what is written in Cliffs Notes: "Consequently, productivity is an expression of the principle of mind-body integration, the ability of the mind to create material abundance for the purpose of enjoying life on earth. But Hank Rearden holds, through much of the story, a mistaken premise that prevents him from recognizing his own moral greatness. He believes the theory that mind and body are split. This viewpoint is known as the mind-body dichotomy—the belief that the mind or soul belongs to a higher world superior to this one, and that earth is ruled by the low instincts of the body. Rearden's liberation from this way of thinking transforms his character." (90) It shows that productivity is the need for the survival of man, since nothing is given to man on earth and all must be created.

As Rearden regards the body as base or ignoble at the beginning, he devalues all its activities. He despises both Dagny and himself for their passionate lovemaking. While discussing the unlimited potential of Rearden Metal, he also says to her that they are a couple of backgrounds and they do not have any spiritual goals or qualities. They are only after material things. In the friendship of Francisco, he learns that material production is an intellectual process and a sublime virtue. In his relationship with Dagny, he learns that sex involves the expression of an individual's inner values. Rearden is attracted by her as she represents the same values of rationality and industrial productivity that he cherishes. When he leaves the idea that the body and its concerns are low, he recognizes his own supreme value. The novel concentrates on some important points about Rearden's family.

Through the character of Rearden, Rand wants to make a point regarding the nature of creative individuals. He is very much similar to the great inventors, writers and artists of history. All these creators like Rearden are motivated primarily by their passionate fascination with their own field of endeavour. All these original thinkers are self-driven and self-actualized. Rand calls Rearden selfish not in the traditional sense but in the sense of being motivated by his own happiness and values. However, Rearden is not consistent in his commitment to himself. He acts selfishly in matters of his marriage, and family life. His wife and other members of his family are able to control him as Rearden feels an obligation to them. He has accepted the code of altruism.

One of Galt's two closest friends is Francisco. The gaiety and enthusiasm that define Francisco's character comes from his view of the world. Human beings who recognize that the rational thought and productive effort alone advance their lives, and who don't place their whims above facts, can expect to attain their goals and live in happiness. Francisco's recognition of this truth is expressed in the two refrains of his childhood. "Let's make it!" was his call to engage in acts of construction. The first expresses an explorer's premise, the second a builder's. Both represent a man to whom reality is open, an individual for whom all roads are cleared and green lights stretch to the horizon.

It is apt to quote here Nathaniel Branden who writes about the novel in *The Literary Method of Ayn Rand:* 'Notwithstanding the austere solemnity of its abstract theme, her novel—as a work of art—projects the laughing, extravagantly imaginative virtuosity of a mind who has never heard that "one is not supposed" to combine such elements as these in a single book. To those who believe that "one is not supposed to" Rand would answer: "Check your premises."' (4) The same is said in the novel. Francisco's characteristic mockery and his use of biting derision are always benevolent and positive. James uses irony as a weapon of destruction, but Francisco uses it to destroy the destroyers and thus clearing the road for the creative.

Rand writes: "Watching them, Dagny thought suddenly of the difference between Francisco and her brother Jim. Both of them smiled derisively. But Francisco seemed to laugh at things because he saw something much greater. Jim laughed as if he wanted to let nothing remain great." (94) Francisco's mockery supports his values. This is proved by a scene from his childhood. Once a professor of literature sees Francisco on top of a pile in a junk yard dismantling the carcass of an automobile, and says to him that a young man of his position should spend his time in library absorbing the culture of the world. Then Francisco replies that he thinks he is doing it. His intention here is not to insult the professor, but to expand the meaning of the term culture to understand the profound value of technology and industrial production. Even when he was young, Francisco concentrated on making a positive point.

In his love for Rearden, Francisco's benevolence is shown. Though he gets insults and a physical blow from Rearden, Francisco does not care. He says to Rearden to understand his right to live. Only when Rearden gets rid of his shackles of guilt and servitude that bind him to the parasites and recognizes his own oral value, Francisco's mission is complete. James Taggart, the main villain in the novel, is far worse than a corrupt businessman who seeks his wealth by being parasites. Like Lillian, he is a nihilist. He always lies to himself and tries to convince himself that he wants to get wealth only to protect the interests of his railroad and to help his friends like Orren Boyle or to serve the public welfare. But in reality, he does not give value to anything. Instead he hates the people who are capable of achieving values and living successfully. This is the reason why during a meeting that leads to the passage of Directive 10-289, which is designed to enslave productive men, he screams involuntarily: "If we are to perish, let's make sure that we all perish together. Let's make sure that we leave them no chance to survive!" (498).

James is shaken after the destruction of Cherryl. This incident brings his real motivation too near to the surface. It is not possible for anyone to tolerate the recognition of his own moral depravity. James has tried to evade this recognition throughout his life. After realizing this, he has lost his mind. Edward W. Younkins in *Atlas Shrugged: A Novel of Human Action* says that in her stylized portraits of the characters in *Atlas Shrugged*, Rand presents no random details and focuses on the essentials to understand each character. By eliminating irrelevant and trivial attributes and actions, her characters become moral projections.

By excluding superficial or accidental facets of a character's personality, Rand makes certain that the attention is not diverted from essential purposes and motives. As a result, says Younkins, the reader is able to gain clear and deep insight into characters such as the self-made martyred industrialist on mixed moral premises (Hank Rearden), the ideal epic heroine (Dagny Taggart), the supremely able man who enjoys an exalted life on earth (Francisco d'Anconia), the brilliant scientist turned moral traitor and looter-politician (Robert Stadler), the envious nihilist death worshipper

(James Taggart), the vacuous power-lustre (Lillian Rearden), and so on.

Atlas Shrugged reminds us that knowledge of agricultural science is needed for the ability to produce food. Cliffs Notes comment: "If man is to resolve various forms of mental illness, he must know psychology, if he is to establish a free society, he must understand the principles of political philosophy. If a man is to avert war, or even personal conflict, he must be able to negotiate his differences, which requires reason. Every value that human life depends on is a product of the reasoning mind. This idea is Ayn Rand's thesis in *Atlas Shrugged."* (993) It is true because every species has its survival instrument. Birds have wigs, antelopes enjoy speed, elephants utilize size, gorillas showcase their strength, and so on, but man can't survive by these means. He does not have wings, strength or speed. Nature endows man with one instrument by means of which to survive—his mind.

In the novel all the thinkers live in accordance with their rational nature. James, Floyd Ferris and other villains seek survival by force, which is an animal's method, not man's. The novel shows various ways in which the great minds are the benefactors of mankind. Through the character of Eddie, Rand also makes it clear that even the individuals of modest intelligence can aspire to lofty goals. He lacks the genius of Dangy, but he knows that if the railroad goes, he will not be rebuilding it. He says: "It's still Taggart Transcontinental. I'll stand by it. Dagny, wherever you go you'll always be able to build a railroad. I couldn't. I don't even want to make a new start. Not any more. Not after what I have seen. You should. I can't. Let me do what I can." (1022)

Eddie's character has a greater significance. He is constant in his devotion to the railroad and also to Dagny. James mocks at him saying: "It's touching—your devotion to Taggart Transcontinental. If you don't look out, you'll turn into one of those real feudal serfs." (18) Eddie's reply is that is what he is. Eddie is, in the words of Rand uses to describe Dagny, a child of the Industrial Revolution. As is mentioned in Cliffs Notes: "The theme of *Atlas Shrugged* is the life-giving nature of rationality, and Eddie is as dedicated to the mind as any of the great thinkers in the story." (94) Though Eddie does not have the power of brain, he is fully rational.

Galt explains that rationality is a commitment to the facts—an inviolable willingness to face reality, no matter how painful, frightening, or unpleasant the truth may be in a specific case. Eddie practices this as perfectly as Galt. His dialogue with James about the Rio Norte Line is an example of that. James says that no one can blame him for the shoddy track or the poor service of Taggart Transcontinental. Eddie likes to fix the track, but James only looks to avoid blame. The thinking of James is ruled by the opinions of others, but Eddie's thoughts are ruled by facts. Eddie's character shows the difference between intelligence and rationality. Intelligence is an intellectual ability and rationality is a method. Robert Stadler has incomparably greater intelligence while Eddie is far more rational.

Stadler tries to convince himself that Galt is dead and he has to be. He says that there is no connection between the prodigy he taught at the Patrick Henry University and the man he now sees. He says to Galt: "You're asking the impossible! Men can't exist your way! You permit no moments of weakness; you don't allow human frailties or human feelings! What do you want us? Rationality twenty-four hours a day, with no loophole, no rest, no escape?" (1024) Though Stadler knows all the words of Galt are true, he does not want to agree with hi. But Eddie does not push the facts aside.

According to the theme of the novel, morality involves an unbreached commitment to the rational requirements of man's life on earth. Such a type of commitment is exhibited by Eddie to the end. For example, when the Taggart Comet breaks down in the Arizona desert, the passengers and the crew leave for a covered wagon, but Eddie refuses to abandon the train. This loyalty is the essence of his moral stature. Dagny and Francisco may rescue Eddie and take him to the valley, where he deserves to be, but it's also possible that they will be unable to find him in the desert and he may die. Eddie's dependence on the strikers is the example of common man's relationship with the creative geniuses.

When the great minds are left to act upon their thoughts, they can create abundance and the common man flourishes. But when the producers are enslaved, they cannot generate prosperity and the common man suffers as a result. Rand sets up a contrast between the heroine, Dagny and her brother, James. Both are businesspeople, but each holds markedly different moral and political theories. Dagny is a model of the spirit and practice of capitalism. She believes in industrial production and profit—hard work and earning large amounts of money. She orders rails from Rearden instead of Orren Boyle because Rearden delivers his product and Boyle does not. Likewise, Dagny will provide freight service to Ellis Wyatt and the Colorado industrialists but not to the destitute economy. Jim, on the other hand, is an example of the spirit and practice of socialism.

James prefers giving chances to the little guy, instead of dealing with those already successful. Just to give some economic opportunity to the impoverished Mexicans, James builds the San Sebastian Line at a cost of millions. While Dagny seeks to earn profit, James sees to serve the public welfare. He says: "Selfish greed for profit is a thing of the past. It has been generally conceded that the interests of the society as a whole must always be placed first in any business undertaking." (29) James does not have a mind of his own. For example, he is afraid to take a chance on Rearden Metal as the product is new and is not yet accepted by society. He says to Dagny: "but no body's ever used it before." (27) But Dagny does not care for what people believe or say. She follows her own judgment. For example, she studies Rearden's formula and examines the results of his testing in order to understand the metal's superiority.

The steady decline of American prosperity reminds Eddie of the oak tree that stood on the Taggart estate when he was a child. The tree was huge and powerful and stood for centuries: "He felt safe in the oak tree's presence: it was a thing that nothing could change or threaten: it was his greatest symbol of strength. One night, lightning struck the oak tree. Eddie saw it next morning. It lay broken in half, and he looked into its trunk as into the mouth of a black tunnel. The trunk was only an empty shell: its heart had rotted away long ago: there was nothing inside—just a thin gray dust that was being dispersed by the whim of the faintest wind. The living power had gone, and the shape it left had not been able to stand without it." (13) Now, Eddie experiences the same feeling when walking into the Taggart Building. Eddie does not find energy of a great living power. But he finds the deadly inner corruption, that is, Taggart.

The oak tree that Eddie remembers serves as an apt metaphor for society's decay. Eddie is reminded that things are not always what they seem to be. The outward appearance of power may not be an accurate indication of inner reality. Both Taggart Transcontinental and the U.S. economy are powerful and seemingly safe through many years, but now they have rotted away. Eddie wonders about the reason for this deterioration. In the description of the valley, Rand shows her ideal world. Francisco plays the role of a playboy and Rearden despises him. Francisco warns Rearden that he must realize and say to his family that he has no moral obligation to support them and that he does so only out of his generosity and kindness. So he deserves their appreciation and thanks.

Francisco says: "Ask yourself where their code is leading you and what it offers you as your final goal. . . . By their own statement you must support them because they cannot survive without you. Consider the obscenity of offering their impotence and their need—their need of you—as a justification for your torture." (422) Rearden is further liberated from the ethical system that has constrained him for so long by the sex speech of Francisco. Francisco makes it clear to Rearden that he is virtuous because of his industriousness, not in spite of it. Rearden must feel a joyous pride for his life-giving achievements and leave any kind of guilt that his family asks him to feel. Rearden is short of words to define his situation, but somehow he knows that he is in need of the sanction that Francisco offers him.

Dagny's romantic attraction to Rearden, the beauty of her appearance and her disappointment at Rearden's indifference are revealed at the party. I strongly believe in the words of Robert James

Bidinotto who says in his *The Revolutionary Philosophy of Atlas Shrugged* (2007), that Rearden is torn by conflicts. He is passionately in love with life and happiness; yet he accepts uncritically the conventional view that his personal desires, such as his love for his work, are subjective, base, and lacking any nobility or moral significance. This belief leaves him morally defenceless against those who plot to destroy his steel mills. Similarly, he views his passion for his mistress, Dagny Taggart, as animalistic and degrading.

This belief, says Bidinotto, leaves him trapped in a loveless marriage to a vicious wife, held by a gray, empty sense of guilt and moral duty. Rearden's rigid formality, and the way he takes Lillian's side in the party offers his own indication that he has same feelings for Dagny. Rearden understands that he has made a mistake in marrying Lillian and feels that his mistake is a lifetime commitment that he intends to honour. Rand contrasts her character to that of Lillian through the bracelet incident. Dagny very much loves the bracelet made of Rearden Metal, because it symbolizes everything she worships, that is, technological innovation, industrial production, and the power of a man's mind in creating progress: "She clasped the metal bracelet on her wrist. She liked the feel of the weight against her skin. Inexplicably, she felt a touch of feminine vanity, the kind she had never experienced before; the desire to be seen wearing this particular ornament." (150) On the other hand, Lillian who claims to have higher spiritual concerns, despises the bracelet as something materialistic.

At some level, Rearden knows that his attraction to Dagny is more than physical. His mind knows her greatness and so his body wants her. He consciously holds the view that mind and body are separate, but he still has an inner belief that the two support each other. Francisco merely makes him recognize what Rearden has always known. Paul Larkin's warning to Rearden shows that the press holds the same moral code as his family. The press writes that Rearden is selfish and antisocial as he is proud of his mills. But Rearden does not care for it and laughs off the attacks of the press, because his great productive ability allows him to feel that he can afford to be tolerant of the media. Yet, Rearden does not recognize the evil of those who attack him for his success. As a result, he does not try to answer the vicious accusations of his family or the false attacks of the press.

The relationship grows between Rearden and Dagny because it is based on the profound values that they share. Both of them love industrialization and man's prosperity on earth. It goes beyond the immediate commitment that they both have to the Rearden Metal and John Galt Line. Similarly, their commitment to the facts and the rejection of the social opinions are their deepest relation. Because of the principles they share and the battle they fight together, it is inevitable that they fall in love. Their views of sex are different and this difference indicates the underlying philosophical difference. Many philosophies and religions teach that only the mind or soul is pure, but the body and its desires are base.

Spark Notes comment: "Rand rejects the mind-body dichotomy that is central to many philosophies and religions. She opposes the idea that the thoughts and achievements of the mind are pure and noble, but the desires of the body are base and immoral, and she presents Dagny as a character who also rejects the idea." Dagny rejects the idea of the split between the mind and body because she recognizes that for a rational man the desires of the body come logically from the understanding and evaluations of the mind. Jim and Cherryl's romance is entirely different. Cherryl chooses Jim because of the values she thinks he represents, but she is wrong about him. Cherryl chooses Jim because of the values she thinks he represents, but she is wrong about him. Jim chooses Cherryl out of his need to destroy. Although he claims to have noble, altruistic goals and a desire to help the "Little guy," his true nature is to destroy the effort and aspirations of others.

In the beginning, the romance between James and Cherryl is motivated by opposite premises. Cherryl is the hero worshipper who sincerely admires great achievement. But James is a nihilist and tries to defeat Dagny and Rearden because of their ability. He cannot destroy the great men as they are so powerful. He can only take his revenge on the little hero worshipper like Cherryl who admires him. This is the reason for his behaviour towards Cherryl. In the plot of the novel, the discovery of the motor is the turning point. Before the discovery, Dagny's only goal is to build the John Galt Line, but now she shifts her energies to discovering the secret of the motor: "It would set the whole country in motion and on fire." (272)

The novel demonstrates the way things work in a mixed economy that is moving towards socialism. Private property exists nominally, but the state is steadily increasing control over its use and distribution. In such a system, Productive businessmen like Rearden and Dan Conway do not have any rights. They are at the mercy of the inferior competitors who have political friends. On the other hand, in a capitalist society, their productive activities would not be restricted by the government bureaucrats and envious competitors. It is thought that capitalism leads to coercive monopoly.

Nathaniel Branden rightly says in his essay, "Common Fallacies About Capitalism": "Now if a company were able to gain and hold a non-coercive monopoly, if it were able to win all the customers in a given field, not by special government-granted privileges, but by sheer productive efficiency—by its ability to keep its costs low and/or to offer a better product than any competitor could—there would be no grounds on which to condemn such a monopoly. On the contrary, the company that achieved it would deserve the highest praise and esteem." (75) It shows that the allegation against capitalism is false.

According to the moral premise of socialism, the strong must serve the weak. Therefore, Rearden's productive company has to be sacrificed to Boyle's unproductive one. Rearden knows it: "He knew that the specific reason behind the Plan was Orren Boyle: He knew that the working of an intricate mechanism, operated by pull, threat, pressure, blackmail—mechanism like an irrational adding machine run amuck and throwing up any chance sum at the whim of any moment—had happened to add up to Boyle's pressure upon these men to extort for him this last piece of plunder." (899) As the government has power over the economy, the level of corruption naturally rises.

Nathanial Branden writes in *Capitalism: The Unknown Ideal* that the cause of the 1929 depression in America was the government's control over public property: "Had men chosen to understand the cause of the crash, the country would have been spared much of the agony that followed. The depression was prolonged for tragically unnecessary years by the same evil that had caused it: government controls and regulations." (81-82) This rise of corruption is because of the state's gaining power to dispense economic favours. It attracts power-seekers like Wesley Mouch and makes incompetent businessmen like James and Boyle to flourish on the competent men like Rearden parasitically. In a free market, customers can choose unrestrictedly among the competitors. They can choose the companies like Rearden's or Conwy's because they get the job done. Edward Wayne Younkins says in *Philosophers* of Capitalism: "The ruling principle of capitalism is justice. Of capitalism is justice. The overall social effect—the fact that individuals and groups who live under capitalism prosper—is simply a by-product or secondary consequence. Political and economic system and institutions which encourage and protect individual rights, freedom and happiness are proper system." (107) But in a state-dominated system, unprincipled people get the favour of power-seeking politicians, brokering corrupt deals that allow them to stay in business by means of legislation. For example, Mouch is an incompetent man. He would not succeed, in a capitalist system where he would have to compete fairly in an open market. But in a socialist system, he can manipulate the coercive power of the state and rise to an influential position in the government.

In the novel, the progressive activities are socialist acts of legislation such as the confiscation of the Rearden ore mines by the government and their distribution to the needy men like Paul. The term, progressive in matters of economic policy, is a euphemism here for the theft of the private properties by the government and the country's gradual decline into dictatorship. The State Science Institute cannot match Rearden's achievement. But it wants to keep his metal off the market so that it will not lose the credibility of the people. Rearden and Dagny struggle hard to complete the John Galt

Line on time. This sets the creative abilities of the two great minds in conflict with the destructive power of the socialist government. Pure capitalism in action is represented by the characters of Rearden and Dagny.

Cliffs Notes comment: "They are innovative businesspeople, like the productive giants of American history Rearden's invention of a new metal and Dagny's recognition of its merits reflect the independent thinking so prevalent among the great American industrialists. Henry Ford, for example, perfected the new technique of mass production, bringing the automobile to millions of customers. Thomas Edison invented an electric lighting system that changed the world and earned him millions of dollars. Pioneering industrialists like George Westinghouse, George Eastman, Andrew Carnegie, James J. Hill, and many others performed similar feats. In more recent times, the great innovators of the computer industry have brought positive changes into the lives of millions with their new products and made fortunes doing so. Rand emphasizes that the greatest capitalists are entrepreneurs with new ideas. In a free country, where Rearden and Dagny would have the liberty to promote this innovation, Rearden Metal would revolutionize industry, improve the general quality of life, and earn millions for Hank Rearden." (32) But unfortunately, Rearden and Dagny do not live in a free country.

The government holds that the individuals must sacrifice themselves for the welfare of the public. When individuals do not come forward for the sacrifice, then the state has the legal power to force them to do so. This premise makes Rearden lose his ore mines using the justification that Rearden is already successful, so someone less successful should be given a chance. Further, the State Science Institute feels that Rearden's selling his metal in the open market poses a threat to it. The institute's response is a smear campaign based on fictitious allegations about the hypothetical problems with Readen Metal.

But as Alan Greenspan writes in his essay, "Antitrust": "The capital market acts as a regulator of prices, not of profits. It leaves an individual producer free to earn as much as he can by lowering his costs and by increasing his efficiency relative to others. Thus, it constitutes the mechanism that generates greater incentives to increased productivity and leads, as a consequence, to a rising standard of living." (68) In *Atlas Shrugged*, Ayn Rand demonstrates that the government violates the rights of the productive people in a socialist system. Consequently, the economy suffers.

Rearden fails to recognize that Paul Larkin is part of the corrupt deal brokered by James and Boyle. However, he finds a trustworthy friend in Ken Danagger. Danagger is a self-made man who like Rearden starts at the bottom of the coal business as a miner and rises to the top by means of his own ability and indomitable work ethic. They used to meet secretly: "They had not discussed that law, at their dinner together, or their motives or the risk they were taking. They had merely talked business, speaking clearly and dryly, as he always spoke at any conference." (355) Rearden and Danagger understand each other not relying on the handouts or the government's coercion. They are the men who make their own ways in the world.

Through the novel, Rand proves that socialism is parasitical. Rearden, Dagny and the great Colorado industrialists have created steel, oil, transportation, and other wonderful inventions. The services and goods they provide make it possible to build and heat homes, construct and fuel automobiles, and participate in many other productive activities. To quote Nathaniel Branden who says in his "The Role of Labour Unions" *Capitalism: The Unknown Ideal*: "If the worker of today produces more than the worker of fifty years ago, it is not because the former exerts more physical effort; quite the contrary: the physical effort required of him is far less. The productive value of his effort has been multiplied many times by the tools and the machines with which he works; they are crucial in determining the economic worth of his services." (84) Consequently, they create jobs for thousands of employees.

Under socialism, they are forced to carry less competent men along with them. The unions of railroad workers clamour for shorter trains that run at low speeds and the government marks these demands law. The union membership is rewarded, but the creator of the line, Dagny is punished. Rearden's situation is even worse as he has to sell to every person or business that wants his product while simultaneously restricting his production. With this scenario, Rand makes a condemnation of socialism. The government compels the great creators to support those who cannot match their achievements, and in this way a socialist government penalizes a man for his hard work and rewards others for their lack of accomplishment. Rand argues that by serving the needy and unproductive does not provide justice to the men and women of accomplishment. Independent men like Wyatt are shackled.

Rather than permit his achievement to be looted in order to support the parasites, Wyatt destroys it. He is both a symbol and a warning: he is a symbol of the great creative and free spirit that tyranny can't subjugate and a warning to those who try to enslave him. "Don't tread on me" was a saying popular at the time of the American Revolution, and Wyatt represents that same spirit of freedom. In the novel, Francisco's money speech also plays an important role. It presents the antithesis of the traditional view that money is the root of all evil.

Francisco reminds one that money is a tool of exchange, which presupposes productive men and their activities. It is shown in the comments in Spark Notes: "Francisco's 'money speech' lays out some critical elements of Rand's philosophy. . . . If a man's ability to be productive is represented by his ability to make money, then money is a moral tool and an indicator of the value of man." Francisco explains that the money a man earns is the symbol of his productive ability and as a result, he gets his moral honour. Francisco asks: "Money is your means of survival. The verdict you pronounce upon the source of your livelihood is the verdict you pronounce upon your life. If the source is corrupt, you have damned your own existence. . . . Money is the product of virtue, but it will not give you virtue and it will not redeem your vices. Money will not give you the unearned, neither in matter nor in spirit. Is this the root of your hatred of money?" (382)

Rearden now has two mistaken ideas that thc industrial production is an unspiritual endeavour and the other is that materialistic concerns are immoral, because only spiritual activities have moral value. Rearden cannot yet see his own towering stature, because of the mistaken ideas. Francisco's intention is to liberate Rearden from his errors and their harmful results in his life. Ayn Rand in her novel asks what happens if the productive men reject demands for service to the parasites. Rand provides the answer through Rearden's transformation. Rearden has come to understand that his productiveness is a great virtue and that the behaviour of his family and the politicians is evil. At his trial, Rearden refuses to accept their moral right to loot his wealth. By withdrawing his tolerance of their actions, he exposes them for what they are—thieves with vicious pretensions to moral rectitude.

Rand shows the cause and effect relationship between events in a country's economy. Now, people such as Lillian, James, Mouch and all the other looters cannot survive on their own. The purpose of the government policies is to ensure that creative, productive people cannot survive too. Rearden now understands the error he has made and its significance. By this Rearden betrayed the code of life by which he has always lived. He has made an enormous error and he knows that he must pay for it, but not Dagny. This is the reason for his signing away the rights to Rearden Metal. He feels free now from the code of death. In the story, Ragnar is a powerful force for justice. His character embodies irony. In order to fight for justice, he's compelled to become a criminal. After talking with Ragnar, Rearden starts to understand that when the law is engaged in robbery, people who want to return stolen goods to their rightful owners must become outlaws.

Unlike Francisco, Wyatt and all other strikers, Dagny is not ready to walk away from the railroad which has given meaning to her life. One of the chapters' titles is formed by Dagny's words to Francisco: "I can't accept what they're all accepting Francisco, it's the thing we thought so monstrous, you and I—the belief that disasters are one's natural fate, to be borne, not fought. I can't accept submission. I can't accept helplessness. I can't accept renunciation. So long as there's a railroad left to run, I'll run it." (584) These words contain the essence of the bond Dagny feels to the railroad and Rearden for his mills. These great producers are willing to bear the torture imposed on them by the dictators in Washington only for the sake of their love.

It is rightly commented in Cliffs Notes: "Ayn Rand emphasizes here that industrial production is just as creative as writing a novel or composing a symphony. Industrial production is also fuelled by love—love for the creation of material abundance and the positive, constructive act of making possible man's life on earth. Such love isn't to be relinquished lightly, which is why Francisco experienced such torment when he chose to leave and is also why Dagny can't yet join him." (59) While Cliffs Notes says about the importance of the story of the motor, in Spark Notes it is seen in a different perspective:

> Rand uses Jeff Allen's detailed account of the chaos at the Twentieth Century Motor Company to illustrate the devastating effects of collectivism. For Rand, the ideas behind the plant's radical management are not just bad ideas, they are pure evil. She intends the plant's story to be an object lesson in the perils of Communism. Under the system at the plant, income was based on need, not performance. Using need as a basis for policy is the system's fundamental flaw, for a number of reasons. First, need as no absolute definitions; what is a need to one person may be a luxury to another. Second, rewarding income based on need removes incentive. If production is separated from income, there is no reason to produce, since a worker will receive income anyway. Finally, ability becomes a liability when those determined to be ablest are given more work but not more income. The biggest winner under such a system is the person with most need and the least ability."

This fact makes it inevitable that a community should dissolve into chaos and mistrust, and that production should cease.

At the Twentieth Century Motor Company, the group used to vote to decide the needs of the individuals, just as the group decided the projected output of each worker based on ability. Consequently, each individual was enslaved to the group and his income was decided by his ability to beg rather than his productive effort. A tramp says to Dagny: "It took us just one meeting to discover that we had become beggars—rotten, whining snivelling, beggars all of us, because no man could claim his pay as his rightful earning, he had no rights and no earnings, his work didn't belong to him, it belonged to 'the family,' and they owed him nothing in return, and the only clam he had on them was his 'need'—so he had to beg in public for relief from his needs, like any lousy moocher, listing all his troubles and miseries, down to his patched drawers and his wife's head colds, hoping that 'the family' would throw him alms." (609)

The workers could not feel pride as their earning money is not the direct result of their hard work. Leonard Peikoff rightly says in *The Ominous Parallels:* 'Nazism like communism dissents private property. This "private property" represented the right of the individual to manage or to speculate with inherited or acquired property as he pleased, without regard for the general interests. German socialism had to overcome this "private," the property is common property. The owner is bound by the people and the Relch to the responsible management of his goods. His legal position is only justified when he satisfies this responsibility to the community.' (18) It is reflected in Twentieth Century Motor Company.

Galt and his friends are not the first group of people to go on strike. Striking workers generally accuse the wealthy and the industrialists of exploitation. They clamour that they gain profits by robbing the true producer of wealth, the manual labourer. But Galt's strike, in contrast, is designed to show that the mind, not physical labour, is the fundamental source of wealth and that the people who perform intellectual work are the true creators of value. Galt stresses the point that a company's long range policies are planned by the inventors or the entrepreneurs. Therefore they are responsible for prosperity. Dagny believes that even the looters want to live and that they are mistaken in their policies. She hopes she can make them realize that their altruist ethics, dictatorial politics, and socialist economics lead them to collapse.

When the looters once realize their mistakes, they step back and allow the producers like Rearden and herself to rebuild the economy. Because of this, Dagny thinks that she must return to her railroad. But the strikers believe that the looters are irrational and they are driven only by the desire to rule men. The strikers think that the looters see the destruction of their policies, yet they are not ready to accept the truth. When reality clashes with their urge to rule and prosper, they try to evade reality instead of questioning their desire. Whatever the consequences may be, they want power. So, they do not accept any kind of evidence that proves the devastating results of their policies and they do not want to change. Galt want to be near Dagny as he knows that she does not win in her battle. It is at this point that the readers cannot decide whether Dagny and Rearden or the strikers are right.

In the novel, Cherryl has a different story. Unlike Rearden, she is still capable of being hurt by James. At the basic level, she is very much similar to Eddie. Both of them have souls as Dagny or Rearden, but they do not have the intellect of such great producers. Cherryl has a pure soul of a hero worshipper and places man at his highest and best. She loves greatness which James wants to destroy. The fifth chapter's title, "Their Brothers' Keepers" refers to the biblical story of Cain and Abel. Rand demonstrates what the religious injunction to be the brother's keeper looks like in practice.

This injunction is embodied by three instances in the chapter. The first instance occurs when the seed grain and the future existence of the Nebraska farmers is seized to feed the starving people of Sand Creek, Illinois. Eugene Lawson says that in this age of enlightenment men realize that they are all brothers' keepers. The second instance occurs when James is desperately in need of holding to the policies of the looters as he can get power with them and he begs Dagny: "Why should you be happy while I suffer? Oh yes, the world is yours, you're the one who has the brains to run it. Then why do you permit suffering in your world? You proclaim the pursuit of happiness, but you doom me to frustration. Don't I have the right to demand any form of happiness I choose? Isn't that a debt which you owe me? Am I not your brother?" (839)

James knows his role in the death of Cherryl and many obstacles he has put in the way of Dagny and he also knows that their policies do not work and so he appeals to obligation of brother to force Dagny into action. The third instance occurs when Philip Rearden, an irresponsible moocher, concerned that his gravy train will end if Rearden retires and vanishes and pleads for a job that he can't successfully perform. His bold request is possible only because he feels justified in arguing that an obligation to one's brother should supersede all other consideration. In all cases, Rand shows that the unproductive try to argue that an individual is obligated to help either his literal brother or his figurative brothers—humanity. She insists that the motive behind this injunction is to enslave the productive to the moochers, who feel that they have biblical license to take what they want.

Francisco has been the protector of Rearden from the beginning. He arms Rearden with the knowledge of his own moral value. Rearden realizes that his love is right and his trust on Francisco the way he always has. In their relationship, as is mentioned in Cliffs Notes, Rand dramatizes the meaning of friendship between rational men. Robert Stadler dramatizes the principle that men seek to live either by mind or force. Stadler necessarily believes that one cannot deal with people with reason and that only force is an effective weapon. He says to Dagny: "The mind? Don't you know how futile it is, the mind against those mindless hordes? Our weapons are so helplessly, laughably childish: through, knowledge, reason, values, and rights! Force is all they know, force, fraud and plunder!" (1023) It shows that he is then driven by the logic of his theory to became a looter and thus becoming a worst enemy to Galt.

Stadler's death is not ironic as it is an exact end dedicated by the logic of his life. He used his mind to serve the brutes and is killed by the weapon that he created in his research. It is created for the looters. Galt knows the logical inevitability of Stadler's end. That is why he does not agree to turn his mind over to them. Dagny, knowing that Galt will be killed by the looters, realizes their true nature. Though the looters try hard to enslave the mind through force, Galt emerges triumphant in his commitment to his intellectual freedom. The power that moves the world is mind and any type of force working to suppress the mind ultimately collapses.

The characters are assessed negatively or positively based on their effort of production. Different social classes are represented among the heroes and the villains of the novel. Among the heroes, Galt and Rearden come from working class background, and Dagny and Francisco are from wealthy families. Among the villains, Fred Kinnan comes from a working class background, but James and Betty Pope are from wealthy families. I totally agree with what is said on Wikipedia: "Rand introduces a theory of sex in *Atlas Shrugged* that is based on her broader ethical and psychological theories. Far from being a debasing animal instinct, sex to Rand is the highest celebration of human values, a physical response to intellectual and spiritual values that give concrete expression to what could otherwise only be experienced in the abstract. This theory of sex is almost identical to that espoused in the platonic dialogue Symposium." Thus, in rejecting the traditional altruistic moral code, Rand also rejects the sexual code that, in her view, is the logical implication of altruism.

The characters who do not have clear purpose find sex without any meaning. This is shown in the contrasting relationships of Rearden with Lillian and Dagny, by the relationships of James with Cherryl and later with Lillian, and finally in the relationship between Dagny and Galt. Illustrations of this theory are found in Dagny's relationship with Francisco. The companies in the novel can be generally divided into two groups: those that are run by hard workingmen who join Galt's movement and the companies owned by looters and moochers. The first group is usually given the name of the owner and the companies owned by looters are given impersonal names like Associated Steel. For example, Rearden's companies are named after him. Wyatt Oil is named after Ellis Wyatt.

Taggart Transcontinental and d'Anconia Copper are named after their founders and are run by their families. James Jerome Hill (1838-1916) was known as the Empire Builder. He built the Great Northern Railway that is in many ways similar to Taggart Transcontinental. Railways in the U.S.A. were facing a decline by 1957, the date of the book's publication. This decline started in the 1920s. Passengers were increasingly switching to road transport. Unlike railways, the road transport was subject to market competition, developing quickly to the benefit of consumers. Air transport was also growing fast, with the restrictions of Government intervention and regulation coming later to the aviation industry. But still, railroads are the most efficient type of transportation over land.

Rand uses many technologies in the novel. Apart from normal technologies, she introduces fictional inventions, including refractor rays, Galt's mirage, Rearden metal, Project X, motors powered by static electricity, and a sophisticated electrical torture device. Erika Holzer comments in *Ayn Rand: My Fiction-Writing Teacher:* "I wanted to steep myself in every imaginable detail about a novel (*Atlas Shrugged*) that had changed—no, clarified and integrated—every important aspect of my life. I wanted to understand from the source—why this novel had the power to transport me to another world, one which, from my very first reading, had made me feel utterly complete." (16) Though *Atlas Shrugged* was a popular success, it was disliked by many critics. It is said that according to a 1991 United States survey by the Library of Congress and the Book of the Month Club, *Atlas Shrugged* was the book that made most difference in readers' lives after the bible.

After its publication, the novel was reviewed by many major newspapers and magazines. The early reviews were mostly negative. They criticized both the book's literary qualities and its political vision. Branden argues that *Atlas Shrugged* encourages emotional repression and self-disowning. Like her other novel, *The Fountainhead*, it contains contradictory messages. He says that the book is the evidence that Rand understood the need for social interaction, but he questions the psychological impact of the novel. But I feel that this criticism is not true. As Howard Dickman of *Reader's Digest* wrote: the novel had the important message of the readers' profound right to be happy.

The libertarian Cato Institute held a joint conference with *The Atlas Society*, an Objectivist organization, to celebrate the fortieth anniversary of the publication of *Atlas Shrugged*. Conservative Associate Justice of the Supreme Court Clarence Thomas states that this novel is one of his favourite novels. The novel's popularity and its influence are well explained on Wikipedia: 'In an article, "Celebrity Rand Fans" in the Objectivist magazine *The New Individualist*, Robert James Bidinotto traces the novel's growing influence among major Hollywood stars, sports champions, and public figures. Chip Mellor of the libertarian Institute for Justice writes that "whether they have adopted her philosophy wholeheartedly or found her writings of more transitory interest, countless individuals working to secure liberty have found inspiration in the works of Ayn Rand."' Thus, with her unique ability to depict heroism, idealism, and romance behind the creativity of the individual, Rand inspires readers to come to the defence of free minds and free markets.

Nathaniel Branden's comments in *My Years with Ayn Rand*: 'I did not think it strange that Ayn Rand should choose to present to the world a new philosophical vision by means of a novel. She had said to me, 'All of the world's major religions have, in effect, their own mythology—tales, parables, stories of various kinds that are intended to dramatize all illustrated abstract values and precepts. Although that is not how the novel stared out in my mind, that is what it developed into—a mythology that concretizes, by means of the actions of its characters, the meaning of my philosophy.'" (199) In a three-month poll of reader selections of the hundred best novels of the twentieth century administered by publisher Modern Liberty, *Atlas Shrugged* was voted number one, ahead of *The Fountainhead*, *Battlefield Earth*, and *The Lord of Rings*.

What is said about her on Wikipedia appears to be inspiring: "Ray Jenkins compares Rand's popularity to that of Hubbard, calling her 'a goddess of a great American cult.' He goes to point out that her works were ignored or deplored by the critics of the day. Literary critic Harold Bloom included her in critical encyclopedia he edited, *American Women Fiction Writers*, vol. Three (Chelsea House, 1998). The C-SPAN television series *American Writers* listed Rand as one of twenty-two surveyed figures of American literature, though primarily mentioning *The Fountainhead* rather than *Atlas Shrugged."* Tom Butler has held *Atlas Shrugged* movie project for months because the actors threatened to go on strike.

After six months of struggling to capture the essence of the book, the script for the upcoming film version of *Atlas Shrugged* has finally been finished. In 2003, The Baldwin Entertainment Group purchased the film rights to the novel, *Atlas Shrugged*. In September 2007, Lions Gate Entertainment has picked up world-wide distribution rights. The screenwriter Randall Wallace has created screenplay from the novel. Angelina Jolie has been confirmed to play the role of Dagny and Brad Pitt is to be cast as John Galt. Both the actors are the fans of Rand's works. Vadim Peralman was hired by Lions Gate to direct the film.

In the novel, the dollar sign also plays an important role. This dollar sign is not merely provocative, it is meant to seal the fact that mankind is ready to submit to elite of technocrats, and their accessories, in a New order, enlightened and instructed by Rand's ideas that the good life is one which has resolved personal worth into exchange value, has left no other bond between a man and man except the naked self-interest and cash-payment. But these words are of Karl Marx. He too admired naked self-interest in its time and place and for much the same reasons as Rand; because he believed it, cleared away the cobwebs of religion and led to prodigies of industrial accomplishment.

It is said that Rand or Marx has created a godless society. But my opinion is that for Rand, an immigrant to the United States and who loved its ideals, this sacred symbol represents the triumph of the creative mind over the state, religion and tradition. It means freedom, mediocrity and its strangling power. The worship of dollar may look unpleasant, but *Atlas Shrugged* depicts what happens when the ethic of the greater good is pursued to its logical ends. It annexes the spirit from an entire nation very effectively. As Adam Smith says: "Rand is a patron of the 21st century entrepreneur because she provides a morality of powerful creation; a person with a Randian frame of mind is opposed in principle to equality if it means sacrificing their dreams for the sake of others. The pursuit of equal rights may be noble, but ultimately suffocates the life-spirit that has always fired human advance." (http://www.butler-bowden.com) He wants to say that self-interest is actually in full accordance with nature and therefore brings the more moral end.

It is strange to note that many businessmen are getting lasting inspiration from the novel, but they do not attain or pursue an understanding of the moral virtue of getting profit. They certainly do not proudly defend their right to practise it freely. Thus most of the admirers of *Atlas Shrugged* proclaim their adoration for the novel, while simultaneously attempting to justify their existence by appealing to the public good that they have led to the shrinking of economic freedom in the last fifty years, just as they did before they read *Atlas Shrugged*. On the occasion of the anniversary of *Atlas Shrugged*, businessmen must reread the book, but in addition to being inspired to greatness by its heroes, they should pay special attention to the book's essence, that is, its radical moral philosophy that has potential to truly change how they look at their lives and enable them to fight successfully for their freedom.

William Thomas writes in *Ayn Rand's Philosophical Stunt Novel:* "Rand's ideas are as fundamental as Nietzsche's, but treatment of them in *Atlas Shrugged* is much more clear, systematic, and comprehensive than in his Zarathustra. Rousseau's *Emily*, along with his epistolary novel *Julie* and other works, has had huge effect in the eighteenth century and since, laying part of the intellectual foundation for the French revolution, for the rise of nationalism and socialism in Europe, and for the Romantic art movement. It is too soon to say what all the effects of *Atlas Shrugged* will be, but it has already given birth, more than any other single work, to the contemporary libertarian movement. It is difficult to recall the lack of confidence that Americans, and the world, had in individual achievement and the free market in the 1960s. But today, there is a robust, worldwide movement in favour of invention and success. When we hear a business entrepreneur lauded as a creator and adventurer, as we often do these days, we are hearing an echo of *Atlas Shrugged* reverberating through the culture." (http://www. objectivistcenter. org) This proves that as philosophy, the novel can be certainly considered a worthy competitor of other great works of philosophy in fiction.

Capitalism as Morality
Capitalism: The Unknown Ideal

Ayn Rand's work of non-fiction, *Capitalism: The Unknown Ideal* is a collection of essays on the moral aspects of capitalism. In the Introduction to the book, Ayn Rand writes: "I want to stress that our primary purpose is not policies or economics as such, but "man's relationship to existence"—and that we advocate capitalism because it is the only system geared to the life of a rational being." (vii) Most of the essays in this book appeared originally in *The Objectivist Newsletter*, others are based on lectures or papers and some of the essays are the answers to the most widely spread fallacies about the economics of capitalism. *Capitalism: The Unknown Ideal* consists of twenty-four essays. Except three pieces by Greenspan, two by Branden, and one by Historian Robert Hessen, the rest of the essays represent Rand's take on capitalism. Rand makes it clear that she is not conservative, classical liberal, or libertarian.

Her approach in these essays is unique by their evasion of the clash between capitalism and altruism. Rand writes about this altruism in *The Romantic Manifesto:* "One of the grimmest monuments to altruism is man's culturally induced selfishness: his willingness to live with himself as with the unknown, to ignore, evade, repress the personal (the non-social) needs of his soul, to know least about the things that matter most, and thus to consign his deepest values to the impotent underground of simplicity and his life to the dreary wasteland of chronic guilt." (16) Capitalism's alleged champions are responsible for the fact that the capitalism is being destroyed without a hearing, without a trial, without any public knowledge of its principles, its nature, its history, or its moral meaning. The book consists of two parts. The first is "Theory and History," which includes essays on inter alia war, the persecution of big business, antitrust, gold and economic freedom, property status of the air-waves, and patents and copyrights.

In "What is Capitalism?" Ayn Rand writes that today's frantic development in the field of technology has a quality reminiscent of the days preceding the economic crash in 1929: "Scientists are abetting the resurgence of a primitive mysticism. In humanities, however, the crash is past and the depression has set in, and the collapse of science is all but complete." (11) Political economics including the advocates of capitalism defined their science as the study of the management or direction or organization. The goal of political economy was assumed to be the study of how to utilize its resources for the common good. The concept of man as a free, independent individual was profoundly alien to the culture of Europe.

The American philosophy of the "Rights of Man" was never grasped fully by European intellectuals. Europe's predominant idea of emancipation consisted of changing the concept that man is a slave of the absolute state embodied by a king. The success of capitalism is explained by the *Encyclopedia Britannica* as follows: "Productive use of the "social" surplus was the special virtue that enabled capitalism to outstrip all prior economic systems." (14) The attitude of most political economists amounts to the unstated implicit postdate: Man is that which fits economic equations. It leads also to a baffling sort of double standard. If they observe a shoemaker, they conclude that he is working in order to make a living; but as political economists, on the tribal premise, they declare that his purpose is to provide society with shoes. Man's essential characteristic is his rational faculty.

"In collective economy public needs enjoy the same sort of built-in priority that private consumption enjoys in a capitalist economy. In the Soviet Union teachers are plentiful, but automobiles are scarce, whereas the opposite condition prevails in the United States." (34) At the end of World War II, Soviet Russia's enemies claimed that thirty million people were doing forced labour in Soviet concentration camps (and were dying of planned malnutrition, human lives being cheaper than food.) That is what the *Encyclopedia Britannica* refers to as "investment in people."

In the second essay, "The Roots War," Ayn Rand discusses the saying that nuclear weapons have made wars too horrible to contemplate. Yet every nation on earth feels, in helpless terror, that such a war might come: 'It is obvious that the ideological root of statism (or collectivism) is the tribal premise of primordial savages who, unable to conceive of individual rights, believed that the tribe is a supreme, omnipotent ruler, that it owns the lives of its members and may sacrifice them whenever it pleases to whatever it deems to be its own "good." (36) Statism—in fact and in principle—is nothing more than gang rule. A dictatorship is a gang devoted to looting the effort of the productive citizens of its own country. Statism needs war; a free country does not. Statism survives by looting; a free country survives by production. In World War II, both Germany and Russia seized and dismantled entire factories in conquered countries, to ship them home.

In "America's Persecuted Minority: Big Business," Rand says how a small group of men were always made to pay for the sins, errors, or failures of any other group. Every movement that seeks to enslave a country needs some minority group as a scapegoat which it can blame for the nation's troubles and use as a justification of its own demands for dictatorial powers. In Soviet Russia, the scapegoat was the bourgeoisie; in Nazi Germany, it was the Jewish people; in America, it is the businessmen. The only proper function of the government of free country, she says, is to act as an agency which protects the individual rights: "The proper functions of a government are: the police, to protect men from criminals; the military forces, to protect men from foreign invaders; and the law courts, to protect men's property and contracts from breach by force or fraud, and to settle disputes among men according to objectively defined laws. These, implicitly, were the political principles on which the Constitution of the United States was based; implicitly, but not explicitly." (47)

In a free market, all prices, wages, and profits are determined—not by the arbitrary whim of the rich or of the poor, but by the law of supply and demand. Rand defines the difference between economic power and political power. Economic power is exercised by means of a positive, by offering men a reward or an incentive. Political power is exercised by means of a negative, by the threat of punishment: "A system of pure, unregulated Laissez-faire capitalism has never yet existed anywhere. What did exist were only so called mixed economics, which means a mixture, in varying degrees, of freedom and controls, of voluntary choice and government coercion, of capitalism and statism. America was the freest country on earth, but elements of statism were present in her economy from the start." (48)

In the essay, "Antitrust," Alan Greenspan discusses how the world of antitrust is reminiscent of Alice's Wonderland. Everything seemingly is, yet apparently is not, simultaneously. It is a world in which competition is landed as the basic axiom and guiding principle, yet too much competition is condemned as cut-throat. Alan Greenspan argues that the ultimate regulator of competition in a free economy is capital market. He says: "The capital market acts as a regulator of prices, not necessarily of profits. It leaves an individual producer free to earn as much as he can by lowering his costs and by increasing his efficiency relative to others." (968)

Nathaniel Branden starts his essay, "Common Fallacies about Capitalism," by condemning the views of Marx: "One of the worst fallacies in the field of economics—propagated by Karl Marx and accepted by almost everyone today, including many businessmen—is the notion that the development of monopolies is an inescapable and intrinsic result of the operation of a free, free unregulated economy. In fact, the exact opposite is true. It is a free market that makes monopolies impossible." (72) Branden continues that a nation-wide depression, such as occurred in the United States in the Thirties, would not have been possible in a fully free society. Throughout most of the 1920s, the government compelled banks to keep interest rates artificially and uneconomically low. As a consequence, money was poured into every sort of speculative venture. Profits were calculated on hysterically exaggerated appraisals of the future earnings of companies. It was like the policy of a man who passes out rubber checks, counting on the hope that he will somehow find a way to obtain the necessary money and to deposit it in the bank before anyone presents his checks for collection.

In his next essay, "The Role of Labour Unions," Nathaniel Branden clears one of the most widespread delusions of the age, 1962. There was a belief that the American worker owes his high standard of living to unions and to humanitarian labour legislation. High productivity depends on machines, inventions, and capital investment which depend on the creativity of individual men. In the 1920s when the labour movement in France and Germany was far more than in the United States, the standard of living of the American worker was greatly superior. It was the consequence of economic freedom. Unions can have value of as a means of keeping members informed of current market conditions, or as a means of bargaining more effectively with employers. Today, Unions enjoy a unique near monopolistic power over many aspects of the economy. They have been able to force wages substantially above their normal market level: "In fact, however, the result of their policy has been (a) a curtailment of production, (b) widespread unemployment, and (c) the penalizing of workers in other industries, as well as the rest of the population." (86)

In the essay, "Publication Education," Branden says that there are no moral grounds whatever for the claim that education is the prerogative of the State. The disgracefully low level of education in America today is the predictable result of State-controlled school system. Only when educational institutions have to compete with one another in the quality of the training they offer, educational standards will necessarily rise. In "Inherited Wealth," Branden opposes the argument that since heir does not work to produce the wealth, he has no inherent right to it. He says that in a free economy, inherited wealth is not an impediment or a threat to those who do not possess it. If an heir is worthy of his money, that is, he uses it productively, he brings more wealth into existence, he raises the general standard of living. If he is not worthy, the only person threatened by it is himself because he will not be able to maintain it for long and he will not be equal to the competition.

In the easy, "Gold and Economic Freedom," Alan Greenspan writes about the hysterical antagonism towards the gold standard becoming one issue which unites statists of all persuasions. What medium of exchange will be acceptable to all participants in an economy is not determined arbitrarily. The term luxury good implies scarcity and high unit value. Having a high unit value, such a good is usually portable; for instance, an ounce of gold is worth a half-ton of pig iron. Prior to World War I, the banking system in the United States was based on gold: "Periodically, as a result of overtly rapid credit expansion, banks became loaned up to the limit of their gold reserves, interest rates rose sharply, new credit cut off, and the economy went into a sharp, but short - lived recession." (99)

Ayn Rand in the essay, "Notes on the History of American Free Enterprise," discusses one of the statists' arguments in favour of government controls. Their notion is that American railroads were built mainly through the financial help of the government and would have been impossible without it. Here Rand quotes from *The Story of American Railroads* by Stewart H. Holbrook: "In a little more than two decades, three transcontinental railroads were built with government help. All three wound up in bankruptcy courts. And thus, when James Jerome Hill said he was going to build a line from the Great Lakes to Puget Sound, without government cash or land grant, even his close friends thought him mad. But his great Northern arrived at Puget Sound without a penny of federal help, nor did it fail." (8-9) The truth is that most of the useless railroads were built, not by men who intended to build a railroad for profit, but by speculators with political pull, who started these ventures for the sole purpose of obtaining money from the government. The solution for this is laissez-faire capitalism, that is, the abolition of all forms of government intervention in production and trade, the separation of State and Economics as the separation of Church and State.

In the next essay, "The Effects of the Industrial Revolution on Women and Children," Robert Hessen speaks about the misconception of child labour. The least understood and most widely misrepresented aspect of the history of capitalism is child labour. During the Industrial Revolution, in fact, capitalism brought an enormous improvement over the condition of children. Ludwig von Mises reminds: "The factory owners did not have the power to compel anybody to take a factory job. They could only hire people who were ready to work for the wages offered to them. . . . These women had nothing to cook with and to feed their children. These children were destitute and starving. Their only refuge was the factory. It saved them, in the strict sense of the term, from death by starvation." (615)

In the essay, "Women and the Industrial Revolution," Robert Hessen opposes the notion that industrial capitalism led to nothing but misery and degradation for women. Mrs. Neff writes that under the system of domestic industry the parents and the children had worked together. But under the factory system, all the members of the family worked in separate departments of the mill, coming home only for food and sleep. After a definite study, Dr. Margaret Hewitt of the University of Exeter concludes that neither of these assumptions proves to have any statistical foundation. Many women worked because their husbands' wages were insufficient to keep the home going and others were widowed or deserted. What factory system offered these women was—not misery and degradation—but a means of survival, of economic independence. Alan Greenspan in his essay, "The Assault on Integrity," writes that the protection of consumer against dishonest and unscrupulous business practices has become a cardinal ingredient of welfare statism. Greenspan argues that a company cannot afford to risk its years of investment by letting down its standards of quality for one moment or one inferior product. Capitalism is based on self-interest and self-esteem and it makes them pay in the marketplace.

Ayn Rand in the essay, "The Prosperity Status of Airwaves," says that any material element or resource which requires the application of human knowledge and effort should be private property. This is particularly true of broadcasting frequencies or waves because they are produced by human action. In those years, when broadcasters had no property rights in radio, the airways were a chaotic no man's land where anyone could use any frequency and jam anyone else. This anarchy is the result of not the property rights but their absence. In her next essay, "Patents and Copyrights," Rand declares that the physical labour of copying is not the source of the object's value, but the value is created by the originator of the idea and may not be used without his consent.

In the essay, "Theory and Practice," Rand speaks about altruism which is different from any people's belief. It teaches sacrifice to others. In "Blind Chaos," Rand advises to learn an important political lesson from the events in Algeria. The people of Algeria were fighting against the French rule. When they won their independence, they fell apart—into rival tribes and armed willayas fighting one another. In the essay, "The Anatomy of Compromise," Rand speaks about the collaboration of the semi-free countries with the communist dictatorships in the United Nations. The United Nations is dedicated to peace, freedom and human rights. But it includes Soviet Russia—the most brutal aggressor. The free countries have nothing to gain from the communist countries. In any compromise between food and poison, it is only death that can win.

Rand in her next essay, "Is Atlas Shrugging?," speaks of a question she has often been asked: Is *Atlas Shrugged* a historical novel. It means that it was a successful prophecy. But she answers that it is not a prophecy of unavoidable destruction, but a manifesto of our power to avoid it. In the essay, "The Pull Peddlers," Rand shows America's foreign policy as irrational. The practical arguments consist of appeals to fear to the effect that their own selfish interest requires that they go bankrupt buying the favour of the under-developed nations who otherwise become a dangerous threat to them. Rand submits an article in the *New York Times* that a non-diplomatic corps of foreign agents has bloomed in lobbying in congress to obtain the passage of legislation of interest to their foreign clients. Russia a not one these foreign interests and is served by registered lobbyists in Washington, but she is merely cashing-in on the situation.

Ayn Rand in her essay, "Extremism" or the Art of Smearing,' condemns the moderates demanding a regulation of extremism without any definition of the term. A large-scale instance in the 1930s was the introduction of the world isolationism into the political vocabulary. The alleged meaning of the term capitalism is intolerance and indictment to violence but the real meaning is capitalism. Thus they destroy the public communications. The notion of compromise is the supreme virtue in a mixed economy. But capitalism requires an uncompromising stand. In the essay, "Conservatism; An Obituary," Rand writes about conservatives and the liberals, stressing the fact that the world is facing a deadly conflict and what we must fight to save the civilization. Politically, the world conflict is the last stage of the struggle between capitalism and statism, the conflict of the individual against the state.

Rand quotes from her *For the New Intellectual* that the world crisis of today is a moral crisis and nothing less than a moral revolution can resolve it—moral revolution to complete the political achievement of the American Revolution. The new intellectual must fight for capitalism, not as practical or an economic issue, but as a moral issue. In her next essay, "The New Fascism: Rule by Consensus," Rand defines the terms socialism, fascism and statism. The dictionary definitions of them are: "Socialism—a theory or system of social organization which advocates the vesting of the ownership and control of the means of production, capital, land etc. in the community as a whole. Fascism—a government system with strong centralized power, permitting no opposition or criticism, controlling all affairs of the nation (industrial, commercial, etc.). . . . Statism the principle or policy of concentrating extensive economic, political, and related controls in the state at the cost of individual liberty." (202)

Both socialism and fascism, which are the two variants of statism, subordinate individual to the collective. There is no ideological trend today. Neither an individual nor a nation can exist without some form of ideology. Rand here quotes from her *The Fascist New Frontier* (1963): "There can be no partnership between armed bureaucrats and defenceless private citizens who have no choice but to obey." (216) In the essay, "The Wreckage of the Consensus," Rand stresses the point that compromise does not lead to general fulfillment, but to general frustration.

She gives the example of the war in Vietnam. It is a cold war where American soldiers were killed on battlefields, not for their families or for any of the Americans. There is no proper solution for the war in Vietnam. To continue it would be senseless and to withdraw from it is one more act towards a world war. One cannot correct a consequence without correcting its cause. This is an example of why we need a policy based on long range principles, i.e., an ideology. A proper solution would be to elect statesmen with a radically different foreign policy, a policy explicitly and proudly dedicated to the defence of America's rights and self-interests. On such a policy they could withdraw from Vietnam at once and the world would have a chance to achieve peace. A voluntary army is the only proper way to defend a free country. The student rebellion at the University of California at Berkeley has profound significance. The University President announces that no student speakers would be allowed to address the meeting. He is dragged off the platform, but it provokes the administration to an act of violence. What follows is a nation-wide publicity and the administration grants most of the rebel's demands.

The unrestricted freedom of speech takes the form of Filthy Language Movement and the F.S.M. begins to lose its following and is eventually dissolved. They are unable to withstand the flood of modern sophistries. So some of them give up and after one or two unintelligible courses, convinced that thinking is a waste of time—and turn into lethargic cynics. Others accept what they hear blindly. These are today's activists. As a part of the ideological conditioning, the rebels attempt to introduce a new variant on an old theme: "If the students commit illegal acts, they will be punished by the courts and must not, therefore, be penalized by the university for the same offence." (26) If such a notion were accepted, individuals would have no right to evaluate the conduct of others. They would have to wait until a court has decreed whether a given man is guilty or innocent. It is the most shameful guild socialism. The goal of an ideological battle is to enlighten the vast, helpless, bewildered majority in the universities—and in the country at large.

In "Requiem for Man," Rand says that the encyclical's position of capitalism is explicit and unequivocal. The encyclical is the manifesto of an impassioned hatred for capitalism. The encyclical judges' specific accusation directed at capitalism reads as the acquiring of temporal goods can lead to the insatiable desire for more, and can make increased power a tempting objective. Advanced nations have a very heavy obligation to help the developing peoples. The superfluous wealth of the rich countries should be placed at the service of poor nations. This demands great generosity and much sacrifice. Rand in "Appendix: Man's Rights," discusses the most revolutionary achievement of the United States of America, the subordination of society to moral law. All previous systems had regarded man as a sacrificial means to the ends of others, and society as an end in itself.

The United States regarded man as an end in himself, and society as a means to the voluntary co-existence of individuals. In her "Appendix: The Nature of Government," Rand again stresses: "A government is the means of placing the retaliatory use of physical force under objective control—i.e., under objectively defined laws." (331) All the essays of the book deal with the political branch of Ayn Rand's philosophy of Objectivism and are appropriate for anyone who seeks to obtain a deeper understanding of her political philosophy beyond reading her novels. Rand begins her section, "What is Capitalism?," by discussing the disintegration of philosophy. The disintegration begins in the nineteenth century and leads to a collapse in the twentieth century. Science, according to Rand, is primitive mysticism. To Rand this is evident in psychology and political economy. The criteria for studying various areas of knowledge come from philosophy. The study of political economy is defined as a study of how scarce resources are used.

Rand explains the political economy clearly: "The clearest evidence of it may be seen in such comparatively young sciences as psychology and political economy. In psychology, one may observe the attempt to study human behaviour without reference to the fact that man is conscious. In political economy, one may observe the attempt to study and devise social systems without reference to man. It is philosophy that defines and establishes the epistemological criteria to guide human knowledge in general and specific science in particular. Political economy came into prominence in the nineteenth century, in the era of philosophy's post-Kantian disintegration, and no one rose to check its premises or challenge its base." (11) Thus political economy accepted as its axioms the fundamental tenets of collectivism.

Rand uses chiaroscuro rhetoric in which she takes on the 1964 *Encyclopedia Britannica*. She quotes: "Capitalism, a term used to denote the economic system that has been dominant in the western world since the breakup of feudalism. Fundamental to any system called capitalist are the relations between private owners of non-personal means of production (land, mines, [industrial plants], etc., (collectively known as capital) and free but capital-less workers, who sell their labour services to employers. . . . The resulting wage bargains determine the proportion in which the total production of society will be shared between the class of labourers and the class of capitalist entrepreneurs." (13-14). It shows that according to Rand there is a moral justification for capitalism, and it is decidedly not altruism. But Britannica has it backward: "Few observers are inclined to find fault with capitalism as an engine of production. Capitalism usually proceeds either from moral or cultural disapproval of certain features of the capitalist system, or from the short-run vicissitudes (crises and depression) with which long-run improvement is interspersed." (31) Capitalism's existence stems from rationality, it protects man's survival qua man, and its ruling principle is justice.

Rand's Objectivist Theory of Value is widespread. Both the Christian era and post-Kantian epistemology are to be blamed for the lack of underpinning capitalism receives. It is proved from the words of Dr. Enrico Peppe: "There has never been a pure capitalism, just variations thereof: Capitalism could not survive in a culture dominated by mysticism and altruism, by the body-soul dichotomy and the tribal premise. No social system (and no human institution or activity of any kind) can survive without a moral base. On the basis of the altruist moralist, Capitalism had to be—and was—damned from the start. For Rand, the quality parties are not the collectivists." (www.intellectual conservative.com) Rand wants to say that the culprits are the Capitalist theoreticians who lack the courage to challenge bad philosophy.

In "Roots of War," Rand says that the threat of nuclear holocaust terrifies many people because they and their leaders feel helpless when confronting war. Majority of the people do not support war. Men always know there is always the possibility of war because they have never rejected the use of physical force to get what they want. This belief comes from the political philosophy of statism, which is also known as collectivism. Leonard Peikoff differentiates this statism, which is also known as collectivism. Leonard Peikoff differentiates this statism from Nazism in *The Ominous Parallels:* "If the term 'statism' designates concentration of power in the state at the expense of individual liberty, the Nazism in politics was a form of statism. In principle, it did not represent a new approach to government; it was a continuation of a political absolutism—the absolute monarchies, the oligarchies, the theocracies, the random tyrannies—which has characterized most of humanist." (16) Thus Statism is the source of both peace and war propaganda. The peace proponents are against war and the threat of nuclear weapons. They do not believe that nations should be permitted to use armed force against one another at the same time and they find nothing wrong with dictatorships.

I agree with Enrico's ten points in this respect: 'Ten points emerge: I. Tribalism and statism hold that men achieve goals by "initiating" force against other men for some notion of public "good." 2. Rand: "Statism is a system of institutionalized violence and perpetual evil war." 3. Statism is a "gang rule." It is not a system conducive to security and peace. 4. Rand: "Statism needs war;

a free country does not. Statism survives by looting; a free country survives by production." 5. The period from the end of Napoleonic power (1815) to the beginnings of World War I—the period the Left abhors because of its unbridled (though not necessarily "pure") capitalism—was a period or relative peace. 6. Rand: "During the nineteenth century, it was free trade that liberated the world . . . wrecking the remnants of feudalism . . . and statist absolute monarchies." 7. War profiteers of mixed economies curry favour with custodians of government largess; in free markets, fortunes from death would not occur. 8. Both Roosevelt and Woodrow Wilson believed that the "benighted" areas of the world needed varying doses of freedom (in FDR's case, four). 9. Rand: "if men want to oppose war it is statism they must oppose." 10. For war to be outlawed, "the rule of force" must cease. Notwithstanding Rand's weaknesses (to come later), this essay should be read and at least acknowledged as appropriate by Libertarians of all wings.' (http://www.intellectualconservative. com) One can say that the essay appears to be fresh today as when it was written.

In the essay, "America's Persecuted Minority: Big Business," Rand looks at the meaning of the word persecution. She considers American businessmen as falling into this category. Persecution is not only the word which describes religious and racial minorities, it also describes businessmen. Businessmen are condemned for their dealings with labour unions and also in the drive for profits. Businessmen are blamed for many problems. Though they are the people who negotiate with labour unions, they are condemned for this behaviour. The businessmen are blamed for the workers' low standard of living. As the businessmen make the decisions that result in corporate actions and profits, they take the blame for the results.

According to Rand, when minority group is being persecuted, there is something more to it. She says: "If you are about minority groups, remember that businessmen are small minority—a very small minority, compared to the total of all the uncivilized hordes on earth. Remember how much you owe to this minority—and what disgraceful persecution it is enduring. Remember also that smallest minority on earth is the individual. Those who deny individual rights cannot claim to be defenders of minorities." (61) Rand's skill is shown by these words. The essay, "Antitrust," by Alan Greenspan, describes the business world with antitrust as a world that welcomes competition, but, if there is too much competition then it is deemed to be cut-throat. Greenspan says that they should review the entire antitrust system. To understand the reason, he says, one must look at the history of the antitrust laws on the economic principles on which they are based.

The popular belief was if business were left free to do as they wanted, it would result in arbitrary power. He says: 'To interpret the railroad history of nineteenth century as "proof" of the failure of a free market, is a disastrous error. The same error—which persists to this day—was the nineteenth century's fear of "truths."'(65) When the railroad was being constructed, they were needed for development and so they were subsidized in the form of land grants. Land grants were based on the fact that there could be no other competing railroads in the area. It is a wonderful essay that attacks antitrust legislation as subjective, harmful and immoral. The essay, "Common Fallacies about Capitalism," authored by Nathaniel Branden comments on some basic economic concepts.

It is rightly said: "He claims it is a fallacy of Marxism and economists to believe you cannot have free economies without the development of monopoly. The term evils of monopoly refer to coercive monopoly. This is a situation where a monopolist is completely independent of the market is setting his price and production policies. It is a situation where competition is impossible and it is a situation only created by government in terms of special licenses, subsidies, actions or some kind of special privileges." (http://www.bookrags.com) Thus Branden begins by asking what prevents the formation of monopolies in a system of laissez-faire capitalism. Branden writes: "Capitalism, by its nature, entails a constant process of motion, of growth, of progress; no one has a vested right to a position if others can do better than he can. When people denounce the free market as 'cruel,' the fact they are decrying is that the market is ruled by a single moral principle: justice." (76) This is the root of their hatred for capitalism.

"Gold and Economic Freedom" is Alan Greenspan's essay on the need for objective currency. Particularly, he considers the role of gold and suggests a return to a 100% gold standard. Until the end of World War II, the gold standard was the mechanism by which the international monetary system functioned. In all transactions and as a means of savings, money functions as the common denominator. The existence of money facilities people to avoid the problems of barter and this in turn promotes the division of labour. The item must be durable to function as a medium of exchange it is usually a metal: "Whether the single medium is gold, silver, seashells, cattle, or tobacco is optional, depending on the context and development of a given economy. In fact, all have been employed, at various times as medium of exchange. Even in the present century, two major commodities, gold and silver, have been used as international media of exchange, with gold becoming the predominant one. Gold having both artistic and functional uses and being relatively scarce, has always been considered a luxury good. It is durable, portable, homogeneous, divisible, and, therefore, has significant advantages over all other media of exchange." (Alan Greenspan, 97) This shows that a single commodity as a medium of exchange is very beneficial for a society. Greenspan wrote this essay before he succumbed to statism (1966). This piece clearly lays out a sound defence of Gold and its necessity for the preservation and integrity of private property which results in freedom.

What Enrico says is true: "His systems based on gold and the mechanism of credit extension based on production. The key is that the process be based on the convertibility of such to gold which is how things were before the organization of the Federal Reserve System in 1913. Before, the short-lived recessions were the rule." (http://www.intellectualconservative.com) In 1927, however, with the Fed's philosophy of international bail- out through paper currency creation in place, the assist given Great Britain because of its gold drain turned sour for all aggregate economies. Greenspan notes: "The 'fed' succeeded: it stopped the gold loss, but it nearly destroyed the economies of the world, in the process. The excess credit which the fed pumped into the economy spilled over into the stock market—triggering a speculative boom. Belatedly Federal Reserve Officials attempted to sop up the excess reserves and finally succeeded in breaking the boom. But it was too late: by 1929, the speculative imbalances had become so overwhelming that the attempt precipitated a sharp retrenching and a consequent demoralizing of business confidence. As a result, the American economy collapsed. Great Britain fared even worse, and rather than absorb the full sequences of her previous folly, she abandoned the gold standard completely in 1931, tearing asunder what remained of the fabric of confidence and including a worldwide series of bank failures." (99-100) As a result, the world economies plunged into the Great Depression of the 1931.

But, under a gold standard, depressions are mostly thwarted. Credit is determined by the tangibility of asset. When this concept is destroyed, as in the case with the issuance of government bonds, the promise-to-pay-through-tax revenues approach yields higher interest rates since financial markets are not in a position to soak these up. Under a solid gold standard (tangibility), government deficit spending is hampered. Greenspan concludes: "The financial policy of the welfare state requires that there be no way for the owners of wealth to protect themselves. This is the shabby secret of the welfare statists' tirades against gold. Deficit spending is simply a scheme for the "hidden" confiscation of wealth. Gold stands in the way of this insidious process. It stands as a protector of property rights. If one grasps this, one has no difficulty in understanding the statists' antagonism toward the gold standard." (101) This essay is a masterpiece frequently quoted elsewhere.

The author of the next essay "The Effect of Industrial Revolution," Hessen examines the role of children and women in the Industrial Revolution. Many children found jobs in factories that showed them a way to survive. The plight of the children was painted in a distorted way by the authors and poets of the time, but the children in the factories did not have hard jobs that were physically demanding. The first labour laws aimed at children working as chimney sweepers in 1788. The first law concerning the factories was to cover parentless children. Hessen writes: "The factory system led to a rise in the general standard of living to rapidly falling urban death rates and decreasing infant mortality—and produced an unprecedented population explosion. In 1750, England's population was six million; it was nine million in 1820, a rate of increase without precedent in any era. The age distribution of the population shifted enormously; the population of children and youths increased sharply. "The proportion of those born in London dying before five years of age" fell from 74.5 percent in 1730-49 to 31.29. Children who hitherto would have died in infancy now had a chance for survival." (110) Thus Hessen justifies the factory system.

In the essay, "The Assault on Integrity," Alan Greenspan comments: "Without some sort of protection, like the Pure Food and Drug Administration, the consumer would be at the mercy of the businessmen who would attempt to pass off unsafe food and products. Greenspan claims the best protection for the consumer is the profits of businessmen. Firms with reputations for being honest and producing good products do better than firms with bad reputations. Firms with bad products or reputations tend to drop in market value. Firms spend years building their reputation and they cannot afford to slip up because the public can turn against them very easily. The reputation of established firms is a force that newer firms have to contend with." (http://www. bookrags.com) Here, Greenspan examines the protection of consumer.

In the essay, "The Property Status of Airwaves," Rand feels that the usage of airwaves requires the definition of some kind of property rights or people would be trying to use the same frequencies jamming each other and she thinks U.S. government has failed in this area: "Collectivists frequently cite the early years of radio as an example of this failure of free enterprise. In those years, when broadcasters had no property rights in radio, no legal protection or recourse, the airways were a chaotic no man's land where anyone could use any frequency he pleased and jam anyone else. Some professional broadcasters tried to divide their frequencies by private agreements, which they would not enforce on others; nor could they fight the interference of stray, maliciously mischievous amateurs. This state of affairs was used, then and now, to urge and justify government control of radio. This is an instance of capitalism taking the blame for the evils of its enemies. The chaos of the airways was an example, not of free enterprise, but of anarchy. It was caused, not by private property rights, but by their absence." (125) Rand shows the Homestead Act and the setting of the western lands in the U.S. as an example of how property rights can be established. Public land was put into private hands when the settlers on the land had worked for it.

The essay, "Patents and Copyrights," is about Rand's views on the necessity and morality of intellectual property rights. As it is said: "There are ways of acknowledging the mental effort that goes into the production of the product or idea. These instruments protect the mind's effort in producing a good or service or idea and are based on the belief that man has the right to what his mind produces. What is produced by mind is called intellectual property. Patents and copyrights protect intellectual property and mean that ideas cannot be copied without the originator's consent. Patents apply to inventions and copyrights apply to ideas. They both protect the mental work and the creativity of the inventor and are one of the reasons people are willing to take risks inventing things." (http://www.bookrags.com) It proves that patents and copyrights are a way of claiming property rights and also they are a way of protecting the results of creative thinking.

The next essay, "Theory and Practice," consists of Rand's views on the invalidity of the mind-body dichotomy, which is also known as the theory-practice dichotomy or the thought-action dichotomy. According to Rand, capitalism is based on altruistic principles and this is one of the grounds on which conservatives try to justify a capitalist society. This means to achieve his goal, the capitalist must be willing to sacrifice. This causes problems because the sacrifice of one individual cannot increase another individual's welfare and this is the reason for the failures. Rand says: "Collectivism does not preach sacrifice as a temporary means to some desirable end. Sacrifice is its end-sacrifice as a way of life. It is man's independence, success, prosperity, and happiness that collectivists wish to destroy." (137) Societies of pre-capitalists were based on the wealthy class exploiting the working classes with little protection of individual rights. But Rand believes capitalism cannot function with slaves. The North fought the South in the Civil War to free the slaves for the economic need of a free labour market. Capitalism, says Rand, was the reason for the end of feudalism and slavery.

In the essay, "Let Us Alone," Rand looks at the origins of the term laissez-faire. She looks at the reign of Louis XIV, whose chief advisor was Colbert. At one point Colbert asked business leaders what he could do to help them and they replied, in French, "Laissez-nous faire" which means "leave us alone." Rand says that the best help the government can give them is to leave them alone and not to interfere in the marketplace. Then they can follow the market signals and do what competition requires instead of what government interference wants. They are not to be constrained by government rules and regulations. Force does not help the marketplace. What is responsible for production and property is the intelligence of man. Government intervention in the marketplace is the use of physical force. Rand says:

> Now consider the fate of England, "the peaceful experiment in socialism," the example of a country that committed suicide by vote: there was no violence, no bloodshed, no terror, merely the throttling process of "democratically" imposed government controls—but observe the present crisis about England's "brain drain," about the fact that the best and the ablest men, particularly the scientists and engineers, are deserting England and running to whatever small remnant of freedom they can find anywhere in today's world. (142)

In "Anatomy of Compromise," Rand discusses the disintegration of an economy. I agree with the saying: "Rand refers to a principle as a general truth. This means there are other things which depend on this general truth. Rand looks at the practical man in this chapter. There are three rules Rand presents. The man with the most consistent behaviour is one who will win when there is a disagreement between groups with the same principles, the more evil or more irrational entity will win. If principles are clearly defined and the groups hold opposite views, the more rational one will win. The more irrational one will win when the principles are hidden and not clearly defined." (http://www.bookrags. com) This shows that when men cease to think in terms of principles and abstractions, economy disintegrates.

In "Is Atlas Shrugging?," Rand compares the events in *Atlas Shrugged* to the events of current times. She poses the question of whether the novel is historic or prophetic and claims that if it is historical, then it has to be prophetic. People commented that current events were like the things discussed in the book: "The political aspects of *Atlas Shrugged* are not its theme, but one of the consequences of its theme. The theme is: the role of the mind in man's existence and, as a corollary, the presentation of a new code of ethics—the morality of rational self-interest." (150) Thus the book presents the conflict between two antagonists with opposing points of view. Rand refers to one as 'reason-individualism-capitalism' and the other as 'mysticism-altruism-collectivism.'

Rand says in *The Virtue of Selfishness:* 'The avowed mystics held the arbitrary, unaccountable "will of God" as the standard of the good and as the validation of their ethics. The neomystics replaced it with "the good of society," thus collapsing into the circularity of a definition such as "the standard of the good is that which is good for society." This meant in logic—and, today, in worldwide practice—that "society" stands above any principle of ethics, since it is its source, standard and criterion of ethics, since "the good" is whatever it wills, whatever it happens to assert as its own welfare and pleasure. . . . And since there is no such entity as "society," since society is only a number of individual men—this meant that some men the majority of any gang that claims to be its spokesman) are ethically entitled to pursue any whims (or any atrocities they desire to pursue, while other men are ethically obliged to spend their lives in the service of that gang's desires.' (177) Here, Rand explains mysticism.

In "Pull Peddlers," Rand looks at the foreign aid program. Foreign aid programs stem from the belief that it is a duty to help under-developed nations. If we do not help them, then they will become a threat to us. So nations help them, even if they risk bankruptcy. The reason for the powerful nations feeling threatened by the underdeveloped nations must be that they are so weak, then they cannot become a threat or they are powerful enough to be a threat. In such a case they should not require foreign aid. According to Rand, neither viewpoint is correct. Rand says societies following the wrong course are using rationalizations in order to try justifying their decisions. Rand feels that there is no consistency in the foreign aid program and the big loser is the United States.

In the essay, '"Extremism," or The Art of Smearing,' Rand examines the concept of smear campaigns. At all levels of government, these are done and are evident during political campaigns. She uses a Republican National Convention as an example of a call for a repudiation of extremism. Rand explains this: "The welfare-statistics hope to eliminate capitalism by smear and silence and to "avoid" dictatorship by "voluntary" compliance, by a policy of bargaining and compromise with the government's growing power." (182) This proves that the people calling for the elimination of extremism do not ever define the word or the activities they wanted eliminated. They kept it going by not explaining any of their reasons for selecting which groups to smear. People are willing to fight for something they strongly believe in. Rand points out various groups like Communist Party, the Ku Klux Klan and the John Birch Society. Nothing links these three groups together though the moderates try hard.

Rand begins the essay, "The Obliteration of Capitalism," by discussing what she means about the smears and how liberals are responsible for statism. She mentions a comment by Governor Romney that we do not have a system of capitalism but one of consumerism. Most of the people who support capitalism give varying definitions of the term. Many feel in capitalism, the producer's role is more important than the consumer's. Many businessmen try to hide the true nature of capitalism by stressing the point that the major part of income goes to labour and the smallest part is profit. They are trying to hide the fact that capitalism is a system based on individual rights. Altruism portrays the system as an evil. Rand says in *The Ayn Rand Lexicon: Objectivism from A to Z:* "Now there is one word—a simple word—which can blast the morality of altruism out of existence and which cannot withstand the word: "Why?" Why must man live for the sake of others? Why must he be a sacrificial animal? Why is that the good? There is no earthily reason for it—and, ladies and gentlemen, in the whole history of philosophy no earthly reason has ever been given. It is only mysticism that can permit moralist to get away with it. It was mysticism, the unearthly, the supernatural, the irrational that has always been called upon to justify it—or, to be exact, to escape the necessity of justification. One does not justify the irrational, one just likes it on faith. What most moralists—and few of their victims—realize is that reason and altruism are incompatible." (5) This is why capitalism and altruism are not compatible.

Rand begins her next essay, "Conservatism: An Obituary," by saying that there is an agreement between conservatives and liberals that there is a fight to save civilization. It is rightly pointed out: "They both agree this is a conflict involving communism but they do not know what to call the other side. What they are really talking about is a conflict between capitalism and statism. Both groups claim their side represents freedom and then they present their programs, which include taxes and various forms of government controls and government programs. These programs and controls are forms of statism. Freedom usually means being free of coercion by government. People still have to work and provide for their livelihood but they do not have coercion from government." (http://www. bookrags.com) Thus conflict involves the struggle between man and state.

Enrico Peppe writes: "She forgives (or rather understands) liberals because they are soft on communism; they think that there is some sort of altruistic message in Marxism. But conservatives, well, that's another story. With alarming prescience (she gave speech at Princeton in 1960), she cuts to the quirk: There are three interrelated arguments used by today's conservatives to justify capitalism, which can best be designated as: the argument from faith—the argument from tradition—the argument from depravity." (http://www.intellectualconservative.com) It shows that both liberals and conservatives and most libertarians accept altruist morality.

To hear prayer offered as the antidote to communism is to assume the enemies of freedom have reason on their side. She states: "The 'conservatives' claim that their case rests on faith, means that there are no rational arguments to support the American system, no rational justification for freedom, justice, property, individual rights, that these rest on a mystic revelation and can be accepted only on faith—that in reason and logic the enemy is right, but men must hold faith as superior to reason." (197) This proves that Rand is strong on this point. The traditionalists claim that the truth of the American system is obvious only because it is chosen by their ancestors. Capitalism may not be that good and indeed the Declaration of Independence may not be that precious, but it is theirs.

As if Rand were speaking directly to George Will on a Chris Mathews segment, she says: 'The argument that we must respect "tradition" as such, respect it merely because it is a "tradition," means that we must accept the values other men have chosen, merely because other men have chosen them—with the necessary implication of: who are we to change them? The affront to a man's self- esteem, in such an argument, and the profound contempt for man's nature are obvious. This leads us to the third—and the worst—argument, used by some "conservatives": the attempt to defend capitalism on the ground of man's depravity. The argument runs as follows: since men are weak, fallible, non-omniscient and innately depraved, no man may be entrusted with the responsibility of being a director and of ruling everybody else; therefore, a free society is the proper way of life for imperfect creatures. Please grasp fully the implications of this argument: since men are depraved, they are not good enough for a dictatorship; freedom is all that they deserve; if they were prefect, they would be worthy of a totalitarian state." (198-99) It shows that Rand does not respect anything only because it is a tradition.

In the essay, "The New Fascism," Rand says that a major point of both socialism and fascism has to do with the ownership and control of property. In socialism, property is owned and controlled publicly. In fascism, property is privately owned but controlled by the government. Property owners cannot control their own property, but also not have any responsibility. Rand believes there is no difference between socialism and fascism in practice and that socialism is more honest of the two systems. This differentiation is shown by Peikoff in *The Ominous Parallels:* "If 'ownership' means the right to determine the use and disposal of material goods, then Nazism endowed the state with every real prerogative of ownership. What the individual retained was merely a formal deed, a contentless deed, which conferred no rights on its holder. Under communism, there is collective ownership of property de jure. Under Nazism, there is the same collective ownership de facto." (18) Thus under both systems, the individual's rights are negated.

Rand begins the essay, "The Wreckage of Consensus," by discussing how compromise is the basis for a mixed economy. The various pressure groups result in a gang mentality as they want position and control in the economy. The result will be basically gang-warfare. Rand views the term cold war, a concept viewed in terms of itself and its negation or opposite. War may not be exactly the same thing as cold war. Warring nations often engage in smear campaigns about atrocities. If the countries know they cannot fight the wares, they do not engage in wars. A non-war occurs when the United States cannot gain from it: 'What is the moral-intellectual state of a country that permits its citizens to stage parades carrying the enemy's—the Vietcong's—flag? Or to collect funds for the enemy on university campuses? What makes this possible? The claim that we are not, allegedly, at war—only at cold war."' (223)

Rand expresses her views on the debacle that was the war in Vietnam. Reading this essay really suggests how she would view the current war in Iraq. The next essay, "The Cashing-in: The Student Rebellion," begins with Rand discussing the student protest at Berkeley in 1964. It results in a group of students protesting a university ban on their protesting on a certain strip of land on campus. This situation is clearly given on bookrags.com: "The result was a three-day struggle that eventually led to the resignation of the Chancellor and university accepting most of protesters' demands. People were amazed this did not end the protest as more was demanded whenever demands were granted. William Peterson, a Professor of Sociology, examined the situation and concluded that the struggle was not over free speech as everyone said. The real issue was power and control. He also looks at the various groups involved and decides their tactics are best described as being Castroite." This is how the result of the student's protest is explained. The next essay, "Alienation" is authored by Nathaniel Branden who examines the issue of alienation. Hegel is the philosopher who introduces the concept of alienation. Man cannot recognize his own alienation because he is lost in the world of social institutions. Karl Marx took the Hegelian concept and applied it to the worker. So he claimed that it was an inevitable part of the division of labour. The worker is separate from the product created by his labour services. This makes him feel he is an object instead of a human being. Because of this alienation, man is searching for an identity. As Branden writes: 'What is responsible for this crisis? What has alienated man and always stated explicitly, but—in their countless disparaging references to "the rationalism of a technological culture," "the vulgar materialism of the West," etc.—the villain in their view of things, the destroyer whom they hold chiefly responsible is not hard to identify. It is capitalism.' (272) Thus Branden explains the cause of the crisis.

This edition includes two articles by Ayn Rand which did not appear in the hardcover edition. They are "The Wreckage of the Consensus," which presents the views of Objectivist on Vietnam and the draft; and "Requiem for Man." It is an answer to the Papal encyclical Progressio Populorum. Rand begins "Requiem for Man" by reiterating her point that capitalism is incompatible with altruism and mysticism. She writes in *For the New Intellectual:* "In politics we are told that America, the greatest, the noblest, freest country on earth, is politically and morally inferior to Russia, the bloodiest dictatorship in history—and that our wealth should be given away to the savages of Asia and Africa, with apologies for the fact that we have produced it while they haven't." (11) Thus Rand expresses her contempt towards dictatorship. She cites an encyclical of Pope Paul VI. It expresses contempt for capitalism. The document is written from the point of view of a mystic- altruist. The system functions on the basis of profit which motivates the economic participants. The system is based on private ownership and functions on the basis of competition. For these bases the system is condemned. A nation functioning on this basis is America.

The fact is that the only way to raise the standard of living is to raise the productivity of labour. When the government sets the objectives to be obtained, then it becomes a totalitarian state. In "Man's Rights," Rand discusses what individual rights are and where they come from. In particular, she argues that rights come from practice. Her next essay, "Nature of Government," contains Rand's view on the government as an agency of force, how the only proper purpose for a government is to safeguard the rights of men, how the only legitimate functions of government are those necessary to preserve individual rights and the necessity for a strong, central government to serve as a final arbiter on the use of retaliatory force. This last point is in contrast to various anarcho-capitalists such as David Friedman and Murray Rothbard.

Alan Greenspan explains how the FED kept inflation down throughout his reign as Chairman. Here is the essence of his philosophy. He, in another essay, explains how corrupt monopolies can exist without the help of the government. Rand herself, while sometimes going overboard on the morality side, makes some very valid points in two of her essays in particular, "The Roots of War" and "Man's Rights." The theme of both is being generous with other people's fortunes. I agree with the comments: "In 'Roots of War,' Rand explains that outside of voluntary charity there are two ways to acquire something: take it, or swap something for it. Conquest or trade. There is no other option. Government is the agent of conquest, capitalism the agent of trade. She also shows the logical progression of each. In a conquest driven society, the pickpocket beats the honest man, but the robber beats the pickpocket, and the murderer beats the robber. Welfare states are not based on altruism, but quite the opposite, and will eventually either collapse or look elsewhere for plunder. In a trade society, those who offer the best value win. In 'Man's Rights' she goes over the same concepts as in 'The Roots of War' but more on the individual's level." (http://www.amazon. com) Rand also discusses how "Right" have gone from claims you have on your own life to claims someone else has on your life, and its potential consequences.

I feel it is apt to quote Younkins who writes in *The Philosophers of Capitalism:* 'It is only an ultimate goal, an end in itself that makes the existence of values possible. Metaphysically, life is only the phenomenon that is an end in itself: a virtue gained and kept by a constant process of action. Epistemologically, the concept of "value" is genetically dependent upon and derived from the antecedent concept of "life." To speak of "values" as apart from "life" is worse than a contradiction in terms. "It is only the concept of "Life" that makes the concept of "Value" possible.' (177) This is proved in *Capitalism: The Unknown Ideal*.

It clearly expresses Rand's political views. As it is said: "She states her views on various subjects in this book ranging from free markets to smear campaigns. This book allows Rand readers to learn the author's views on various economic and political subjects as she freely states her views and positions on various issues without having to do it within the framework of a story. Most of the chapter selections come from newsletters and articles which the author wrote or collected over the years. This is a much more direct and easy way for the reader to learn Rand's philosophy than to read." (http://www.bookrags.com) .This shows that for Rand, the only sound way to define capitalism is the axiology of Objectivism. Her critics may talk about her lack of academic pedigree and her dogmatism poses problems, but they are only detractors.

Enrico Peppe is right when he says: 'There is also the talk about her "cult" following. What? There's no "cult" around Strauss? These are non-issues. Rand's book and the other non-fiction collections cleared away the cobwebs in many a person's head. There are still "pure" Randists around. There are many more recovering Randians. There can be found everywhere—in schools, think tanks, in the military, some even at a Friday night Steak and Ale fest. The great majority are imbued with the concept that freedom is most desirable. That is a good thing. The book under review—its ideas—its impact—played no small part. This is not to say that there isn't major problem concerning the innards of Rand's philosophic outlook. It must be stated that the writings pro or con, related to Rand, the person, and Rand, the champion of her own "objectivism," have been intellectually wanting.' (http://www. intellectualconservative.com) Here, Rand's philosophic outlook is made clear.

George Smith in his *Atheism, Ayn Rand, and Other Heresies*, writes that there has appeared relatively little in the way of competent reflection of Ayn Rand as philosopher. Robert Bass, in a fine piece, *The Rights and Wrongs of Ayn Rand*, concludes: "She . . . constantly uses and relies upon the generic 'man.' For example (in Rand's words), 'Productiveness is the recognition . . . that productive work is the road of man's unlimited achievement and calls upon the highest attributes of his characters.' While it is certainly true that without productive work, the human species would perish, it does not follow that every (mature) human being must engage in productive work in order to survive . . . (conversely) . . . if . . . man is meant to apply directly to the individual, the statement is simply false (as a generalization)." (http://www.intellectualconservative.com) Their comments are absolutely true. A summative judgment on Rand and her book must be made in positive terms. She has certainly contributed, whether she likes it or not, to the literature of the Libertarian Movement. Her general philosophy is comprehensive and her defence of capitalism and freedom are certainly novel.

Den Uul and Rasmussen in their *The Philosophic Thought of Ayn Rand* bring it home: "Rand attempts to combine an essentially classical or premodern view of man with a modern political doctrine: that is to say, an Aristotelian view of man's nature is integrated with a liberal political doctrine. The argument . . . is that freedom of action in society is a function of what is proper to living a . . . good life . . . what is necessary for the fulfillment of our human potential. There have been other intellectuals who have held a basically classical view of man and who were also political liberals. But no one else has shown the connection between these two outlooks as explicitly and successfully as Rand." (http://www. intellectualconservative.com) Thus Rand insists on the point that productivity and capitalism go hand in hand though it is not always the case. One need not create anything of any worth to anybody whatsoever to create great wealth in this day and age. In our civilization wealth has always been created not from economic expansion or creation of a tangible good or service abuts through manipulation. Playing the currencies market in Malaysia by creating panic in its currencies so that it would drastically decline so by strengthening the dollar with decreasing U.S. exports and jobs is often the nature of today's capitalism. In the eighteenth century, capitalism although usually uncaring was about expanding the national pool of wealth. This is not only apathy for others but total disregard for the foundation that allows wealth to be created.

Rand says that empathy inherently leads to the rich being taken down to the level of the poor and that is the real goal of social reformers. The same is explained in these statements: "if so then how come that those social reformers who argued about the poor's plight in the 1800s have helped create a system that workers are grossly better off than they were in the 1800s while the rich are even richer? For all the talk about supply side economics, what is ignored is the even more important demand side economics. If demand is low, then industries don't create even if supply of investment capital is high, if demand is high then investment capital usually suffers little because there is a continuous flow of money going back to industries. Progressive reforms hence led to a middle class that could consume quantities of products to fuel industries whose products are intended for those same workers, such as automobiles, household appliances and other forms of technology." (http://www. members.tripod.com) Rand wants to say that apathy can be aright because empathy is evil.

Christopher in the article, "A book of lists and not for a true small business" writes: "The author spends time so much time with lists of 'Why', 'How', 'If, and 'What' that there was no substance. The book becomes list, after list, after list. I was patient hoping that this rhetoric would cease and I would be given examples and how-to, but no. In fact, I got a little depressed answering not to 'Do you have a map of the floodplain for your office?' and 'Where are your extra diskettes to back up your critical data?' 'Do you have extra potable water if you are stranded in your office' for upon a corporate and executive level risk planning background have little context to a small business. May be I misunderstood the author's meaning of small business or her definition of small company, but the examples she cites are from large corporate companies. The operational and business management structures she suggests are so out of context that I started to question if her stated ownership of past small business was actually true." (http://www.audible.com) But I feel it is not an objective review, but a personal ideological attack. The statements of the review are totally baseless and do not have any justification for them. The wonderful essays of the book cover a lot of practical issues associated with a free market capitalism.

This collection of essays proves that Rand is a brilliant thinker. Her way of exposing the moral fallacies behind the current altruistic or collectivist philosophy is amazing. Many people do have the same feeling as Rand, but they fail to express them in words or they may have been conditioned to suppress by their culture. But Rand is bold enough to put her ideas into words. The book can be treated as an educational piece of literature. Very often freedom fails to make the moral case and makes the mistake of defending freedom and capitalism from the perspective of altruism by saying that it is the best economic system for the common good. But Ayn Rand points out that though the fact is true, it is secondary.

Primarily, capitalism is the only political and economic system that is compatible with individual rights and proclaims that is a true moral virtue. It is apt to quote Mimi Reisel Gladstein who writes in *The New Ayn Rand Companion:* "Rand acted on her commitment to capitalism, in 1940, by working full time for the election of Wendell Willkie. Willkie characterized himself as a defender of the free enterprise system, and in Rand's mind, it was important to counter the growing collectivism that Franklin D. Roosevelt represented. It was during this campaign that Rand came to the conclusion that those who called themselves conservatives and supporters of capitalism were often the poorest advocates for what they believed in." (11) This book can be regarded primarily a treatise on the moral aspects of capitalism.

Rights of Man philosophy is often described as an American philosophy. In fact, it has only one particular application in the U.S.A. In "Roots of War," she says: "Let those who are actually concerned with peace observe that capitalism gave mankind the longest period of peace in history—a period during which there were no wars involving the entire civilized world—from the end of the Napoleonic wars in 1815 to the outbreak of World War I in 1914." (38) Rand means that capitalism provides the longest period of peace in history. In 1815, even Britain was still ruled by its gentry. The U.S.A. was on the other side with its attack on the British Empire in 1812-14. The 1914-18 was blamed in monarchist Germany and Czarist Russia. Yet Russia and the Prussian monarch were peace makers in 1815, and they allowed capitalist development in the interim.

In an article, "What a load of nonsense," it is written: "Readers of this work should note that both its author and its defenders engage in the same technique: attacking the motives and 'psycho-epistemologies' of those who have anything negative to say about either 'capitalism' or the book itself. Ayn Rand was so clearly not a 'philosopher' that I hesitate to use that word in the same sentence as her name. She was an anti-philosopher, a propagandist, a cult leader, a demagogue, a self-appointed Messiah of 'Capitalism', an ill-educated and ill-read megalomaniac who knew little economics and even less philosophy. They were, and are, much more able defenders of 'capitalism' than she and the hard fact is that people who misspell 'capitalism' are thereby indicating unfamiliarity with them." (http://www.amazon.com) But I think those who actually read the book would have grasped the essential statement of Rand that she is not primarily an advocate of Capitalism, but of reason. Capitalism is only the natural conclusion.

The book is an example of historical evidence with philosophical reasoning. It may appear strange, but Rand presents series of arguments backed up with historical evidence that spans the nation's history prove their point. D.C. Lewis is right when he says in the article, "Capitalism is Right": "Never, even once in America's history, did free enterprise ever cause ANY of the economic problems that have plagued this country. From the railroads, to the child labour laws, to anti-trust regulations . . . all were caused by Government regulation and interference in the free market. It is a conclusion that one must read and study to believe." (www.amazon.com) Rand is still influential whatever the controversies surround her life and thought. For anyone, she is the phase they go through when first coming to understanding their rights as individuals.

The book is widely considered a well thought one. It is a reasonable interpretation of true free market capitalism. Nathaniel Branden asserts it in his essay, "Common Fallacies about Capitalism": "When people denounce the free market as 'cruel,' the fact they are decrying is that the market is ruled by a single moral principle: justice. And that is the root of their hatred for capitalism." (76) It is clear that those who rate this book as poor are those who fail to understand that the failure of capitalism is not capitalism itself, but the inadequacy of those who claim to uphold it. It is proved from the words: "Capitalism, when followed accordingly, is an excellent means of braining about prosperity and progress. However, given the common businessmen who cuts corners in order to cut costs, who fail to uphold the standards of proper human resource management, we live in a society where sweatshops and wretched poverty exits. I know first hand what it is like to starve. I have first-hand experience with the collectivist ideal. Many of you seem to be jaded by your middle class/upper middle class 'intellectual' life styles. I believe in Capitalism. It has made me who I am today: A 20 year old Jamaican female entering graduate school in 2009 now standing at the Undergraduate level at GWU. It is your bias and misunderstanding that has brought you to such a brash conclusion. I have always believed that, those who have not experienced something, can have no rightful opinion on it." (http://www.barnesandnoblesoul.com) This proves that many people fail to understand the real nature of capitalism.

The fame of the book rests on Rand's surprising connection that capitalism is a system morally superior to any other. It is built on personal freedom delivering astounding wealth and yet it remains the most misunderstood system of political economy. What made her write the book is that she was confounded by the fact that young people blame capitalism for every societal ill. It is not surprising as they have not lived under any other system. At the time Rand was writing, there were promoters of socialism and communism, but capitalist ideas seemed to be held up as evil. Edward Wayne Younkins quotes Mises in *The Philosophers of Capitalism* about socialism: "Mises demonstrated that even with perfect information, the central planners in socialism cannot rationally calculate how to combine resources to render efficient production (Ebeling 1991). They can only grope in the dark; as Mises put it, socialism is 'planned chaos,' an irrational endeavour that must leach off and mimic capitalism to provide even a subsistence standard of living to its citizens." (165) This analysis is true. Rand being an American immigrant who witnessed the misery of economy, in Russia, resolved to be the defender of capitalism at an early age.

Rand attacks the *Encyclopedia Britannica*, usually considered a source of objective information. She had discovered that its entry described capitalism simply as another way in which a society organizes itself to produce a 'social surplus.' It did not mention that wealth is created by individual minds. Instead, wealth is described as an impersonal aggregate produced by the allocation of resources.

In Rand's view there is no such thing as a social surplus. Wealth is created by an individual and so it belongs to him:

> To see wealth as some social good produced by the tribe was 'morally obscene' In her words, When 'the common good' of society is regarded as something apart from and superior to the individual good of its members, it means that the good of some men takes precedence over the good of others, with those others consigned to the status of sacrificial animals. When the gold of majority overrides individual rights, Rand observes, you may as well have no rights at all, since what you are left with, taken to its logical conclusion, are regimes like the former Soviet Union, where 'the greater good of all' meant misery for almost every individual. In Soviet Union people were told to bear many hardships in the service of achieving some vision of a prosperous, industrialized state. Tough conditions were only temporary; soon they would overtake the capitalist West. But while they waited for tractors and generators, the government was spending fortunes on putting men into space. (http://www.citiwire.com)

Thus Rand notes that in a communist society everything gained comes at the expense of something else.

Rand says that capitalism is based on the objectivist theory of value. The value of an object is a combination of reason and labour. In the hands of a human being, even a rock which is only a lump can be made into a useful weapon. But he must first conceive of the rock as a weapon. To sharpen the stone, through reason, he must discover that a sharp edge is more useful. Then by applying labour, he sharpens the stone and thus value is created. Rand explains the same in "Patents and Copyrights": 'Those who observe the spectacle of the progressive collapse of patents—the spectacle of mediocrity scrambling to cash—I note the achievements of genius—and who understand its implications, will understand why in the closing paragraphs of Chapter VII, Part II, of *Atlas Shrugged*, one of the guiltiest men is the passenger who said: "Why should Rearden be only one permitted to manufacture Rearden metal?"' (133-34). Most of people cannot produce everything they require for living.

As it is said: "One human may not be better at shaping flint into arrowheads. Another may have acquired the skill to turn mud into pottery. If the first wants a pot to cook in, he may trade an arrowhead for a pot. The central feature of free trade is that each participant feels they have traded an object of *lesser value* for that of *higher value*. The arrowhead is not very useful for cooking so the first human feels he obtained a more valuable object. Conversely, the second human will have a hard time hunting buffalo with a piece of pottery, so to him the arrowhead is of more value than a pot." (http://www.wikipedia.com) Thus skills differ from one person to another.

The Objectivist philosopher Andrew Bernstein in his book, *The Capitalist Manifesto: The Historic, Economic and Philosophic Case for Laissez-Faire* (2005), argues that capitalism in its pure form is the most moral and political social system. In the context of sports, he writes a novel celebrating individual excellence, *Heart of a Pagan*. He writes: "The Capitalist Manifesto defends capitalism as the world's most moral and practical social system. This book is written for the rational mind, whether the reader is a professional intellectual or an intelligent layman. It makes the case for individual rights and freedom in terms intelligible to all rational men. The key to explaining capitalism's unparalleled economic success is dual: to show that it alone is the system that guarantees individual liberties, and to demonstrate that political liberty is an indispensable requirement of man's life on earth." (http://wwwandrewbernstein.com) This is proved in *Capitalism: The Unknown Ideal*.

Rand argues that the motive force of history is ideas. Finally, the course of human events is controlled by intellectuals. For example, in her second essay "Roots of War," in *Capitalism: The Unknown Ideal*, Rand declares: "Just as the destruction of capitalism and the rise of the totalitarian state were not caused by business or labour or any economic interests, but by the dominant statist ideology of the intellectuals—so the resurgence of the doctrines of military conquest and armed crusades for political "Ideas" were the product of the same intellectuals' belief that "the good" is to be achieved by force." (40) In the same essay she says that it was collectivist intellectuals, but not economic interest that pushed America into involvement in both World Wars.

Rand is true to her principles in opposing the military draft and the American involvement in Vietnam. However, Rand and her followers focused in the contribution of collectivists to militarism and neglected the other side of the coin, the contribution militarism, war, and imperialism have made to advance the power of government. Rand is a political thinker, a good ethicist and an epistemologist, but not a metaphysician at all. In her fields, she may have benefitted from closer attention to the writings of Blanshard, whom she respected most in spite of some disagreements. From the *Letters of Ayn Rand*, one can know that when *Reason and Goodness* was published, Blanshard sent her a signed copy of it.

Rand's philosophy is an attempt at grounding her defence of capitalism in ethics, epistemology, and metaphysics. Further when she wanders from her strengths, it becomes gradually less successful. Hoke writes in the article, "Unlearn What You Have Learned" in *Capitalism: The Unknown Ideal*: "This book dispels all of the myths our public school education system and other liberal groups have put out for years. It also embraces Capitalism as not only the best economic model but also the only ethical one in existence. If you read this with open mind there are many things you will take away from it. Some of the myths that will be dispelled are: Monopolies are always bad, Unions protect workers, War is good for business, and many more." (http://www. amazon.com)

This book as an interesting relic of the past is worth reading though Rand's confident sense of her own rightness with little respect for the opposing views may be a little annoying for some readers. Some critics say that she uses outdated words such as "altruists" to represent the forces of evil who would overburden the poor and that she protests the American business community far too much. Americans have seen many of the abuses come to pass that Rand, writing in 1946, claims would never happen if free enterprise were just left to its own devices, so many of her arguments will be lost on a modern reader. B. David H. Miller says in the article, "A Utopian Ideal": "back in the '60s, it was controversial simply to argue that capitalism was revolutionary. Times have changed. Nowadays it would require an invincible ignorance to believe that socialism can compete economically with capitalism. And to believe that socialism is morally superior to capitalism, now that everyone knows the truth about actually existing socialism in the former Soviet Union, would be morally depraved. Intellectually, the battle is over. Capitalism has won; socialism has lost. Capitalism is no longer an "unknown" ideal. Our new historical situation makes it possible to look more clearly at Ayn Rand's political writings. Rand was unquestionably right about the moral and economic superiority of capitalism." This shows that capitalism has won over socialism.

The book is mainly based on America's founding principles and an understanding of the fact that America's abundance was created by the productive genius of free men who pursue their own personal interest, and the making of their own private fortunes, but it is not created by public sacrifice to the common good. As Xenocrates writes in the article, "At Whose Expense?": "If you resent the fact that your life is your own responsibility and no one else's, then you will not like this book. This will account for the less than perfect overall rating this book inevitably will acquire as there are many among the masses who just cannot accept that they might have to be accountable for their own decisions. Such thoughts clearly do not speak to the quality of the book, rather frustration with the ideals; an understandable and anticipated response to a book of this nature. Anyone seeking to understand the logical and objective ideals of laissez-faire capitalists will discover all they are searching for with this book and I highly recommend this to readers and critical thinkers of all views of economic thought." This proves that Rand is one of the rare writers who not only drew in readers with her novels, but also created a philosophical movement with them.

Capitalism: The Unknown Ideal provides the reader the intellectual background to understand the basis of America's principles of liberty and economics. The readers can also understand what has crept into America and that it has implications on the problems America is facing today. This kind of book must be prescribed in high schools and colleges. Rand explains this in "Theory and Practice": "Prior to the American Revolution, through centuries of feudalism and monarchy, the interests of the rich lay in the expropriation, enslavement, and misery of the rest of the people. A society, therefore, where the interests of the rich require general freedom, unrestricted productiveness, and the protection of individual rights, should have been hailed as an ideal system by anyone whose goal is man's well being." (136) Thus the book will reinforce what is to be American and why they should feel proud of their culture and heritage.

Regardless of one's beliefs, one should read this book and one should understand this side of the coin. As Karen says: "This book is so rational and so true in stating the cause & effect of the last 100 years of the US and its failing economy. Even though this book is over 40 years old it rings as true, if not more so. We are seeing our country falling into socialism/communism run by statist who wants to export our wealth and redistribute it as they see fit. Every US citizen should read this book. It's about time we start to understand why our country's production and development have slowed to a crawl since 1890." (http://www. audible.com) It proves that this book is definitely accessible to all. But I think that those who are just getting familiar with the non-fiction works of Ayn Rand will find many of the essays in *The Virtue of Selfishness* and *Capitalism: The Unknown Ideal* to be more interesting to start. In the latter, Ayn Rand in clear English sets out what exactly capitalism means to the ordinary person and dismantles the entire case for socialism and the anti-capitalism. This book is frequently reprinted and it is a perennial favourite among high school students.

Spawning Criticism

Rand is neither a classical empiricist like Hume nor a classical rationalist like Plato (428/427 BC-348/347 BC), a Greek philosopher, or Descartes (1596-1650), a French philosopher. Like Descartes or John Locke (1632-1704), Rand also considers her ideas to be different from foundationalism (a belief in a strict adherence to a set of basic principles), realism, or representationalism (the philosophical position that the world we see in conscious experience is not the real world itself, but merely a miniature virtual-reality replica of that world in an internal representation). Rand's Objectivist epistemology is fully developed in her *Introduction to Objectivist Epistemology* (1979). In her view, concepts are man-made. Rand presents her theory of Concept Formation in *Introduction to Objectivist Epistemology*. They are objective: "products of a cognitive method of classification whose processes must be performed by man, but whose content is dictated by reality." (54)

We need a code of values with "man's life" as its standard. Rand identifies three cardinal values: Reason, Purpose, and Self-esteem, with the corresponding virtues of Rationality, Productiveness, and Pride. Rational men, says Rand, approach one another as traders, offering values they have created in exchange for the values they seek, each appealing to the rationality and self-interest of the other. When men recognize this and formulate their goals accordingly, their interests do not conflict and all the benefits of social existence are possible. This requires, she says in *The Virtue of Selfishness* (1964) that the identification of rights, "moral principle[s] defining and sanctioning a man's freedom of action in a social context." (124)

The Objectivist theory of art flows from its epistemology, by way of psycho-epistemology. It is proved from the words of Louis

Torres and Michelle Marder Kamhi in *What Art is* (2000): 'According to Rand, an artist's style is not only the "product of his own psycho-epistemology" but also by implication, a projection of his view of man's consciousness, of its efficacy or impotence, of its proper method and "level of functioning." She offers no evidence in support of this sweeping assertion.' (57) For Marxism art is part of the superstructure of society. As the Russian Marxist critic George Plekhanov (1857-1918) puts it, the social mentality of an age is conditioned by that age's social relations. Every writer, individually placed in society, responds to a general history from his own particular standpoint, making sense of it in his own concrete terms. Literature is not merely the passive reflection of the economic base.

Each element of a society's superstructure—art, law, politics, religion—has its own internal evolution. It cannot be reduced to a mere expression of the class struggle or the state of the economy. As Leon Trotsky (1879-1924) says in *Literature and Revolution* (1924), art has a very high degree of autonomy. And yet Marxism holds that art is determined by the mode of production. Engels remarks that art has a more complex relationship to ideology than law and political theory. But the French Marxist theorist Louis Althusser argues that art cannot be reduced to ideology. But it has a particular relationship to it. Ideology signifies the imaginary ways of man's experience of the real world. In this way, art does not make us understand the truth which ideology conceals, since Althusser holds that knowledge of capitalism which *Marx's Das Capital* (2000) rather than Dickens's *Hard Times* (1853) allows us.

Science gives the conceptual knowledge of a situation, but art gives us the experience of that situation. Objectivism defines "art" as a "selective re-creation of reality according to an artist's metaphysical value-judgments. As Torres and Kamhi write in *What Art Is:* "Once again, Rand's position is comparable to that of Louis Arnaud Reid, who held that the greatest art deals with values that are "profound and lofty and broad and far-reaching in the complexity of their implications," the greater the values, and the more of greater values we have, provided they are united into one coherent or meaning of art is primary, and no work can be judged great that is neither profound nor complex in its meaning." (59) According to this view, objectivism regards art as a way of presenting abstractions concretely, in perceptual form. Objectivism does not regard art as propagandistic. Rand writes in *The Art of Fiction* (2000): "To master the art of writing you have to be conscious of why you are doing things—but do not edit yourself while writing. Just as you cannot change the horse in the middle of a stream, so you cannot change premises in the middle of writing. When you write, you have to rely on your sub-conscious, you cannot doubt yourself and edit every sentence as it came out." (4) Thus art stems from an artist's sense of life which is preconception and largely emotional.

Rand believes that Romanticism is the highest school of literary art, as she understands that the Romanticists brought to art the primacy of values which are the source of emotions. A great deal of emotional intensity was projected in the work of the Romanticists and reactions of their audiences, as well as a great deal of imagination, originality, excitement, and all the other consequences of a value-oriented view of life. It is rightly remarked: "The term "romanticism," however, is often affiliated with emotionalism, to which Objectivism is completely opposed. Historically, many romantic artists were philosophically subjectivist. Most Objectivists who are also artists subscribe to what they call romantic realism, which is how Ayn Rand labelled her own work. The Fountainhead Café, a coffee shop in New York City is inspired by Objectivism. The sign reads "Eat Objectively, Live Rich." Rand places her theory in the context of the triumph of Romanticism over Classicism.

In both fiction and non-fiction writing, Rand offered private courses. *Ayn Rand: A Sense of Life* (1997) serves as proof of her influence. It is an Academy Award nominated documentary about her life. Her novels and essays present an internally consistent world view. They express an all-encompassing philosophical system. Rand shows her characters in different perspectives. From this quality she can be regarded as a postmodernist. Postmodernism explores multidimensional characters in literature. Peter Barry says in *Beginning Theory* (1995) that the term 'postmodernism' was used in the 1930s, but its current sense and vogue can be said to have begun with Jean-Francois Lyotard's *The Postmodern Condition: A Report on Knowledge* (1979). Barry continues: "For Lyotard the Enlightenment whose project Habermas wishes to continue is simply one of the would-be authoritative 'overarching', 'totalizing' explanations of things like Christianity, Marxism, or the myth of scientific progress. These 'metanarratives' ['super-narratives'], which purport to explain and censure are really illusions, fostered in order to smother difference, opposition, and plurality." (86) It means that Lyotard's definition of postmodernism is the incredulity towards metanarratives.

Brian McHale writes in *Postmodernist Fiction* (1987) that the dominant of postmodernist fiction is ontological, that is, it deploys strategies which engage the questions like 'which work is this?' and 'What is to be done in it?' He brings about the similarities of science fiction and postmodernist fiction: "Indeed it is perhaps like ontological genre *par excellence*. We can think of science fiction as postmodernism's non-canonized "low art" double, its sister genre. Darko Suvin has defined science-fiction genre as "literature of cognitive estrangement." (59) Rand also introduces science fiction in her *Atlas Shrugged* by creating the Galt Gutch where the strikers live. Postmodernism also includes historical fantasy. McHale says: "Postmodernist apocryphal history is often fantastic history at the same time" (95) He continues: "Postmodernist fiction shares with classic modernist fiction an affinity for cinema (and more recently for television), drawing upon its models and raw materials." (128) Thus all the four novels of Rand were made into films.

In her multi-dimensional characterization, Rand too is a postmodernist. *We the Living* is the story of three characters—Kira, Adrei and Leo. The three characters represent three different attitudes to the oppression of communism. Kira represents the ideal woman who can withstand all obstacles. Andrei, a man of powerful character, is ruined because of choosing the wrong side of the communist party. Leo is an idealist who comes out of his illusion about the political system, and continues his struggle due to his uncompromising nature towards life. In *Atlas Shrugged*, her heroine is completely incapable of guilt. Fundamental guilt does not mean the ability to judge one's own actions and regret a wrong action, if one commits it. Fundamental guilt means that man is evil and guilty by nature.

Rand says: "It is the concept of original sin that my heroine, or I, or any Objectivist, is incapable of accepting or of ever experiencing emotionally. It is the concept of original sin that negates morality. If man is guilty by nature, he has no choice about it. If he has no choice, the issue does not belong in the field of morality. Morality pertains only to the sphere of man's free will—only to those actions which are open to his choice. To consider man guilty by nature is a contradiction in terms. My heroine would be capable of experiencing guilt about a specific action. Only, being a woman of high moral stature and self-esteem, she would see to it that she never earned any guilt by her actions." (http://www.ellenspacenet/ar-pboy.html) It means that her actions are totally moral manner and, therefore, she does not accept an unearned guilt.

Edward W. Younkins points out that Rand's characters are persons in whom certain characteristics and behaviours are pinpointed more consistently and sharply than in typical human beings. Russel A. Potter in his *Spectacular Vernaculars: hip-hop and the Politics of Postmodernism* (1995) explains about the postmodern theorists: "For instance, postmodern theorists have spent a great deal of time talking about the ways in which identity, far from being reducible to essentialized categories such as race, class, and gender, is in fact more of a patchwork of overlapping—and in some cases, conflicting—identities." (13) This quality is very much like that of Rand's own.

Rand believes that in order to be in control of one's life, one has to have a purpose—a productive purpose. James and Dagny's characters prove this. Rand says: "Hitler and Stalin, to name two tyrants, were in control of their own lives but they did not have a clear purpose. Both of them ended as literal psychotics. They were men who lacked self-esteem and, therefore, hated all of existence. Their psychology, in effect, is summarized in *Atlas Shrugged* in the character of James Taggart. The man who has no purpose, but has to act, acts to destroy others." (http://ellenspacenet/ar-pboy.html) This means that he has no productive or creative purpose.

Reason, man's tool of knowledge, enables him to perceive the facts of reality. As Rand says, emotions are not tools of cognition. One need not ignore emotions, but one should merely keep them in their place. An emotion is an automatic response, an effect, not a cause. There is no necessary clash. Rand says: "His emotions are not his enemies; they are his means of enjoying life. But they are not his guide; the guide is his mind." (http://ellenspacenet/ar-pboy.html) It means that there is no dichotomy between man's reason and his emotions—provided he observes their proper relationship. For Rand, friendship, family life and human relationships are not primary in a man's life. Women as well as men should organize their lives around work. If a man places his own productive work first, there is no conflict between his work and his enjoyment of human relationships. She says: "What is proper for a man is proper for a woman. The basic principles are the same. There is no particular work which is specifically feminine. Women can choose their work according to their own purpose and premises in the same manner as men do." (http://ellenspacenet/ar-pboy.html) This makes Rand's stand clear that women can choose their purpose as it is the case with men.

Ursula Tidd says in *Simone de Beauvoir* (2004): 'Beauvoir starts out with the statement that woman is a transcendent being who, like man, should live as an authentic subject and allow others to do the same (Lundgren-Gothlin 1996: 184)." (53) It shows that Beauvoir too holds the same opinion as Rand. Rand believes that a woman who chooses to devote herself to home and family instead of a career is impractical, because a home cannot be a full-time occupation, except when her children are young. However, if she wants a family and wants to make that her career, at least for a while, it would be proper—if she approaches it as a career, that is, if she studies that subject, if she defines the rules and principles by which she wants to bring up her children, if she approaches her task in an intellectual manner. It is a very responsible task, but only when treated as a science, not a as a mere emotional indulgence.

According to Rand the only man capable of experiencing a profound romantic love is the man driven by passion for his work, because love is an expression of self-esteem, of the deepest values in a man's or a woman's character. Rand does not consider herself a feminist. She believes that women are equal to men in all aspects except in physical strength. Ursula Tidd writes in *Simone de Beauvoir* (2004): "Beauvoir accepts that there are certain minor physiological and biological differences . . . that the valuing of these differences between women and men should justify the oppression of women and their traditional status as second class citizens in patriarchal society." (52) These words echo Rand's opinion.

The feminist literary criticism, the product of the women's movement, dates back to 1960s as people increasingly adopted the perception that women are oppressed in a male-centred society. The feminist movement is rooted in the West and especially in the reform movement of the 19th century. The organized movement is dated from the first women's rights convention at Seneca Falls, New York in 1848. Emmeline Pankhurst was one of the founders of the suffragette movement and aimed to reveal the institutional sexism in British society, through the Women's Social and Political Union. Over a century and a half the movement has included diverse perspectives on discrimination against women. Early feminists and primary feminist movements are called the first-wave and feminists after about 1960 the second wave.

Though there is third wave, it s not agreed by the feminists as they haven't felt it necessary and beneficial. Like ocean waves, each wave comes on top of the one before and so they are called waves. In K.M. Newton's *Twentieth-Century Literary Theory* (1988) it is said that according to Josephine Donovan for feminist criticism there can be no separation between the aesthetic and the moral aspects of literary texts even if this means judging adversely works as central to Western civilization as Homer's *Odyssey* (1178

BC), Dante Alighierie's *Divine Comedy* (1306-21), and *Goethe's Faust* (1808): "Another important concern of feminist criticism is women's writing. Elaine Showalter advocates 'gynocriticism', in which the concerns of the woman as writer are central. She argues that the 'woman as reader' approach of critics such as those in the 'image of women' school is restrictive in that it concentrates on male views of woman." (263) Here, Showalter's concern is woman as writer.

A very important supporting factor in modern feminism is the publication of *Sex and Temperament in Three Primitive Societies* (1935), a book by anthropologist Margaret Mead. In it the women are shown to be dominant in the Tohambull tribe. The earliest works on the women question criticized the restrictive role of women without saying that men are to be blamed.

One of the few books that can be called feminist is Mary Wollstonecraft's *A Vindication of the Rights of Woman* (1972). As Susan Alice Watkins, Marisa Rueda and Marta Rodriguez write about Wollstonecraft in their *Feminism for Beginners* (1992): "Her demands for an end to the double standards of male and female behaviour, for woman's rights to independent work education, civil and political life still form the basis of feminism today." (16) However, by modern standards, her metaphor of women as nobility, the elite of society, fragile and in danger of moral sloth does not look like a feminist argument.

Wollstonecraft holds that both women and men contributed to this situation and women have power over men. Mead's work inspired the belief that European ideas of masculinity and femininity were very much cultural than instinctive. Hans Berten says in *Literary Theory; The Basics* (2004) that feminism has been hard on the impersonalists: "In their use of autobiographical material, female academics have followed a trend set earlier by female writers such as the American poets Sylvia Plath (1932-1963), Anne Sexton (1928-1974) and Adrienne Rich (1929). Since the mid-1960s women writers drawing on their personal experiences, have increasingly brought female sexuality, female anguish, childbirth, mothering, rape, and other specifically female themes into their work." (101) Thus Berten concentrates on the personal element in the writings of women.

The name feminism suggests a single ideology, but in reality the movement has many subgroups. Feminist ideology has been compelled to move in different directions to achieve its goals because of historical precedents, the current legal status of women in certain countries, and other factors. Consequently, many kinds of feminism arose. Peter Barry says in *Beginning Theory* that the representation of women in literature, then, was felt to be one of the most important forms of socialization. A major division in feminism is concerned with disagreements about the amount and type of theory that should feature in it. One of these is Anglo-American version of feminism. The Anglo-Americans, says Barry, seem to accept the conventions of literary realism and treat literature as a series of representations of women's lives and experience which can be measured and evaluated against reality.

It is written in *Twentieth-Century Literary Theory* of Newton in Western tradition, the female stereotypes symbolize either the spiritual or the material, good or evil: "Under the category of the good-woman stereotypes, that is, those who serve the interests of the hero, are the patient wife, the mother/martyr, and the lady. In the bad or evil category are deviants who reject or do not properly serve men or his interests: the old maid/career woman, the witch/lesbian, the shrew or domineering mother/wife." (266) It shows that several masterpieces of the Western tradition rely upon the stereotypes of woman.

Hans Berten in his *Literary Theory: The Basics* says that feminist critics showed how the literary representations of women repeated familiar cultural stereotypes such as women as immoral and dangerous or the women as cute but helpless and so on. Sandra M. Gilbert and Susan Gubar aptly quote Virginia Woolf in *The Mad Woman in the Attic:* 'Before we women can write, declared Virginia Woolf, we must "kill" the "angel in the house." In other words, women must kill the aesthetic ideal through which they themselves have been "killed" into art.' (17) Berten wants to say that female writers, too, were regularly found to have succumbed to the lure of stereotypical representations. On the other hand, Swift, Pope, and others represented women as inescapably monstrous.

As Gilbert says in *The Mad Woman in the Attic* (2000): "Yet despite the obstacles presented by those twin images of angel and monster, despite the sterility and anxieties of authorship from which women have suffered, generations of texts have been possible for female writers." (44) Significantly, the conflict between these two women is fought out in enclosures which have been packed with enchanted magic glass. Gilbert and Gubar say in *The Man Woman in the Attic:* 'Here, wielding as weapons the tools patriarchy suggests that women use to kill themselves into art, the two women literally try to kill each other with art. Shadow fights shadow, image destroys image in the crystal prison, as if the "fiend" of Aurora's mother's portrait should plot to destroy the "angel" who is another one of her selves.' (36-37) Here, the authors show how women kill themselves into art.

One type of feminism, Radical feminism, feels, says Susan Alice Watkins in *Feminism for Beginners:* "We radical feminists see the problem as patriarchy—a whole system of male power over women. Male rulers, male military, political and religious establishments, male trade unions and the male-dominated left are all apart of the patriarchy . . . reinforcing—and reinforced by—the power of individual men over women and children within their families." (120) It shows that patriarchy is the root cause of many serious social problems. This situation is well explained by Elaine Showalter in *The Female Malady* (1987): 'Female intellectual inferiority could be understood as the result of reproductive specialization, and the "womanly" traits of self-sacrifice and service so convenient for the comfort of a patriarchal society could be defended in evolutionary terms as essential for the survival and improvement of the race.' (122) This type of feminism was popular in the second wave, though it is not prominent today.

However, when people use the word 'feminism' they mean Radical feminism. Western women feel that gender oppression is the root oppression that they face, but in other parts of the world, women are able to trace their oppression to their race or economic status instead of their status as females. In the nineteenth-century romantic operas, women's escape from the bondage of femininity into an empowering and violent madness was a popular theme. Elaine Showalter writes in *The Female Malady:* "Given the pervasive cultural association of women and madness, it is not surprising that madwoman has become as emblematic a figure for contemporary feminists as she was for Mary Wollstonecraft in 1797." (4) This shows how contemporary feminists represented women.

To find the female perspective on insanity, says Showalter, one must turn to Victorian women's diaries and novels: "These texts present female insanity in its social contexts, and as a reaction to the limitations of the feminine role itself. Unmarried middle-class women, for example, were widely considered a social problem by the Victorians. Stigmatized by terms like "redundant," "superfluous," and "odd," they were also regarded as peculiarly subject to mental disorders" (61). It shows that the family life, boredom, and patriarchal protectivism are destroying women's capacity to dream or to act. Showalter puts forward the argument of Florence Nightingale in *The Female Malady:* "If women are to be saved, Nightingale argues, they must first be awakened from their infantile unconsciousness. Women must be able to suffer if they are to grow." (65) It proves that experiencing frustration is a privilege that may lead to action.

Another fragmentation, says Hans Breten in *Basics of Literary Theory*, would ultimately destabilize a specifically British offshoot of feminism: Marxist feminism: "From a Marxist perspective, history is dominated by a struggle between social classes that will only end when a truly classless society has been achieved. Given the fact that throughout history women have been collectively denied important rights, it was almost inevitable that a Marxist feminism would emerge that saw women as constituting a seriously underprivileged class." (102) Thus Marxist feminism considers women as underprivileged class. It is written in *Twentieth-Century Literary Theory* edited by Newton: "Elaine Showalter advocates 'gynocriticism', in which the concerns of the woman as writer are central. She argues that the 'woman as reader' approach of critics such as those in the 'images of women,' school is restrictive in that it concentrates on male views of women." (263) Thus Showalter advocates gynocriticism. Showalter continues that representatives of the formal Female Aesthetic, such as Dorothy Richardson and Virginia Woolf, begin to think in terms of male and female sentences, and divide their work into 'masculine' journalism and 'feminine' fictions.

Another sect, Althusserian feminism, says Breten, examines how literary texts and films hail their readers or audience and position them with regard to gender. He questions: "Into what position does a text, a film, a rock video or a commercial try to manoeuvre us through specific strategies of narration, specific shots, images, and other forms of representation? How do they persuade a female audience to accept a liberal humanist ideology that so clearly disadvantages them?" (103) All these show that there are diversions among different types of feminism. Some Radical feminists advocate a complete separation of male and female in society and culture. Other feminists hold feminism to be one movement of liberation among many others, each affecting the other such as Gender Feminism, French Feminism, Pop Feminism, and Liberal Feminism. However, Showalter writes in *The Female Malady* that Darwinian feminists wrote about the psychological consequences of feminist rebellion: "In a few celebrated cases, radical women who challenged the norms of feminine conduct were actually committed to lunatic asylums." (146) Thus madness is the result of social position of women.

Many leaders of feminism have been women, but all women are not feminists. Interestingly, in Charlotte Bronte's *The Professor* we find a male narrator. Gilbert says in *The Mad Woman in the Attic:* "In this world of passive doll-like women and ferociously overbearing men, Bronte's male narrator plays from the first a curiously androgynous part. In his yearnings toward women he is conventionally masculine." (319) But some feminists feel that men should not be the leaders of feminist movement as men have been socialized to aggressively seek position of power within a leadership hierarchy; they would apply this tendency to feminist organization. As a result, even the feminist movement would become a male-controlled movement and it does not fulfil the feminist ideal of representing women. Beauvoir links the class struggle with the feminist struggle for equality. Ursula Tidd says in *Simone de Beauvoir:* "She accepts the temporary exclusion of men from the political process on the grounds that women have to analyse their own specific oppression apart from men and also because, even if men are also in certain ways victims of the patriarchal system, they nevertheless profit from it and internalize its ideology." (77) It proves that many of the feminists accept and seek support of men in their movement.

The other diversions of feminism are described by Barry in *Beginning Theory:* "While the definitive works in the so-called 'Anglo-American' tradition appeared in the late 1970s, the British 'socialist feminist' tradition produced its key works in the mid-1980s and remains active and influential. In contrast to the Americans (if not, as we have just argued, to the British) the work of 'French' feminism is more overtly theoretical, taking as its starting point the insights of major post-structuralists, especially Lacan, Foucault and Derrida." (125) Though feminism has been a movement mainly in Western countries, some advances have been made in non-Western countries. Feminists hope that their movement will have an equal effect on the other countries in the 21st century. As the movement has been dominated by white women, many black feminists criticize the movement. Western society is not relevant to the lives of black women.

In postcolonial feminism, it is the key idea. Many black women prefer the term womanism for their views. Feminists are sometimes wary of the transsexuals, and the sharing of water is considered to be a virtue, as it represents the giving of life-sustaining respite from the heat and weariness of travel. Notably, Christ usually made followers of those who gave him water to drink. In this case, the Golden One's giving water to Equality 7-2521 accompanies her conversion into obedience of him.

As she has mind of her own, she does not blindly follow the authorities. She is more than a beautiful young woman. Her inner beauty can be recognized externally. Equality knows her virtues even before speaking to her. She gleans from her fearless eyes and her derisive mannerisms reveal that she is proud, with an inner reverence that comes only from an unbroken independence of spirit. To pursue her goals, like Equality, the Golden One too violates the customs of the society. Later, she talks to him as fearlessly as he does. She does not mind the social approval. Her personal values mean everything for her. She tells him in the forest: "We wish to be damned with you, rather than blessed with all our brothers. Do as you please with us, but do not send away from you." (83)

What Barbara Barden says about Rand in *The Passion of Ayn Rand* can be applied to her heroine: 'The human qualities she [Rand] cared about were, she believed, specifically masculine attributes, above all, purposefulness and strength. She would later insist that she had never regretted being a woman, but "it was hero worship from the first." And she would later define femininity as "hero worship." Man, she would say, is defined by his relationship to reality; woman—by her relationship to man. Far into old age, she would comment about herself proudly, "I'm a hero worshipper.' (18) Thus like Rand, the Golden One is a hero worshipper. From most of the women gatherings, transsexual women are excluded and they are rejected by some feminists as they believe that no one born male can understand the oppression faced by women. It is proved by the words in *Twentieth-Century Literary Theory* by K.M. Newton: "Women in literature written by men are for the most part seen as Others, as objects, of interest only insofar as they serve to detract from the goals of the male protagonist. Such literature is alien from a female point of view because it denies her essential selfhood" (264). On the other hand, the transsexual women are quick to retort and assert their gender identity; they faced many struggles such as that for legal recognition. This discrimination against gender-variant people is the other face of heterosexism and patriarchy.

Feminism has brought out many changes in Western society including women's suffrage, employment of women with equal pay and the right to initiate divorce proceedings. Some feminists feel that there is still much to be done in this field and others believe that they have already won the battle. In Western societies today, no one questions the right of women to vote or own land. It is a strange concept for the women just hundred years ago. Breten writes in *Basics of Literary Theory:* "Feminism seeks to change the power relations between men and women that prevail under what in the late 1960s and the 1970s usually was called patriarchy, a term that referred to the (almost) complete domination of men in Western society (and Beyond)." (96) This proves that feminism, from the beginning, fights against patriarchy.

Many feminists still struggle to achieve their goals. Feminists are proponents of using "Ms." They also stress on using gender-inclusive language. For example, they use humanity in place of mankind and "he or she" instead of he when the gender is unknown. Feminists often desire the change in language in order to promote an equal and respectful treatment of women. This is to change language which has been viewed by some feminists as imbued with sexism. It directly affects the perception of reality. Feminists of other languages many not insist on gendered pronoun and do not feel it important to change language. But English has become more universal in this issue of language. This is expressed by Breten too in *Basics of Literary Theory:* "We have now all been brought within the capitalist orbit, so that politics all over the Western world looks more or less the same—and we have all become part of an international English-speaking, mass culture. But maybe that is exactly why difference is so appealing." (104) This comment shows the effect of English on feminism. The nature of heterosexual relationships in Western and other societies is affected by feminism and it has some negative consequences.

In these relationships, there has been a change in the power relationship between men and women. In such conditions, women and men have had to accustom to new situations which sometimes cause confusions about identity. The system of marriage has also suffered as some women have the opinion that marriage is an institution that oppresses women. They have successfully created change towards equality in the West, but there is still a very long way to get true equality. According to statistics, women own only one percent of the world's wealth, and earn ten percent of the world's income, though they make up 49 percent of the population. In matters of childcare and housework, women work longer than men in both the industrialized and developing world.

Rand feels that America represents freedom and it is true, but that freedom is not extended to women. It is proved by the statement of Susan Alice Watkins and others in *Feminism for Beginners:* "At the end of the war, 4 out of 5 women in the US wanted to keep their jobs in peacetime. Men thought different. Job segregation returned with a vengeance. In the 50s women were constantly brainwashed by ads, movies and vulgarized psychoanalysis to stay home and be happy housewives." (97) If we take into account the statistics, America is the last country to offer the right to vote for women. As Susan and others say in *Feminism for Beginners:* "Increasing numbers of college-educated women in the US and Europe now had raised expectations. They felt equal—but in practice still found themselves trapped in the traditional secondary role of looking after men and striving for their attention and approval" (103). It shows that even now their condition has not changed. Even her Objectivism is blind to the conditions of women.

The same is the case with Western literature. Josephine Donovan says about women in *Twentieth-Century Literary Theory* edited by Newton: "They are objects, who are used to facilitate, explain away, or redeem the projects of men. Western projects of redemption almost always depend upon a salvific woman" (267). Showalter says in *The Female Malady:* "American nervousness was alarmingly frequent "among the well-to-do and the intellectual, and especially among those in the professions and in the higher walks of business life, who are in deadly earnest in the race for place and power." (135) This proves that many of the neurotic patients in America are intellectual women.

The number of women in all of the world's legislative bodies is much less than the number of men. According to 1985 statistics, Finland had the largest percentage of women in national legislature at approximately 32 percent. Currently, Sweden has just 9 percent. Wales, while not an independent country has 50% of its members being women. In much of the third world, women are considered as property, and have no legal rights in practice. Most feminists believe discrimination against women still exists in North American and European nations, as well as worldwide. Berten says in his *Basics of Literary Theory;* "Black Marxist feminists, for instance, were too quick to point out that black female writers had to cope not only with biases based on gender, but also with an equal crippling racial bias and that an approach that failed to take race into account would never be able to do justice to the work of black female writers." (103-4) Here, he says about the problems faced by the black feminist writers.

There are many ideas within the movement regarding the severity of current problems. Extremes on the one hand include some radical feminists such as Mary Daly who argues that the world would be better off with dramatically fewer men. There are also dissidents, such as Christina Hoff Sommers of Camille Paglia, who identify themselves as feminists but who accuse the movement of anti-male prejudices. Many feminists question the use of the feminist label as applying to these individuals. The feminist movement in the 21st century has its goal of improving the situation of women in non-Western countries. Feminists do not like to take men as participants in their movement. Kaja Silvermen (1992) argues that, masculinity impinges with such force upon femininity (that) to effect a large-scale reconfiguration of male identification and desire would, at the very least, permit female subjectively to be lived differently than it is at present. Calvin Thomas (2000) points out that this would most likely require feminist-informed men. In February 2003, second year English student Adam Webster was selected as their Women's Officer.

Some of the feminists do not agree with the view that men are equally oppressed under patriarchy, other feminists especially third-wave feminists agree that men are similarly oppressed and that gender equality means oppression of neither gender. Some argue that feminism makes men to be oppressed. Many sociologists reject it, but those who make this claim note that males die from suicide four times more frequently than females attempting suicide in the U.S. Even the global statistics are similar. Efforts have been made to curb sexual harassment against women in the workplace, but in resolving disputes, the concern is shown towards women and it has become an indirect discrimination. Since the 1990s, proving sexual harassment in the United States has been made much more difficult by Supreme Court decisions. Postcolonial feminists criticize Western forms of feminism, notably radical feminism and its universalization of female experience.

Feminist movement hardly affected Objectivism which is an individualist philosophy. It is rightly said that Objectivism holds that each person is a rational animal and that all individuals deserve to be free to make their own choices in life unless they initiate force against others. In its concepts of moral virtues or fundamental value, it does not distinguish between men and women. Because it rejects traditional restrictions on women and regards productive work as a virtue for women as well as men, Objectivism shares many of the views of classical, individualist feminism. This can be seen in the portrait of business executive Dagny Taggart in *Atlas Shrugged*, for example. In addition, Objectivists support the idea that a woman has right to abortion, as it is an extension of the individual's general rights to control the uses of her own body.

Ayn Rand herself rejected the label "feminist" declaring herself a "male chauvinist": 'In addition to her philosophical views per se, she had a view of sexual psychology that ascribed distinctive "masculine" and "feminine" attitudes to healthy men and women respectively. She argued that sexually, women should desire to engage in "hero worship," and that this required having at least one man to whom they could each look up. . . . There are strong strands of collectivism in today's feminism. These strands of thought treat men and women as hostile classes. Some infamously ascribe radically different thought patterns to men and women as such.

Objectivism rejects group-think of this sort, and holds that each individual should be jugged based on character, actions, and ability, not merely on the person's sex. Rand called herself a "male chauvinist" because she admired the many great men of history, to whom all of civilization owes so much.' (http://www.objectivist center.com) This proves that Rand is an anti-feminist.

Feminism was a logical topic for Objectivists. Rand had created female characters of unsurpassed independence and moral strength. In the Sixties, her *Objectivist Newsletter* (1958) had run a largely favourable review of Betty Friedan's *The Feminine Mystique*. It is said: "Rand believes that the most authentic human mode of being is the instrumental mode, and the instrumental mode is dedicated to the rational awareness of the world and to practical activity to produce desired effects. But it is men who are defined in relation to reality, with the relation being the instrumental one. If women, insofar as they are human beings, must relate to the world instrumentally, but insofar as they are women need not seek relations with the world but only with other people (men), then femininity is a defect in authentic humanity. This may be the saddest expression of Rand's Artistotelianism, because Rand's view seems to parallel Aristotle's theory that the female is a defective and ill-formed male." (13) (http://folk.uio.no/thomas/po/sexual-approaches.html) This proves Rand's definition of femininity as worship of masculinity.

In Barbara Braden's biography of Rand, Braden observes that, according to Rand: "Man . . . is defined by his relationship to reality; woman—by her relationship to man." (18) Nathaniel Branden's comments, both in his essay "Was Ayn Rand a Feminist?" and in his psychological work provide the clearest hints of Rand's views that women are important to men at philosophical level. In the life and novels of Rand, modernity's search for the heroic woman may very well have reached fruition. The let down of *We the Living* for some critics is Rand's shabby treatment of the leading lady, Kira. In all her works, the heroine is shown willing to the consumed by anyone and everyone without having the slightest thought of her self-respect. Be it Dagny or Dominique or Kira, each of these ladies, say the critics, has a trait to fall into the abyss of self-depravity. But in the opinion of Rand, sex is not physical, but an intellectual union. They are willing to do anything and everything for the love of their lives, even if it means destroying themselves in the process.

Feminists question the Golden one's subservience to Equality 7-2521 in *Anthem*. Rand might answer that the Golden One by bowing before Equality 7-2521, is just acknowledging the perfection in him and offering him herself as equality perfect. Sandra M. Gilbert and Susan Gubar say in *The Mad Woman in the Attic:* "Like the metaphor of literary paternity itself, the corollary notion that the chief creature man has generated is woman, has a long and complex history. From Eve, Minerva, Sophia, and Galatea onward, after all, patriarchal mythology defines women as created by, from, and for men, the children of male brains, ribs and ingenuity." (12) Hence, Rand here appears to mimic the biblical story of Adam and Eve, in which Eve springs from Adam's rib and is, in a certain sense, an extension of her husband.

Feminists also object to the naming of the Golden One who has now been named twice by her mate, and who apparently has no independent sense of self-worth. However, the Golden One is an active participant in the new world and that her part is to make the world beautiful and to endow her children with a sense of individualism. It is interesting that Liberty 5-3000 is referred to throughout the novel as the Golden One, the name assigned by Equality to her, but her name for him does not appear again. Feminists argue that this disparity shows the fundamental inequality in Rand's view of men and women. But Rand might say that the issue is entirely stylistic. After all, Equality is writing the test, and so if he incorporates the name assigned by the Golden One to him, it would not appear meaningful. Another significant incident is the offering of water to Equality. It symbolizes the Golden One's taking the role of a caretaker. This image is found very often in the Judaeo-Christian Bible. According to the New Testament, Jesus Christ often asked and received water from townspeople. Hamilton in *Historicism* (2007) comments that the woman is a historicizer: "To that extent she is much an impetus to progress as he, albeit an ironic one. From Milton's Eve, with her prophetic dreams, to the woman of D.H. Lawrence's *The Rainbow*, she activates male dissatisfaction from her subordinate position because she sees the *particular* advantages of a progress he can only idealize and spiritualize." (167) Rand holds the same opinion.

The character of the Golden One, like that of Equality, displays an important principle about Rand's theory of human nature. Rand thinks that independent persons form their own values. The Golden One loves Equality 7-2521 because his genius and proud independence cause him to stand out from the crowd. She chooses Equality 7-2521 for her own reasons and in defiance of social regulations. Her independent evaluation is responsible for the vitality of her emotional life in contrast to the dry existence of her peers. Because other members of society mindlessly conform that they have no passions of their own. Nothing means that much to the other members of the society because they have surrendered their minds to the state. The Golden One repudiates such a course of action emphatically. Society's beliefs are insufficient to shake her confidence in her own judgment, and this is what makes her a heroine.

The Golden One is originally proud, but her originality is at odds with her subservience to Equality. Her willingness to accept the new names that Equality gives her shows that she has broader willingness to accept the identity he gives her. Her underdevelopment is because of the fact that Rand presents her character as the only other example of goodness in a collective society. She is introduced by Rand, as the pinnacle of feminine power and wisdom. Feminists often criticize Rand for her view of women.

They argue that Rand dehumanizes and subjugates women to the will of men. I think it is apt to quote Barbara Branden who explains Rand's feeling about it in *The Passion of Ayn Rand*: 'In childhood, and all of her life, it appears that her most intense scorn was reserved for women. The scorn was evident in her recollections of childhood, and, equality, it is the impression of many of the people who knew her in later years. Even before adolescence, she was what she later called "an anti-feminist, I regarded men as a super value.'" (17) However, Rand believes that the success of women is in their innate wisdom and in their physical beauty.

In *We the Living* Kira's strong desire to be an engineer. Rand writes: "she stood watching her eyes wide, her lips smiling. A young man with a tanned face and a pipe in the corner of his mouth, walked swiftly up the narrow planks in the perilous framework, and the movements of his hands were brusque, precise, implacable like the blows of a hammer. He did not know how long she had been standing there. She had forgotten all but the work before her. Then, suddenly, her world returning to her with a jolt, in blinding second of clear, sharp perception—as if new eyes were taking a first glance at a new world and saw it as she had forgotten to see it—she wondered, astonished, why she was not there, on the scaffolding, giving orders like the man with the pipe, what reason could possibly keep her from work, her life work, her only desire." (323-24) Kira's thoughts are very well reflected in this book.

One can notice that Kira gets what she wants; though Lydia says she does not understand how Kira manages that. When Kira slips away from church and is returned home hours later by the police, she is never again sent to church. When her nanny buys a book Kira does not like, she throws it out of the window and her next books are those that Kira will approve. When her family returns to Petrograd, Kira announces that the she plans to attend the Technological Institute to study engineering. Her cousin tells her that she is being selfish by choosing that route because there are other careers better suited to women. In *The Fountainhead* Dominique has always been provoked by violence. Her lifelessness after the explosion is part of her rebirth. With the destruction of the building comes the destruction of her resistance to the world. The reader can understand later that Dominique's cutting herself in the car is her final act of machismo. The violence in the destruction of the building heals her and consoles her with Roark, the man she loves.

Rand describes Dominique: "She wore a gray suit: the contrast between its tailored severity and her appearance was deliberately exorbitant—and strangely elegant. She let the fingertips of one hand rest on the railing, a narrow hand ending the straight imperious line of her arm. She had gray eyes that were not ovals, but too long, rectangular cuts edged by parallel lines of lashes; she had an air of cold serenity and an exquisitely vicious mouth." (111) This description shows that she has more masculine qualities. She speaks her mind with no regard for the opinion of her audience. After writing a report on slums, her uncompromising attitude and refusal to identify herself with one camp or the other parallels Roark's self-possessed withdrawal from society.

Among the few women characters in the novel, Catherine Halsey is a victim of Toohey. The only passion of her life is her love for Keating. Katie illustrates an important aspect of Ayn Rand's philosophy. Her sweetness, innocence, and good nature are inadequate to protect her from Toohey's evil. A lack of independent thinking is what dooms Katie's attempt to gain love and happiness. Dagny Taggart in *Atlas Shrugged* as an engineer is not concerned with the public's fears and beliefs, but she is concerned only with the facts of the metal and its capabilities. By taking the full responsibility for the metal's performance, Dagny stakes her future on her own judgment.

Rand can also be considered a new historicist. New historicism explores new voice in literature. Among Russians writers, Rand's voice seems lonely. She negates history, politics, feminism, and anthropology in her works. According to Peter Barry's *Beginning Theory*, the term new historicism was coined by the American critic Stephen Greenblatt whose work *Renaissance Self-Fascinating: From More to Shakespeare* (1980) is usually regarded as its beginning. New historicism is a method based on the parallel reading of literary and non-literary texts, usually of the same historical period. It means a new historical essay will place the literary text within the frame of a non-literary text. The text and co-text used will be seen as expressions of the same historical moment.

Paul Hamilton explains New Historicism in his *Historicism*: "'New Historicism', though, is a label usually applied to a body of critical work on the English Renaissance, most conveniently and persuasively represented by the writings of Stephen Greenblatt." (131) It shows that new historicism is seen in the works of Greenblatt. Barry differentiates the 'new' from the 'old' historicism : "The practice of giving 'equal weighting' to literary and non-literary material is the first and major difference between the 'new' and the 'old' historicism we could cite E.M.W. Tillyard's *The Elizabethan World Picture* (1943) and *Shakespeare's History Plays* (1944), books against which new historicism frequently defines itself." (174) Thus, new historicism is a historicist rather than a historical movement.

Paul Hamilton answers the question what is new historicism in his *Historicism:* "Again and again, critics stage and confront an unavoidable mirroring of the present in the past and the dialectical struggle for objectivity which ensues. Attempts towards the struggle vary. For some, it represents the chance to take political initiatives, to appropriate polemically classical texts from the repressive ideologies they have been used to bolster in the past." (143) The right of any discourse to undermine a received hegemony, says Hamilton, colludes with market economics: "The ingenious exchange and articulations of power recorded by new historicists must, by their own argument, operate within their own work as it writes contemporary history as well as that of their chosen period or research. Greenblatt's art over its economic base." (146) Thus the new historicists, apart from writing about contemporary history, deal with their own chosen research.

It is, Barry continues, resolutely anti-establishment, always implicitly on the side of liberal ideals of personal freedom and accepting and celebrating all forms of difference and deviance. It is in this aspect that Rand is a new historicist. Her answer for the question that what she thinks of her antagonists' contention that the moral and political principles of Objectivism place her outside the mainstream of American thought proves this: "I don't acknowledge or recognize such a concept as a mainstream of thought. That might be appropriate to a dictatorship, to a collectivist society in which thought is controlled and in which there exists a collective mainstream—of slogans, not of thought. There is no such thing in America. There never was. However, I have heard that expression used for the purpose of barring from public communication any innovator, any non-conformist, anyone who has anything original to offer. I am an innovator. This is a term of distinction, a term of honour, rather than something to hide or apologize for. Anyone who has new or valuable ideas to offer stands outside the intellectual status quo. But the status quo is not a stream, let alone a mainstream. It is a stagnant swamp. It is the innovators who carry mankind forward." (http://elenspacenet/ ar-pboy.html) Thus Rand herself approves that she is an innovator.

Rand is a supporter of capitalism in a communist country like Russia. She proves in *Atlas Shrugged* that in a state-dominated system, unprincipled people get the favour of power-seeking politicians, brokering corrupt deals that allow them to stay in business by means of legislation. It is shown in the character of Mouch. Through the episode of the twentieth century Motor she shows the drawback of communism. First, Rand uses it to demonstrate the consequence of communism in practice. The primary question raised by a communist system is how an individual's needs can be determined if a group permits each individual to determine his or her own needs, the group faces the daunting task of having to satisfy every person's desires. Rand shows that the problem here is not that people are unscrupulous, but the problem is in such a case, there is no way to achieve objectivity. Undoubtedly hers is a new voice in Russia.

For the question that she has been quoted as saying, the cross is the symbol of torture, of the sacrifice of the ideal to the non-ideal and that she prefers the dollar sing. Rand says: "I never said that. . . . It is the symbol, clearly explained in the story, of free trade and, therefore, of a free mind. A free mind and a free economy are corollaries. One can't exist without the other." (http://ellenspacenet/ar-pboy.html) It shows that far Rand the dollar sign, as the symbol of the currency of a free mind. More than that, as to the historical origin of the dollar sign, although it has never been proved, one can conclude that it stands for the initials of the United States.

Rand's development and her philosophy are much more clearly placed in historical perspective in *Ayn Rand: The Russian Radical* (1995) by Chris Mathew Sciabarra. He writes: "What must be recognized here is Rand's use of dialectical method was essential to her Historical formulation of Objectivist principles, as was her original synthesis in the realm of content. In constructing a philosophy, every philosopher develops a certain content through the use of a specific method. In the seamless conjunction of a realist-individualist-libertarian content with a radical, dialectical method, Rand forged new system of thought worthy of comprehensive, scholarly examination." (20) It proves that in many ways, Rand was a veritable radical for capitalism.

Douwe Fokkema Elrud Ibsch writes in *Theories of Literature in the Twentieth Century:* "Here it may help to recall the original meaning of the word "dialectic," which is derived from a Greek word meaning "to carry on a discussion." Statement (thesis) and counterstatement (antithesis) may give rise to a certain conclusion (synthesis). Under favourable conditions the conclusion can be considered as belonging to a higher level. The conclusion, of course, may serve again as the starting point or first statement in a new discussion." (82-83) Thus Ibsch defines the word dialectic.

Sciabarra gives an example of Rand's rejection of formal dualism, i.e., her policy of consistently rejecting false alternatives in every branch of philosophy like altruism vs. hedonism in ethics, and statism vs. anarchism in politics and so on. Objectivism is just as much a revolt against the latter. Sciabarra finds evidence to say that throughout her life Rand was a Russian thinker: "Although she rejected both the mysticism of Russia's religious traditions and the secular collectivism of the Russian Marxists, she nonetheless remained a profoundly *Russian* thinker. Rand's Russian nature was not reflected merely in her heavy foreign accent or in the length of her novels. She was Russian in more fundamental ways. In the sweeping character of her generalizations, and in her passionate commitment to the practical realization of her ideals, Rand was fully within the Russian literary and philosophic tradition." (10) It shows that her views appear to be evolved in response to the dualities that she confronted in Russia.

Rand tends to think of the problems of life as problems about large wholes. Some people today think racist thoughts cannot be eliminated unless the system itself is changed. This is why Rand is considered a radical thinker. Her way of thinking more or less requires her to call for change in the system as a system, changes that would alter every aspect of life. Ayn Rand's novels blend two distinct genres. She follows the tradition of the Russian philosophical novelists like Tolstoy and Dostoevsky. But she is also Romantic in the tradition of Victor Hugo with her rich plots. Millions of readers have recognized that Rand's novels present a revolutionary view of morality and politics. However, very few of them have understood the foundations of her philosophic system. All these characteristics prove Rand to be a new historicist.

She says in the interview for the *Playboy*: "When one is certain that one's choice is final, then marriage is a desirable state. But this does not mean that any relationship based on less than total certainty is improper. I think the question of an affair or a marriage depends on the knowledge and the position of the two persons involved and should be left up to them. Either is moral, provided only that both parties take the relationship seriously and that it is based on values." (http://elenspacenet/ar-pboy.html) It proves that for Rand if a man has no clearly defined value he is not able to appreciate another person.

While speaking about art, Rand argues for the liberation of art from politics. In her stress on liberty of art, she can be treated as a postcolonial writer as postcolonialism argues for the liberty of a set of people or a race. The ancestry of this postcolonial criticism, according to Peter Barry, can be traced to Frantz Fanon's *The Wretched of the Earth* (1961) that voiced cultural resistance to France's African empire. The criticism, says Hamilton, emerges from the resulting portrait of an absolute power capitalizing on or colonizing all forms of cultural diversity: "Greenblatt's resistance to this, however, given his Foucauldian scepticism of enlightened reason, can only be expressed colonizing it on his own critical terms, showing a similar disrespect for its native interests, inhabiting it and articulating it without subscribing to its ends." (132) We can conclude that his critical momentum takes him to the heart of the problem with which postcolonial theory begins.

Ratna Kapur in his work *Erotic Justice: Law and the New Politics of Postcolonialism*, rightly points out in his introduction: "Each chapter challenges the dominant narratives of modernity that do not pay attention to the uneven development and variously disadvantaged histories of nations, races, communities and peoples. It is a challenge that does not consider imperialism as a thing of the past, but observes that colonialism's methods of domination are reproduced in different ways in the present, in and through the techniques of liberalism and through the different course of rights." (7) Here, he describes the methods of colonialism. As Hamilton writes in *Historicism:* "With its emphasis on an epistemological break between colonizer and colonized, postcolonialism renews the postmodern questioning of historicism. . . . Obviously the failure to treat subject peoples equally reflects on the ideals of justice possessed by the ruling society. If on the other hand, justice is abandoned and the colonized are defined as inferior or irredeemably 'other', the effects on the colonizers can still be disconcerting." (152) It shows that the discontinuities between the interests of colonizer and colonized make a coherent history of their exchanges virtually impossible.

Kapur shows here how James Mill justifies colonialism: "James Mill's logic is sometime regarded as an argument for the permanent segregation of India and of the natives. In the light of India's extreme difference, it is relegated to the primitive end of the civilization spectrum, regarded as incapable of being entitled to self-government." (24) But Rand protests colonialism of any form. This colonialism need not be political colonialism, but it may be ideological colonialism. She is against the Russian Marxist colonialism in other countries. She feels it as an ideological colonialism. She proves this in her *The Fountainhead* through the character of Toohey. Apart from his cult activities, Toohey seeks to establish dictatorship in America. The forces of collectivism are represented by his character.

As Tiffany K. Ng remarks Toohey is a Marxist intellectual, preaching communism to the masses, he desires to control editorial policy of the Wynand papers. Toohey makes *The Banner* his platform and hopes to spread the ideas necessary to establish a totalitarian state in America. In *Atlas Shrugged* James Taggart's character too represents collectivism. Taggart supports the doctrines of altruism and collectivism because they enable him to attack and enslave the productive men that he hates. He recognizes that the consistent application of these theories leads inevitably to natural socialism and communism, which are totalitarian dictatorships that imprison and exterminate the independent minds that he loathes. The acts of mass destruction wrecked by such collectivist murderers as Adolf Hitler, Joseph Stalin, Mao Tse-Tung, and Pol Pot are real life examples of the same nihilism that drives the actions of Taggart. This characteristic of detesting the ideological colonialism makes one consider Rand a postcolonial writer.

Rand once said that she does not refer to politics, but her literature cannot be called apolitical. From this we can conclude that Rand too is a postcolonial writer. Rand profoundly opposes the philosophy of hedonism. It is said hedonism is the doctrine which holds that the good is whatever gives you pleasure. Rand says: "My philosophy is the opposite of hedonism. I hold that one cannot achieve happiness by random, arbitrary or subjective means. One can achieve happiness only on the basis of rational values." (http://elenspacenet/ar-pboy.html) By this she does not mean whatever a man may arbitrarily or blindly declare to be rational are rational values. It is the science of ethics, to define for men what a rational standard is.

Rand believes that the kind of man who spends his time running after women is a man who despises himself. This type of man is reversing cause and effect in regard to sex. Sex is an expression of a man's self-esteem, of his own self-value. But the man who does not value himself tries to reverse this process. She most emphatically advocates black-and-white view of the world: "It means good and evil. Before you can identify anything as gray, as middle of the road, you have to know what is black and what is white, because gray is merely a mixture of the two. And when you have established that one alternative is good and the other is evil, there is no justification for the choice of a mixture." (http://elenspacenet/ar-pboy.html) This shows that she does not believe in the mixture of good and evil.

Then she speaks about Christ, who in terms of the Christian philosophy is the human ideal. He personifies that men should strive to emulate: "Yet, according to the Christian mythology, he died on the cross not for his own sins but for the sins of the non-ideal people. In other words, a man of perfect virtue was sacrificed for men who are vicious and who are expected or supposed to accept that sacrifice. If I were a Christian, nothing could make me more indignant than that: the notion of sacrificing the ideal to the non-ideal, or virtue to vice. And it is in the name of that symbol that men are asked to sacrifice themselves for their inferiors. That is precisely how the symbolism is used." (http://elenspacenet/ar-pboy.html) This is the torture Rand means.

Rand does not consider charity a moral duty. There is nothing wrong in helping other people, if and when they are worthy of the help and one can afford to help them. For her, compassion is proper only towards those who are innocent victims, but not against the principles of Objectivism. It depends on the circumstances. She says that she would step in the way of a bullet if it were aimed at her husband. She does not take it as self-sacrifice to die protecting that which she values if the value is great enough and we do not care to exist without it. This applies to any sacrifice for those whom one loves.

She cannot say if Objectivism as a philosophy will eventually sweep the world. Men have free will and it has always been the most rational philosophy. It is from this perspective that she would say that Objectivism will win. She is critical of the world as she sees it today. Through her books, she makes radical proposals for changing not merely the shape of society, but the very way in which most men work, think and love. But she is hopeful about man's future Collectivism, but freedom and individualism, and their political expression, capitalism, have not yet been discovered. Men will have time to discover them. It is rightly said: "Look at modern art and literature with their image of man as a helpless, mindless creature doomed to failure, frustration and destruction. This may be the collectivists' psychological confession, but it is not an image of man." (http://elenspacenet/ar-pboy.html) If it were, we would never have risen from the cave.

Sciabarra in *Ayn Rand: The Russian Radical* observes: "Objectivism is a seamless conjunction of method and content—of a dialectical method and a realist-egoist-individualist-libertarian content." (381) This unique synthesis, linking a multilevel, dialectical analysis to a libertarian politics is Rand's most important contribution to twentieth-century radical social theory. To pursue one's long-range interests rationally, one functions as neither master nor slave. Rand vividly illustrates these themes in her novel *The Fountainhead*, in which the Nietzschean kind of egoists are contrasted with self-sufficient Roark. Sciabarra continues: "For Nietzsche, Apollo and Dionysus embodied opposing metaphysical principles. In 1969, Rand would reiterate this Nietzschean symbolism in her assessment of New Left counterculture. In Rand's view, Nietzsche had used the symbols of Greek tragedy to express a false dichotomy between reason and emotion. But Rand saw Nietzsche's archetypes as appropriate symbols for what happens when reason and emotion are disconnected." (33) Thus Sciabarra differentiates Rand from Nietzsche.

Sciabarra's attempt is to elucidate Rand's thought to thinkers within the tradition of Continental philosophy. Sciabarra's work is not for the European audience, because Rand herself disliked contemporary Anglo-American philosophy. Sciabarra points out that the rejection of dualism is an important theme in her work. Rand certainly rejects a number of important dichotomies. Two of the most memorable passages in *Atlas Shrugged* are Francisco's speeches on sex and on money. In one of them he depicts that sex is at the same time a physical pleasure and a moral choice that embodies one's deepest values. In the other, he characterizes money both as the symbol of greed and as profoundly moral and noble. Virtue for Rand is defined in terms of its conduciveness to life.

In an article, Peter Saint Andre writes that part from the influence of the Russian philosopher, N.O. Lossky, Rand was influenced by the writer and theorist Yevgeny Zamyatin (1884-1937). He says Rand's thought was not a-historical, but that it was deeply affected by the philosophy and culture of the Silver Age in Russia. Other than Gorky, Yevgeny Zamyatin was the most influential writer in Russia in the years immediately following the Russian Revolution. Today Zamyatin is best-known for his dystopian novel *We* (1921). It is proved by the statement of Andre that Zamyatin is also an unjustly neglected master of the school of experimental modernism which flourished in Russia until the early 1920s.

His novel, *We* is a satirical critique of the Russian revolution which he had supported: "It is a novel which deserves to be much better known. In a totally regulated society where people are known by numbers, two lovers embody irrational urges towards which the state is hostile. The novel was tragically prophetic of the Stalinism which was to come. It is written in a dazzlingly poetic and experimental style, and it was quite clearly the model for both Aldous Huxley's *Brave New World* (1932) and George Orwell's *Nineteen Eighty-Four* (1949)." (http:// www.montex.co.uk.com) These characteristics apply to Rand's *We the Living*.

When Rand was in college, Zamyatin had greatest fame and influence in Petersburg. At that time, he was hero to writers and was admired for his fierce independence and literary individualism. He was the only writer in Russia to resist collectivism and conformity. He was a highly philosophical presence in Petersburg. Though Rand never mentions Zamyatin, she might have read some of his stories and essays. There are some striking similarities between their views and works. Zamyatin's influence on Rand is seen throughout *Anthem*—in their negative treatment of the realization of utopian ideals and the presentation of their philosophical beliefs in their works. Both the authors stress the need for human individuality and the word 'I' as its representation. In *Anthem*, the hero is a scientist who writes his story in a secret diary. The individual soul is oppressed by the collective. The protagonist rediscovers his soul through the intervention of the heroine.

These similarities may be because of Zamyatin's influence on Rand or both of them may have been influenced by a third source. They may have used common literary devices like the narrative as diary and theme as depicting a woman as the inspiration for a man's spiritual awakening. But there are significant differences between the two novels: "One difference is that *Anthem* ends optimistically with the protagonist escaping from the collectivist society and vowing to bring about a renaissance of civilization, whereas *We* ends with the spiritual death of the protagonist D-503 when he undergoes a forced fantasiectomy that removes his budding soul, with the capture and perhaps imminent capital punishment of D-503's lover I-330 for her subversive activities, and with success of the revolt of I-330's Mephis in doubt. Yet this difference is non-essential, since Zamyatin's aesthetic purpose was not the portrayal of an ideal but he continued questioning of assumptions and the inculcation of such an attitude in his readers; the ambiguities present at the end of *We* are quite in line with this purpose." (http://www.books. stpeter.im/rand/zamyatin-rand.html) Thus one cannot say that both the novels are entirely alike.

Another difference between the two dystopias is that in *We*, D-503 begins to question the received wisdom and to discover his soul only after being confronted by the femme fatale I-330, who tempts him intellectually. In *Anthem*, no one among the citizenry or from outside can tempt Equality 7-2521. The conflict in *We* is often seen as a kind of Hegelian dialectic between the thesis of Apollonian reason in the form of the Single State and the antithesis of Dionysian emotion in the form of the Mephis. Unlike *Anthem*, there are two opposing societies present in *We*. These differences point out each writer's view of human nature.

This difference is seen in the stylistic approaches of the authors. As Saint Andre says: "We leave the reader in a state of suspense and uncertainty, with battles still raging in the streets, I-330 and other Mephis leaders in captivity and awaiting execution, and D-503 spiritually lobotomized but still alive. *Anthem* ends far from the corruption of the city, high in the mountains where Equality 7-2521 and Liberty 5-3000 have discovered a house still standing from the Unmentionable Times, filled with books of ancient wisdom that Equality samples and then shares with Liberty, much as Eve shared the fruit of knowledge with Adam. The two of them essentially decide to found a new race of men that will wipe the slate clean and begin the world over again based on a holy reverence for the individual soul, for this god, this one word: 'I'." (http://www.books.stpeter.im/rand/zamyatin-rand.html) Therefore, Rand and Zamyatin are similar in their purpose.

Zamyatin is equally vexed up with the thoughtless game of hyper-plot to be found in novels of pure adventure. He argues that they reflect only one colour in the contemporary spectrum and that "to reflect the entire spectrum, the dynamics of the adventure novel must be invested with a philosophic synthesis on one kind or another" (106) Ayn Rand seems to follow this. Zamyatin says: "The purpose of art, including literature, is not to reflect life but to organize it, to build it" (130) Zamyatin sees Synthetism or Neo-realism as a way to overcome the struggle between two artistic methods—romanticism and realism. Similarly, Rand too sees her own aesthetic as a synthesis of realism and romanticism.

As it is said there are some similarities between Zamyatin's descriptions of Petersburg in his essays and Rand's descriptions in *We the Living*. For instance, both Zamyatin and Rand stress that Petersburg is a "he" whereas Moscow is a "she" (Zamyatin, 132 and Rand, 259). Zamyatin says that "Petersburg is all straight lines, all geometry and logic" (Zamyatin, 69) and Rand celebrates the fact that "its facets are cut clearly, sharply; they are deliberate, perfect with the straight-forward perfection of man's work" (229).

But these appear to be mere surface similarities based on the common reality of the city.

In the fictional essay "The New Utopia" by Jerome K. Jerome—quite popular in Russia around the turn of the twentieth century—the description of the society has a number of features familiar from *We* and *Anthem:* individuals have numbers rather than names, the family has been outlawed in favour of government-controlled breeding, and so on. Both Zamyatin and Rand may have been influenced by his writings. Another possible influence is Dostoevsky's *Notes from Underground.* In spite of the differences, between *We* and *Anthem*, there are interesting similarities between statements made by Zamyatin and Rand on literary style and the creative process. However, Zamyatin's plot-development is much more instinctive than Rand's. However, Rand's style may have been influenced by Zamyatin as also of Nietzsche, Hugo, Dostoevsky, and many others. For Zamyatin, the dialectical process of never-ending revolutions applies even to society. Revolution is everywhere, in everything and there is no final revolution. In Rand's *The Fountainhead* three autobiographical sentences are found from Roark on the same topic: "I inherit nothing. I stand at the end of no tradition. I may, perhaps, stand at the beginning of one." (24-25)

According to Rand, by the use of reason, humans can discover new resources and find how to use existing resources more efficiently. Rand writes in "The Cashing-in: The Student Rebellion," that our age is witnessing the ultimate climax, the cashing-in on a long process of destruction, at the end of the road laid out by Kant. Ever since Kant divorced reason from reality, his intellectual descendants have been diligently widening the breach. She says: "It has been said that Kant's dichotomy led to two lines of Kantian philosophers, both accepting his basic premises, but choosing opposite sides: those who chose reason, abandoning reality—and those who chose reality, abandoning reason. The first delivered the world to the second." (247) They had reduced philosophy into existentialism declaring: "Since this is reason, to hell with it!"

Stephen Cox has done a great service to liberty lovers with his biography, *The Woman and the Dynamo: Isabel Paterson and the Idea of America* (2004). He writes: "Without a doubt, she was one of the most important political writers of the twentieth century. Among the many measures of this importance is the fact that Paterson probably had greater influence on Ayn Rand than any of her other contemporaries. Together, these two women were the major inspiration for contemporary radical capitalist thought. Isabel Paterson and Ayn Rand are the two godmothers of the American Individualist movement." (http://www.aynrandlexicon.com) This Cox sees as another angle of Ayn Rand as a political writer.

Paterson was obviously an important source for Rand on many aspects of American history and government. Rand herself wrote that she had learned many important ideas from Paterson, in a letter dated 8 May 1948. These ideas seem to have been factual, but as Cox writes in *The Woman and the Dynamo*: "*We the Living* is an anticommunist novel, but its treatment of alternatives to communism, of political ideas in general, is sketchy, to say the least. It is a novel of psychological individualism. In succeeding years, Rand worked her way from a continental version of individualism influenced by Nietzsche to an American individualism grounded in a political theory of natural and equal rights." (221) Thus Rand's ideas were shifting significantly during the period of their first acquaintance.

In many of Rand's private philosophical journal entries throughout much of the 1930s, some traces of the distinctively Nietzschean can be seen. As it is said: "Rand argues for free will, and, even more importantly, she comes out in favour of what Nietzsche contemptuously called the Aristotlianism of morals, i.e., an ethics based squarely on logic and generalization. Rand simultaneously and explicitly rejected any need for what she called a history of ethics—and what Nietzsche called his genealogy of morals—only a very Aristotelian system of ethics which would stand or fall on its own merits. Even in the original edition of *We the Living*, Rand's heroine first gives voice to John Galt's "A is A," Rand's intended tribute to Aristotle in *Atlas Shrugged*, by saying that Steel is steel and Numbers are numbers. There is thus no reason to doubt Rand's own reports of admiring both Aristotle's logic and Nietzsche's heroic sensibility as early as her teens." (http://www.aynrandlexicon.com) It shows Cox's strong belief that Paterson was crucial to the development of Rand's belief in natural and equal rights.

Even before meeting Paterson, in a letter dated 12 Aug. 1936, Rand wrote to a reader who argued for the idea of umpired individualism: "I believe more firmly than in any Ten Commandments that the State exists only and exclusively to serve the individual." (35) Rand had still not met Paterson or her other political friends. Yet, she was an advocate of both economic and personal liberties. One can agree with the idea that capitalism in its extreme, without any checks and bounds, will be very bad. It is proved in China. It has adopted capitalism but does not have a democratic framework to keep its ills at bay and look how people are suffering. Her personal sufferings in Russia made her go to the other extreme of the scale. K. Balachander also said so in an interview: "Ayn Rand is far too intelligent to not understand that altruism is useful. Corporate Social Responsibility could be a good countervailing force to the ill-effects of capitalism—sort of like the bridle on the runaway capitalist horse. Every single human-created system causes problems—religion, for example, has killed far more human begins compared to every other scourge combined and it continues to kill." (http://www.aynrandlexicon.com) This is how Balachander justifies the opinion of Rand.

In the early 1970s, Rand's philosophy, Objectivism calmly spread. A few years later, perhaps, the time would arrive to begin political action. But without having the patience to wait, they held a founding convention in 1972 and created the U.S. Libertarian party. They began to run candidates for president and vice-president of the United States. In the 1972 presidential election, their candidate won one electoral vote. Though they did not get very far, they helped to educate many about the existence of Libertarianism, and many people read about Rand's ideas. So gradually thinker Russia seems to have realized the virtues of anti-collectivism as Medvedev has been playing the leading role even though the president has far more constitutional powers than the Prime Minister. It is stated in *The Hindu*: "Nevertheless, the Duumvirate has established credible division of authority, ending a long tradition of concentration of power in the hands of one ruler in the Kremlin that has hampered effective government. The emergence of two centres of power also helps to create checks and balances that have been conspicuously absent in the Russian system." (29 May 2009) This indicates the real separation of power.

Rand was not the only anti-collectivist writer of her generation, but she distinguished herself from most of them, however, by her realization that collectivism wasn't just an offence to human rights; it didn't even work. As several scholars have pointed out, however, the strange thing about this society, and about the totalitarian society in George Orwell's more famous novel *1984* (1949), is that it somehow survives with its technology intact. Throughout the existence of the Soviet Union, Western "experts" insisted that the communist experiment might still be considered successful, in some sense, because of its supposed advances in the economic sphere. They believed it was possible to trade personal liberty for economic efficiency. Rand knew that they were wrong. She knew that no person or group or persons can ever know to be successful in planning other people's lives. In *Anthem*, a council of state-appointed experts decides on the lifework of Equality 7-2521, who has a brilliant scientific mind. It sentences him to a career of street sweeping. This is Rand's way of asking: "How do you plan for the welfare of everyone when you cannot decide what is right for any particular person?" (30)

When Equality 7-2521 discovers the electric light, the planners try to prohibit its use: "'This would wreck the Plans of the World Council," said Unanimity 2-9913, "and without the Plans of the World Council the sun cannot rise.'" (73-74) That is what happens in every collectivist society. Rand gives an instance here. An individual will not be restricted to leave their house simply because he may commit a violent crime. Similarly, we should not restrict business simply because they may commit fraud. Capitalism applies the same principle to both, and insists on the same rigorous punishment in the case of violations. Rand's objectivism claims that man survives by means of mind contrasts with the claims of the two dominant philosophical schools of modern western culture, Marxism and Christianity. The Marxists hold that human beings produce economic value by manual labour. It implies that muscle power, not brain power, crates wealth. The idea conveyed through *Atlas Shrugged* is that mind must be free. To stifle the research of Galt or Rearden people like Floyd Ferris or Wesley Mouch placed a gun between the great mind and the facts that is studies. This is the reason why the freest countries are the most advanced, and why the brutal dictatorships are in terrible poverty. Ragnar Dannnesjkold tells Rearden that he wants to destroy Robinhood, the man who, according to legend, stole from the rich and gave to the poor. But Ragnar steals from the poor to give to the rich, i.e., he steals from the parasites to give goods back to the men who produced them.

In her fundamental beliefs Rand can be compared to Marx. For Rand, a person's goal is to use labour of workers to create something. She hates Marxism because it lacks the motivating factor as a person will not be rewarded for doing something worthwhile. She says that in Marxism the most needy gets the most. Therefore, under Marxism people are not motivated to create things as they will not be rewarded for it. For Marx, self-actualization is realized through the creation of physical items. A person is motivated to create products to see his ego in the object. Marx's goal is to create a system where this happens as efficiently as possible. So, both Marx and Rand believe that through achievements, a person realizes himself.

Rand and Marx differ only in their analysis of the problem. Marx holds that the problem with capitalism is that the means of production will be kept in the hands of a few rich. Hence, labour will be dissatisfied and people are disqualified from the tools to do meaningful work. For Rand, the problem lies in the ethical system which tells the achievers that they should serve those who do not achieve. It puts barrier after barrier in the way of those who seek self-realization through creation. Ursula Tidd is right when he says in *Simone de Beauvoir*: "Marx focused on the economic organization of society (the base) and argued that all aspects of life were, ultimately explicable through underlying economic relations." (18) This school of thought was founded by Karl Marx (1818-1883), a German philosopher, and Friedrich Engels (1820-1895), a German sociologist.

Peter Barry says that Marx and Engels called their economic theories Communism. They believe in the state ownership of industry, transport, etc. rather than private ownership. Lenin argued, says Barry, that literature must become an instrument of the party. Barry distinguishes the two streams of Marxism: "Steiner calls the two main streams of Marxist criticism, the Engelsian kind, which stresses the necessary freedom of art from direct political determinism, and the 'Leninist' which insists on the need for art to be explicitly committed in the political cause of the Left." (160) But both their views appear to support that good art always has a degree of form prevailing economic circumstances.

In K.M. Newton's selection *Twentieth-Century Literary Theory* it is said that the Vulgar Marxism of the 1930s views that there is a straightforward deterministic relation between bases and super structure, so that literary texts are seen as casually determined by the economic base. An example of this rigid kind of Marxist criticism is Christopher Caudwell's *Illusion and Reality* (1946). Newton writes: "Marxist literary theory starts from the assumption that literature must be understood in relation to historical and social reality as interpreted from a Marxist standpoint." (85) The current Marxist thinking has been influenced by the work of the French theoretician Louis Althusser. He offers, says Barry, ways of by-passing the crude base/superstructure model without giving up the Marxist thinking altogether. Althusser's views represent the revisionist Marxism.

It is mentioned about Althusser in Newton's *Twentieth-Century Literary Theory*: "He rejects the so-called 'vulgar' Marxist view that works of art are wholly determined by socio-economic forces and argues that they have 'relative autonomy' and are 'over-determined', that is, determined by a complex network of factors." (241) Thus revisionist Marxism rethinks and repackages the basic concepts in a more flexible form. The aim of Marxist criticism is to understand ideologies—the ideas, values and feelings by which men experience their societies at various times. It is continued in *Twentieth-Century Literary Theory* that Marxism can incorporate within itself all other forms of thought: "In contrast to the anti-interpretative tendency of much structuralist and post-structuralist influenced criticism, he supports an interpretative critical approach in which Marxism functions as the 'master code'." (242) This is how Marxism functions.

Both Rand and Marx regard the governmental form as the means of repression and they seek a change. Rand stresses that paid labour should be free and should never be forced. In this she agrees with Marx's distaste for coerced labour. It is interesting that these two extreme views agree on their fundamental belief of human self-realization, but they differ in their theories on how to achieve that goal. Terry Eagleton in his *Marxism and Literary Criticism* rightly says that an interesting parallel is Marx and Rand's analysis of social change. For Marx, there is the "mode of production" or "base"; from the base, the "relations of production" arise; and to defend these relations of production, there emerges a "superstructure" of ideas justifying what exists.

For Marx, social changes should be traced from the base; new means of production lead to changing property roles and status relations; which lead to new philosophies. For Rand, we can see the entire process reversed: changes originate at the level of the superstructure, when prevailing philosophical ideas fall into disfavour; these ideational changes prompt the re-organization of the relations of production, which finally lead to a new way of life and production. A changed set of social relations between the capitalist class who owns the means of production, and the proletarian class whose labour power the capitalist buys for profit leads to new ways of productive organization. Marxism regards the proletarian class as the economic base or infrastructure and from this a superstructure emerges. The superstructure consists of political, religious, ethical, aesthetic and other forms of social consciousness which is called ideology by Marxism.

It is explained by Douwe Fokkema Elrud Ibsch in *Theories of Literature in the Twentieth Century:* "It is not the consciousness of men that determines their being, but on the contrary their social being, that determines their consciousness. At a certain stage of their development the material forces of production in society come into conflict with the existing relations of production or, to mention the legal expression, the property relations within which they have been at work. From the conditions for the development of the forces of production these propriety relations become their fetters. Then a period of social revolution begins." (84) With this change in the economic basis the entire superstructure is transformed. Later comes the neo-Marxism developed by Th. W. Adorno, Walter Benjamin and Lucien Goldmann. Ibsch says in *Theory of Literature in the Twentieth Century:* "It is necessary to make a distinction between those who accept the Marxist canon as definite truth and those who regard it merely as a source of inspiration, particularly in the study of Marxist literary criticism." (115-16) Here, Ibsch wants to say that there is a difference between Marxists and those who are only inspired by the ideas of Marx.

In recent theory there has been a shift of emphasis towards the reader. In "Reception Theory and Reader-Response Criticism" of *Twentieth-Century Literary Theory* edited by K.M. Newton, it is said that in both reception theory and reader-response criticism the role of the reader is seen as crucial. The leading figure in reception theory is Hans Robert Jauss: "Jauss criticizes two opposite extremes in literary theory: formalism, with its lack of a historical dimension, and Marxist criticism with its view of the literary text as a purely historical product. He uses Gadamer's concept of a 'fusion of horizons', in which a fusion takes place between the past experiences that are embodied in the text and the interest of its present-day literary text and how it is perceived at different stages in history up until the present." (219) The reader-response critics, such as Bleich and Fish start from the premise that the object has no separate existence from the subject and they have explored the implications of this for literary criticism.

When asked, Rand dismisses the question of whether she is a philosopher or a novelist. She claims in *For the New Intellectual*: "every novelist is a philosopher . . . [whose only choice is] whether he holds his philosophical convictions consciously or subconsciously" (vii). Writing philosophy differs from that of artistic creation. Philosophic inquiry requires critical reflection in checking the accuracy of statements, in verifying underlying assumptions. Yet, advocates of Rand's philosophy rarely question her approach of deriving a system of philosophy from works of fiction, as Nathaniel Branden has recently noted that this combining of two different sorts of literary texts was an error in the development of Objectivism.

It is rightly pointed out: "Not only are art and philosophy two very different media of expression, requiring radically different creative approaches, each requires a very different frame of mind on the part of readers/viewers. Historically, these two literary forms have typically been combined for the purpose of proselytizing political or religious doctrine. This is why so-called docudramas often offend our sense of history. I would suggest that it was this combining of fiction and philosophy that made Objectivism susceptible to charges by critics of overstatement and melodramatic simplification. Fictional depictions are after all, dramatizations: "The myth of Prometheus, martyred for heroism, runs through all of Rand's novels. . . . [H]eroes are punished, if not defeated, by a corrupt society." (105 Journal, 1996) That IOS Journal report acknowledged that this is how many Objectivists respond to Rand's novels, explaining that this was a theme "driven by fiction's requirements for a different method—one that does not rely upon caricature and melodrama, which are inherent in the process of artistic selectivity." (http://www.aynrand.org) However, Rand's skill lies in the fusion of fiction and philosophy.

Her novels reveal the skill of a craftsman carving into rock new architectural forms. The images of the novels evoke a sense of reality where individuals can succeed in their efforts to form matter, rebuild their surroundings, and remake themselves. After reading about her version of the world order, anyone can realize the virtue of selfishness. In her economics, Adam Smith's philosophy is found. If people are provided with a free environment, they can improve and create things that make their lives better. Objectivism teaches one not to be ashamed of one's wealth creating ability. Thus, it prevents guilt at being smart. Preventing the guilt helps one to be happier. However, objectivism cannot say what makes us happy or how to pursue that happiness because it is a subjective question and in the point Objectivism cannot assist. It really can only tell us not to be guilty about pursuing the happiness if it does not harm another.

Rand has taught that the fundamental interests of individuals do not conflict when people respect the right of others to pursue their own lives and when they do not seek the gain possession of other's property through legalized force. Against the backdrop of today's conflicts, such a vision of human benevolence and social peace will continue to exercise a wide appeal. Today, the businessmen are frustrated as their earnings are drained away through taxation, their creative visions are restrained by government regulations, and their productive labours portrayed in the entertainment media as the work of villains who make themselves rich by stealing from the poor.

When the literature of the twentieth century has been engulfed by the wave of Naturalism, her novels are an outstanding exception. This can be proved from the words of Nathaniel Branden in *The Literary Method of Ayn Rand:* "she is a *Romantic Realist*. "Romantic"—because her work is concerned with *values*, with the essential, the abstract, the universal in human life, and with the projection of man as a heroic being. "Realist"—because the values she selects pertain to this earth and to man's actual nature, and because the issues with which she deals are the crucial and fundamental ones of our age. Her novels do not represent a flight into mystical fantasy or into the historical past or into concerns that have little if any bearing on man's actual existence. Her heroes are not knights, gladiators or adventurers in some impossible kingdom, but engineers, scientists, industrialists, men who belong on earth, men who function in modern society." (3) Thus her novels are both a continuation of the Romantic tradition and a significant departure from the mainstream of that tradition.

In order to justify her secular individualistic view of man and morality, Ayn Rand elaborated the system of thought, "Objectivism." It addresses issues of philosophy usually left to advanced academics. However, Objectivism is dismissed by academic scholars for a few reasons. Rand looked at the world in a different perspective, and she has long puzzled the intellectuals. Academic world has antagonism towards her views as they fail to understand that she was an individualist but not a subjectivist, an absolutist but not a dogmatist. They have ignored that she had given her original solutions to such intractable problems as how to ground values in facts. But even in academic world her ideas are accepted. For example, university fellowships and a subgroup within the American Philosophical Association to study Objectivism prove this. A legacy in defence of reason and freedom is left by Rand. It serves as a guidepost for the American spirit and it is relevant today when America and what it stands for are under assault.

Rand's Objectivism, as a philosophical system, is technically incomplete in many areas. Despite the neglect of Objectivism by academic, their studies, too, can benefit from serious consideration of the arguments Rand sketched. To be culturally literary in America means knowing about Ayn Rand and Objectivism. I feel that there is no other writer who could more readily cut through to the essence of an issue, explain it, resolve it, and impress the reader with the necessity that everyone understands it. She shows how and why philosophical ideas matter in our personal lives, in movie theatres, book stores and in parliament or Congress. Millions of Rand's readers may seek the spiritual and intellectual guidance in Christianity, Judaism, or in other secular philosophical systems, but never find it. That guidance is provided in Rand's work. During a period when Socialism, Fascism or Communism was pregnant in almost every nation in the West, she is courageous enough to swim against the tide of her time. As a result, she has been ignored by the philosophers and the political scientists, but she has a strong cult following and nearly every young person has, at least, a flirtation with her ideas.

Conclusion

It is truly said: "Against the backdrop of a state that grows ever larger and a chorus of muckrakers that grows ever louder, Rand's call for self-assertion by businessmen will continue to attract ever more adherents. But most of all, Ayn Rand will continue to appeal to idealistic young people, who have always been the greatest course for her audience. Hearing in their classrooms that truth is a social construct, that reason is sophistry, that morality is service to the public interest, the politics is group conflict—and that art is either rage, mockery, or emotional self-expression—young people will continue to turn to Ayn Rand." (http://www.objectivist.com)

In October 1964, Rand is said to have received a letter from L. Quiney Mumford, Librarian of Congress, inviting her to place her manuscripts and personal papers in the library. Though she responded positively, Rand never formalized her acceptance. After her death, her papers and manuscripts were left to Peikoff. In 1991, Peikoff decided to donate a portion of her manuscripts to the Library. However, he returned two pagers of *The Fountainhead* as a memento. It is said: "In 1998, Peikoff mentioned in a newspaper interview that he still had the two pages. The Library subsequently threatened legal action against him. The government claimed that the pages were of the materials he had donated, and thus were the property of the Library.

In 2002, Peikoff acquiesced and turned over the pages, rather than fight the Library in court. The remainder of Rand's papers are in private hands. A large portion of them are in the possession of the Ayn Rand Institute Archives. The books, letters and Journals of Ayn Rand have been published based on these materials. Another group of Rand manuscripts, consisting of draft versions of many of her non-fiction articles, were in the possession of Robert Hessen.

When Hessen announced that he would sell these manuscripts at an auction in 1998, Peikoff disputed Hessen's ownership of the papers. However, no legal action was filed. The auction was allowed to proceed, and included both Hessen's materials and some of Rand's papers that belonged to Barbara Branden. This material is now in the hands of various private collectors." (http://www.aynrandlexicon.com)

Inspired by Objectivism, a coffee shop in New York City is named as 'The Fountainhead Café.' The sign reads "Eat Objectively, Live Rich," Edward Wayne Younkins says rightly in *Philosophers of Capitalism:* "Since Rand's death, the estate of Ayn Rand has continued to issue a number of editorial collections of Rand's writings. These books have—to varying degrees—aided scholars in their attempt to trace the development of Rand's thought." (190) A website, namely "Randex," updates a list of recent media references to Rand or her work. In the summer of 2007, BioShock, an award-winning video game was released. It is built around a story influenced by Rand's philosophy and *Atlas Shrugged*. Rand appears on a 33 cent U.S. postage stamp, which debuted 22 April 1999 in New York City. Objectivism has remained popular on college campuses, with many student groups deciding to promote and study the philosophy of Objectivism spread across the U.S., Australia, Canada, Israel, the Netherlands, New Zealand and Norway.

Rand is not found in the comprehensive academic reference texts, the Oxford Companion to Philosophy or the Cambridge Dictionary of Philosophy. A lengthy article on Rand appears in the Internet Encyclopedia of Philosophy. She has an entry forthcoming in the Stanford Encyclopedia of Philosophy and a brief entry in the Routledge Encyclopedia of Philosophy which features the following passage: "The influence of Rand's ideas was strongest among college students in the U.S.A. but attracted little attention from academic philosophers. . . . Rand's political theory is of little interest. Its unremitting hostility towards the state and taxation sits inconsistently with a rejection of anarchism, and her attempts to resolve the difficulty are ill-thought out and unsystematic. Allan

Gotthelf (chairman of the Ayn Rand Society) responded unfavourably to this entry and came to her defence. He and other scholars have argued for more academic study of Objectivism, viewing Rand's philosophy as a unique and intellectually interesting defence of classical liberalism that is worth debating. Despite the claims of critics such as William F. Buckley, who called her philosophy "stillborn," Ayn Rand's books remain popular, selling over 400,000 copies per year." (http://www.lrb.co.uk.com)

If we see the recent economic turmoil in America, we come to the conclusion that Rand's prophesy about it in *Capitalism: The Unknown Ideal* comes true. The present state of economy reminds one of the depressions in America in 1929. The present condition is explained in *The Hindu*: "In the United States, Dow Jones slipped below 8000 in the very week President Barack Obama took office, the automobile industry continues its spiral (Toyota has already displaced GM as the world's largest automarker) and in one day in January, some leading companies announced shedding 72,000 jobs." (4 February 2009) The same condition prevails in Russia. The crisis, as stated in *The Hindu* had badly hit Russia as the rouble plunged 25 cent to the dollar. It is said: "Finance Minister Alexei Kudrin said 2009 would be the worst year for the Russian economy since World War II, with the budget deficit touching the $70-billion mark." (*The Hindu*, 2 May 2009)

Rand is everywhere on the internet: stickers, coasters, car number plates, CDs featuring a Randian 'Concerto of Deliverance' at starshipaurora.com. Randians can meet 'at least' four thousand other, it is claimed, through the Objectivist dating agency at theatlasphere.com, which last January carried an ad for Ayn Rand social evening at a New York City restaurant called Proter's. Professional philosophers can join the Ayn Rand Studies, which was founded in 1999, and continues to run out of New York University. A paper by Slavoj Zizek is another highlight. In 2001, the Anthem Foundation for Objectivist Research is said to have established a $300,000 fellowship in the philosophy department at the University of Texas at Austin. Austin's current Anthem fellow is the author of, among other things, a paper called 'Money Can Buy Happiness'. Fellowships have also been established at the University of Pittsburgh and Ashland University in Ohio.

Rand's ideas could withstand fierce opposition and influenced our culture and politics. It is because those ideas convey her bright vision of an Atlas society composed of rational and responsible individualists. She will continue to leave her ineffaceable stamp on our future. The continued refusal of the intelligentsia to recognize her, merely serves to make her accomplishment all the more remarkable. I believe the words that when the dust has settled, a few decades or centuries from now, one assumes that Keynes and Galbraith, Marx and Rawls, Dreiser and Lewis and Sinclair—all of the thinkers and writers of the failed Left—will have been consigned to oblivion and the names that are honoured will be Hayek, Popper, Friedman, Orwell and Ayn Rand.

Bibliography

Aksyonov, Vassily. *Generations of Warmth*. New York: Vintage, 1994.

Amsden, Diana Avery, *An Index to Ayn Rand's "Atlas Shrugged."* New York: Diana Avery Amsden, 1983.

Andre, Peter Saint. *Journal of Ayn Rand Studies*, 4.2 (2003): 285-304.

Ashcroft, Bill, Gareth Griffiths, Helen Tiffin. *Empire Writes Back*. Minneapolis: University of Minnesota Press, 2001.

Aune, James Arnt. *Selling the Free Market: The Rhetoric of Economic Correctness*. New York: Guilford Press, 2001.

Badwar, Neera K. *Is Virtue Only a Means to Happiness?* New York: The Objectivist Centre, 2001.

Baker, James J. *Ayn Rand*. USA: Twayne, 1987.

Baring, Maurice. *An Outline of Russian Literature*. New York: Nova Science, 2006.

Barker, Adele Marie. *A History of Women's Writing in Russia*. Cambridge University Press: Jehanne M. Gheith, 2002.

Barry, Norman P. *On Classical Liberalism and Libertarianism*. New York: St. Martin's Press, 1987.

Barry, Peter. *Beginning Theory*. UK: Manchester University Press, 1995.

Barthes, Roland. *Mythologies*. London: Random House, 1957.

Bateson, F.W. *The Cambridge Bibliography of English Literature*. Vol 3. UK: Cambridge University Press, 1940.

Beheric, Patrick. "A Defence of Collectivism." *Gopher*, 1999. (http://www.geocities.com/c_ansertoAnthem.html)

Berliner, Michael S. ed. *Letters of Ayn Rand*. New York: Plume, 1995.

Bernstein, Andrew. *Ayn Rand for Beginners*, Hanover, New Hampshire: Steerforth Press of America, 2005.

_____. *The Capitalist Manifesto: The Historic, Economic and Philosophic Case for Laissez-Faire*. Lanham, Maryland: University of Press of America, 2005.

_____. Objectivism in One Lesson: An Introduction to the Philosophy of Ayn Rand. Lanham, Maryland: Hamilton Books, 2009.

Berten, Hans. *Literary Theory: The Basics*. London: Routledge, 2004.

Biddle, Craig. *Loving Life: The Morality or Self-Interest and the Facts that Support it*. Glen Allen Press, 2002.

Bidinotto, Robert James. "The Revolutionary Philosophy of *Atlas Shrugged.*" *The Atlas Society*. Washington DC: Connecticut, 2007. (www.objectivistcentre.org.com)

Binswanger, Harry. *Introduction to Objectivist Epistemology*. New York: Penguin, 1979.

_____. *Ayn Rand Lexicon: Objectivism from A to Z*. New York: New York American Library, 1986.

_____. *The Biological Basis of Teleological Concepts*. Los Angeles: Ayn Rand Institute Press, 1990.

Bishop, Lloyd. *In Defence of Altruism: Inadequacies of Ayn Rand's Ethics and Psychological Egoism*. New Orleans: University Press of the South, 2001.

Borovsky, Robert Leach Victor. *A History of Russian Theatre*. UK: Cambridge University Press, 1999.

Boumel, Adam, "A Fight for Ego." (http://www.termpapers.com/Termpapers/Miscellaneous/A_Fight_for_Ego.sc.html)

Bowden, Tom Butler, *Nicholas Brealy*. UK: London, 2003.

Branden, Barbara. *The Passion of Ayn Rand*. New York: Anchor, 1986.

Branden, Nathaniel. *Who Is Ayn Rand?*. Paperback Library, 1964.

_____. "Answer to Ayn Rand: Part 1 to 2." *The Objectivist*, 16 Oct. 1968.

_____. *Breaking Free*. USA: Bantam Doubleday Dell, 1970.

_____. *Psychology of Romantic Love: Romantic Love in an Anti-Romantic Age*. New York: Penguin, 1980.

_____. *The Romantic Love Question & Answer Book*. Los Angeles: J.P. Tarcher, 1982.

_____. *Honouring the Self: Self-Esteem and Personal Transformation*. Los Angeles: J.P. Tarcher, 1983.

_____. "The Benefits and Hazards of the Philosophy of Ayn Rand: A Personal Statement," *Journal of Humanistic Psychology*, 24 (1984): 39-64.

_____. *How to Raise Your Self-Esteem: The Proven Action-Oriented Approach to Greater Self-Respect & Self-Confidence*. USA: Bantam Hardcover edition, 1987.

_____. *Taking Responsibility: Self-Reliance & the Accountable Life*. New York: Fireside, 1997.

_____. *A Women's Self-Esteem: Struggles and Triumphs in the Search for Identity*. USA: Jossey-Bass, 1998.

_____. *Self-Esteem at Work: How Confident People make Powerful Companies*. USA: Jossey-Bass, 1998.

_____. *The Art of Living Consciously: The Power of Awareness to Transform Everyday Life*. NY: Fireside and Colophon, 1999.

_____. *Self-Esteem Everyday: Reflections on Self-Esteem and Spirituality*. New York: Fireside and Colophon, 1998.

_____. *The Moral Revolution in Atlas Shrugged*. New York: Poughkeepsie, 1999.

_____. "Who Owns Objectivist?" *TDO*, 25 Dec. 1999.

_____. *The Literary Method of Ayn Rand*. USA: The Atlas Society, 2000.

_____. *The Psychology of Self-Esteem: A Revolutionary Approach to Self-Understanding That Launched a New Era in Modern Psychology*. USA: Jossey-Bass, 2001.

_____. Devers Branden and Ayn Rand. Exercised Part 4 of Pre-Final version of Judgment Day. 1 June 2007 (nathanielbranden.com).

Britting, Jeff. *Ayn Rand*. New York: Overlook Duckworth, 2004.

Bulgakov, Micheal Afanasovich, Michael Karpelson. *The Master and Margarita*. Lulu Press: Michael Karpelson, 2006.

Burns, Jennifer. *Goddess of the Market: Ayn Rand and the American Right*. New York: Oxford University Press, 1975.

Caplan, Bryan. 1991. (http://economics.gmu.ed/bcaplan/atlas.html)

Capitalism: The Only Moral Economy. David Matthew Press. Wichita, KS. (2001) (http://www.aynrand.org/site/pageServer?Pagename_education_contests_aswinner_2001)

Cederholm, Mark. "The Objectivist Trilogy" (www.plerssen.com)

Change, Yosun. "Musings on Atlas Shrugged." 30 Aug. 2005. (http://atlasshruggednovel.blogspot.com)

Chesterton, G.K. *The Everlasting Man*. Objective Systems, CAN, 2006.

Childs, Roy A., Jr., Taylor, Joan Kennedy, ed. *Liberty against Power*. San Francisco: Fox & and Wilkes, 1994.

Clyman, Toby W. and Diana Greene, ed. *Women Writers in Russian Literature*. Greenwood: Praeger, 1996.

Coloman, Rani. Rev2. 19 February 2001. (http://www.ninetyandnine.com/Archives/20010219/review2.htm)

Cookinham, Frederick. *The Age of Rand; Imagining an Objectivist Future World*. USA: iUniverse, 2005.

Cornwell, Neil. *Reference Guide to Russian Literature*. USA: Fitzroy Dearborn, 1998.

Copleton, Frederick. *A History of Philosophy*. Kent: Burns & Oats, 1996.

Cox, Stephen. "Ayn Rand: Theory versus Creative Life," *Journal of Libertarian Studies*. 8 (1) (1986): 19-29.

_____. *Anthem: An Appreciation*. San Diego (www.atlassociety.org.com)

_____. *The Woman and the Dynamo*, New Jersey: Transaction, 2004.

Den Uly, Douglas, Douglas B. Rasmussen. "Nozick on the Randian Argument." *The Personalist*, 59 (1978): 184-205.

_____, ed. *The Philosophical Thought of Ayn Rand*. USA: Board of Trustees of the University of Illinois, 1984.

Den Uly, Douglas J. *"The Fountainhead": An American Novel*. New York: Twayne, 1999.

Dickens, Charles. *Hard Times*. New York: Barnes and Noble, 2004.

Doherty, Brian. *Radicals for Capitalism: A Freewheeling History of the Modern American Libertarian Movement*, New York: Public Affairs, 2007.

Dokupil, Susanna. *"Atlas Shrugged:* An American Apocalyptic Tale." 8 Feb. 2004. (http://americansfuture.org/doublethink/2004/02/atlas_shrugged_an_american _apocaly ptic_tale/)

Donna. *Ayn Rand and Business*. USA: Texere, 2001.

Dragon, Top. Rev. "Highly Recommended." (Centennial Edition Hard Cover). USA, 6 Aug. 2009.

Dubb, Ruth. Rev. "One Small Voice, Mine." (Alexandria, V A United States), 4 Oct. 2001. (http://www.amazon.com/gp/cdp/member reviews/AN7IJ6YQ4Q0OP?ie=UTF8 &sort_by=MostRecentReview)

Eagleton, Terry. *Marxism and Literary Criticism*. New York: Methuen, 1976.

Efron, Robert. "Biology without Consciousness—and Its Consequences," *Perspectives in Biology and Medicine*, 2 (1067), (1).

Ellis, Albert. *Are Capitalism, Objectivism and Libertarianism Religions? Yes!* Santa Barbara, California: Walden There, 2006.

Fleming, Thomas. *The Morality of Everyday Life*. Colombia: University of Missouri Press, 2004.

Forman, Frank. "Ayn Rand and Natural Rights," *The Metaphysics of Liberty*. Theory and Decision Library, Series A. New York: Kluwer Academic, 1989.

Fromm, Eric. *Escape from Freedom*. New York: Holt, Rinehart and Winston, 1941.

_____. *Man for Himself*. Great Britain: Taylor & Francis Group, 1971.

Gilbert, Sandra M., Susan Gubar. *The Madwoman in the Attic*. London: Yale University Press, 2000.

Gladstein, Mimi Reisel. *The New Ayn Rand Companion*. USA: Greenwood Press, 1999.

_____. *Atlas Shrugged: Manifesto of the Mind*. New York: Twayne, 2000.

Gordon, Philip. "The Exroflective Hero: A Look at Ayn Rand," *Journal of Popular Culture*, 10 (4) (1977): 701-10.

Gotthelf, Allan. *On Ayn Rand*. Belmont, California: Wadsworth, 1999.

Hamilton, Paul. *Historicism*. London: Routledge, 2007.

Hammer, Richard. Rev. *Formulations* (Winter 1995-96). (http://libertariannation.org/a/f32h5.html)

Harrison, Charles, Paul Wood. ed. *Art in Theory, 1900-2000: An Anthology of Changing Ideas*. USA: Blackwell, 1993.

Harryman, David, ed. *Journals of Ayn Rand*. New York: Plume, 1999.

Hegel, George Wilhelm Friedrich. *The Philosophy of Fine Art*. Theommes Continuum, 1999.

Heller, Anne. *Ayn Rand and the World She Made*. New York: Doubleday, 2009.

Hessen, Robert. "Objectivist, 1962-1976," ed. Lora Ronald & Henry William Langton. *The Conservative Press in Twentieth-Century America*. Westport, Connecticut: Greenwood, 1999, 349-56.

Hicks, Stephen. "Ayn Rand and Contemporary Business Ethics," *Journal of Accounting, Ethics and Public Policy*, 3 (1) (2003): 1-26.

Holzer, Erika. *Double Crossing*. USA: G.P. Putnam's, 1920.

_____. *Eye for an Eye*, USA: Tor, 1993.

_____. *Ayn Rand: My Fiction Writing Teacher*. California: Madison Press, 2005.

Hornstein, Alan D. "The Trials of Howard Roark," Vol 23, no. 4 (1999). (http://tarlton.law.utexas.edu.html)

Hospers, John. *An Individualist Philosophical Analysis*, New Jersey: Prentice-Hall, 1967.

Hudgins, Edmund L. rev. "Atlas Shrugged as a Prophecy." (http://www.objectivistcenter.org/cth-1990-Rand_pro.aspx)

Hudgins, Edward. *An Objectivist Secular Reader*. Washington, DC: The Atlas Society, 2008.

Ibsch, Douwe Fokkema Elrud. *Theories of Literature in the Twentieth Century*. Hyderabad: Orient Longman, 1978.

Jefferson, Thomas, Sam Fink Jefferson. *Declaration of Independence*. USA: Scholastic, 2002.

Johnson, Donald Leslie. *The Fountainheads: Wright, Rand, the FBI and Hollywood*. Jefferson, North Carolina: McFarland, 2005.

Kate, Lady. Rev. "Brilliant, very flawed work by brilliant, very flawed woman." Middleton, NJ, USA, 3 February 2003.

Kelley, David. *The Evidences of the Senses: A Realist Theory of Perception*. Louisiana: Louisiana State University Press, 1986.

_____. Rev. "Unrugged Individualism: The Selfish Basis of Benevolence." New York; Poughkeepsie, 1996.

_____. *A Theory of Abstraction*. Poughkeepsie, New York: The Objectivist Centre, 1999.

_____. *The Contested Legacy of Ayn Rand: Truth and Toleration in Objectivism*. 2nd ed. New Transaction Publishers, 2001.

Kirkpatrick, Jerry. *In Defence of Advertising: Arguments from Reason, Ethical Egoism and Laissez-Faire Capitalism*. West Port, CT: Greenwood, 1994.

Klaier, Glenn. *The Last Day*. New York: Warner, 1998.

Knapp, Shoshena Miligram. *Ayn Rand's Draft: The Labours of a Literary Genius*. Connecticut Second Renaissance Books, 1998.

Kropotkin, P. *Ideals and Realities in Russian Literature*. USA: Alfred A. Knopf, 1905.

Levina, David E. rev. "Brilliant despite stilted dialogue." Peekskill, NY, 9 March 2001.

_____. rev. "Library Journal—A Public Scandal." (http://search.barnesandnobel.com/capitalism/AynRand/e/9780451147950)

Long, Roderick T. *Reason and Value: Rand versus Aristotle*. Poughkeepsie, New York: The Objectivist Centre, 2000.

Lukas, George. *The Theory of Novel*. Berlin: P. Cassirer, 1920.

Lyotard, Jean-Francois. *The Postmodern Condition: A Report on Knowledge*. England: Manchester University Press, 1979.

Machan, Tibor R. "Nozick and Rand on Property Rights," *The Personalist*, 58 (1977): 192-95.

_____. *Ayn Rand*. New York: Peter Long, 2000.

_____, ed. *Ayn Rand at 100*. New Delhi, India: Pragun, 2006.

Maloney, Ryan. 5 October 2000 http://www.vu.union.edu/~concordy/20001005/ae4.html

Marx, Karl. *Theories of Surplus Value*. New York: Prometheus, 1999.

_____. *Das Capital*. Washington DC: Regnery, 2000.

Mayhew, Robert, *Ayn Rand and Song of Russia*. Scarecrow Press, 1947.

_____. *Ayn Rand's Marginalia: Her Critical Comments on the Writings of over 20 Authors*. Connecticut: Second Renaissance Books, 1995.

_____, ed. *Essays on Ayn Rand's "We the Living."* USA: Lexington, 2004.

_____, ed. *Essays on Ayn Rand's "Anthem."* USA: Lexington, 2005.

_____, ed. *Ayn Rand: The Best of Her Q & A*. New York: New American Library, 2005.

_____, ed. *Essays on Ayn Rand's "The Fountainhead."* Lanham: Lexington, 2007.

McHale, Brian. *Postmodernist Fiction*. London: Routledge, 1987.

McQuillan, Martin. *Paul de Man*. London: Routledge, 2001.

Mehta, Neil. 1999-2000. http://www.4freeessays.com/essays/1016. schtml

Merrill, Ronald E. *With Charity toward None: An Analysis of Ayn Rand's Philosophy*. New Jersey: Adam's, 1972.

_____. *The Ideas of Ayn Rand*. La Sale, Illinois: Open Court, 1991.

Mirsky, DS. Francis James Whitfield. *A History of Russian Literature*. New York: Northwestern University Press, 1958.

More, Thomas. *Utopia*. United Kingdom: The Press Syndicate of the University of Cambridge, 1989.

Morrissey, Edward. *The Wall Street Journal*. 10 Oct. 2007. (http://www.captainquarterblog.com/mt/archives/014620php)

Morrison, Simon Alexander. *Russian Opera and the Symbolists Movement*. London: University of California Press, 2002.

Newton, K.M. *Twentieth-Century Literary Theory*. London: MacMillan Education, 1988.

Ng, Tiffany K. "Who Shall Rule the Soul?" (http://www.angelfire.com/tn/tifni/misc/fountainhead.html)

Nietzsche, Friedrich. *Thus Spake Zarathustra: Book for All and None*. Germany: Ernst Schmeitzner, Orrin, C. Judd, 2000. (http://www.brothersjudd.com/index.cfm/fuseaction/reviews.detail/book_id/7 68/Andam/htm)

Nozick, Robert. "On the Randian Argument," *The Personalist*, 52 (1971): 282-304.

O'Neil, Patrick M. "Ayn Rand and the Is-Ought Problem," *Journal of Libertarian Studies*, 7 (1) (1983): 81-99.

Paul, Ellen Frankel, Fred D. Miller Jr., Jeffrey Paul. *Objectivism, Subjectivism and Relativism in Ethics*. United Kingdom: The Press Syndicate of the University of Cambridge, 2008.

Paxton, Michael, *Ayn Rand: A Sense of Life: The Companion Book*. Utach: Gibbs Smith, 1998.

Peikoff, Leonard. *The Ominous Parallels*. New York: Penguin, 1982.

_____. *Objectivism: The Philosophy of Ayn Rand*. New York: Penguin, 1991.

_____. *The DIM Hypothesis: The Epistemological Mechanism by Which Philosophy Shapes*, Connecticut: Second Renaissance Books, 2004.

Perrin, Vincent. *Ayn Rand: First Descriptive Bibliography*. Quill & Brush, 1990.

Plasil, Ellen. *Therapist*. New York: St. Martin's/Marek, 1985.

Plato. *The Republic*. Middlesex: The Echo Library, 2006.

Podritske, Marlee, Peter Schwartz., ed. *Objectively Speaking: Ayn Rand Interviewed*. Maryland: Lexington Books, 2009.

Potter, Russel A. *Spectacular Vernaculars: Hip-Hop and the Politics of postmodernism*. US: State University of New York Press, 1995.

Rader, Scott. Rev. 24 April 2000 (http://www.scottarder.net/aynrand.html)

Raimondo, Justin. *Reclaiming the American Right: The Lost Legacy of the Conservative Movement*. Burlingame, California: Centre for Liberation Studies, 1993.

Ramana. "The Woman Who Launched a Movement." 2 August 2008. (http://dukkipati.blogspost.com)

Rand, Ayn. *For the New Intellectual*. USA: Penguin Group, 1961.

_____. *We the Living*. New York: New American Library, 1936.

_____. *Anthem*. New York: New American Library, 1938.

_____. *The Fountainhead*. New York: New American Library, 1943.

_____. *Atlas Shrugged*. New York: New American Library, 1957.

_____. *Capitalism: The Unknown Ideal*. New York: New American Library, 1967.

_____. *The Virtue of Selfishness: A New Concept of Egoism*. New York: The New American Library, 1964.

_____. "To Whom It May Concern." *The Objectivist*, May 1968.

_____. *The Romantic Manifesto*. New York: New American Library, 1971.

_____. *The Night of the January 16th*. New York: American Library, 1971.

_____. *The New Left: The Anti-Industrial Revolution*. New York: New American Library, 1971.

_____. *Philosophy: Who Needs It?* USA: New American Library, 1974.

_____. *Introduction to Objectivist Epistemology*. United States: New American Library 1979.

_____. *Voice of Reason*. USA: Penguin, 1990.

_____. *Russian Writings on Hollywood*. California: Marinadel Ray, 1999.

_____. *The Art of Fiction*. New York: Plume, 2000.

_____. *The Art of Non-Fiction*. New York: Plume, 2001.

Rasmussen, Douglas, "Essentialism, Values and Rights: The Objectivist Case for the Free Society," *The Libertarian Reader*. New Jersey: Rowman & Littlefield, 1982.

Riesman, George, *Capitalism: A Treatise on Economics*. Ottawa, Illinois: Jameson, 1996.

Richman, Sheldon. "Neglected Fritch Anniversary," Jan. 1997. (http://www.fff.org/comment/ed109a.asp)

Rius. *Marx for Beginners*. Great Britain: Writers and Readers Publishing Cooperative, 1977.

Rivera, David Allen. "*Atlas Shrugged*—Final Warning: A History of the New World Order." 2007 (http://www.real-debt-elimination.com/FinalWarning-a-history-of-thenewWorldOrder)

Rousseau, Jean-Jacques. *Confessions*. USA: Oxford University Press, 2000.

Robbins, John W. *Without Prayer: Ayn Rand and the Close of Her System*. Hobbs, New Mexico: Trinity Foundation, 1997.

Ryan, Scott. *Objectivism and the Corruption of Rationality: A Critique of Ayn Rand's Epistemology*. USA: Writers Club Press, 1995.

Sciabarra, Chris Matthew, *Ayn Rand: The Russian Radical*. University Park PA: The Pennsylvania State University Press, 1995.

_____. *Ayn Rand: Her Life and Thought*, Poughkeepsie, New York: The Atlas Society, 1996.

_____. "A Renaissance in Rand Scholarship," *Reason Papers*, 1998, 23: 132-59.

_____. *Feminine Interpretations of Ayn Rand*. University Park: Pennsylvania University Press, 1999.

_____. *Ayn Rand, Homosexuality and Human Liberation*, Cape Town, South Africa: Leap Publishing, 2003.

Seddon, Fred. *Ayn Rand, Objectivists and the History of Philosophy*. Lanham, Maryland University Press of America, 2003.

Sharma, Vivek. Atlanta, GA USA (http://desicritics.org/2006/04/21/001213.php)

Shelmer, Michael, *Why People Believe Weird Things*. USA: W.H. Freeman, 1997.

Showalter, Elaine. *The Female Malady*. London: Vintage Press, 1987.

Sid[ney], Greenberg. *Ayn Rand and Alienation: The Platonic Idealism of the Objectivist Ethics and a Rational Alternative*. San Francisco: Self-Published, 1977.

Simpson, Brian. *Markets Don't Fail*. Maryland: Lexington, 2005.

Sinyavsky. *Good Night!* New York: Viking, 1984.

Smith, George. *Atheism, Ayn Rand and Other Heresies*, New York: Prometheus Press, 1991.

Smith, George H. "Belief and Knowledge: Ayn Rand's Theory of Knowledge," *Why Atheism?* Buffalo, New York: Prometheus, 2000.

Smith, Tara. *Moral Rights and Political Freedom*. USA: University Press of America, 1997.

_____. *Viable Values: A Study of Life as the Root and Reward of Morality*. Lanham: Rowman & Littlefield, 2000.

_____. *Ayn Rand's Normative Ethics: The Virtuous Egoist*. USA: Cambridge University Press, 2006.

Sobran, Joseph. Rev. "Mussolini Shrugged: Ayn Rand Revived." 27 January 1989 (http://findarticles.com/p/articles/mi_m1282/is_nl_v41/ai_6975836/pg_4)

Stockton, Sharon. "Engineering Fascism: Ayn Rand, Ezra Pound and the Virile Hero," *The Economics of Fantasy: Rape in Twentieth-Century Literature*. Columbus, Ohio: Ohio State University Press, (2006), 48-70.

Sures, Mary Ann, Charles Sures. *Facets of Ayn Rand*, Blackstone Audiobooks, 2003.

Tidd, Ursula, *Simone de Beauvoir*, London: Routledge, 2004.

Toffler, Alvin. Ayn Rand: Interview. *Playboy*, 1964.

Thomas, William. Ayn Rand's *Philosophical Stunt Novel*. 1992 (http://www.objectivistcenter.org/cth-1992-Stunt_novel.aspx)

_____. "Ayn Rand: Radical for Capitalism," Bryan-Paul Forst & Jeffrey Sikkenga, ed. *History of American Political Thought*. Maryland: Lexington, 2003.

Torres, Louis, Michelle Marder Kamhi, ed. *What Art Is: the Aesthetic Theory of Ayn Rand*. Illinois: Open Court Publishing Co., 2000.

Touchstone, Kathleen. *Then Athena Said: Unilateral Transfers and the Transformation of Objectivist Ethics*. Maryland: University Press of America, 2006.

Trifonov, Yury. *The House on the Embankment*. Illinois, Northwestern University Press, 1976.

Tucker, Alan. "Steve Mallory: Objectivist Ideal for the Struggling Artist," 2001.

Valliant, James S. *The Passion of Ayn Rand's Critics*. Texas: Durban, 2005.

Walker, Jeff. *The Ayn Rand Cult*. Illinois: Carus, 1999.

Watkins, Susan Alice, Mrisa Rueda, Marta Rodriguez, *Feminism for Beginners*. Cambridge: Icon, 1992.

Wieder, Charles. rev. "Who is Dagny Taggart?" *Objectivity, 1998.*

Wortham, Anne. *The Other Side of Racism: A Philosophical Study of Black Race Consciousness*. Columbus, Ohio: Ohio State University Press, 1981.

Wyrick, Deborah. *Fann for Beginners*. Chennai: Orient Longman, 2003.

Younkins, Edward Wayne. *Philosophers of Capitalism*. London: Routledge, 2001.

_____, ed. *Ayn Rand's "Atlas Shrugged": A Philosophical and Literary Companion*. USA: Ashgate, 2007.

_____. "*Atlas Shrugged* in a Business School." http://solohq.solopassion.com/Articles/Younkins/Atlas-Shrugged-in-Business-School. shtml

_____. *Champions of a Free Society: Ideas of Capitalism's Philosophers and Economists*. Maryland: Lexington, 2007.

Zamyatin. *Journal of Ayn Rand Studies*. 4.2 (Spring 2000); 285-304. http://www.objectivistcenter.org/cth1346Feminism_and_Objectivism.aspx

http://folk.uio.no/thomas/po/sexual-approaches.html